The Meanings of Magic

Polygons: Cultural Diversities and Intersections
General Editor: **Lieve Spaas**, *Professor of French Cultural Studies, Kingston University, UK*

Volume 1
Reynard the Fox: Social Engagement and Cultural Metamorphoses in the Beast Epic from the Middle Ages to the Present
Edited by Kenneth Varty

Volume 2
Echoes of Narcissus
Edited by Lieve Spaas in association with Trista Selous

Volume 3
Human Nature and the French Revolution: From the Enlightenment to the Napoleonic Code
Xavier Martin
Translated from the French by Patrick Corcoran

Volume 4
Secret Spaces, Forbidden Places: Rethinking Culture
Edited by Fran Lloyd and Catherine O'Brien

Volume 5
Relative Points of View: Linguistic Representations of Culture
Edited by Magda Stroi´nska

Volume 6
Expanding Suburbia: Reviewing Suburban Narratives
Edited by Roger Webster

Volume 7
Cultures of Exile: Images of Displacement
Edited by Wendy Everett and Peter Wagstaff

Volume 8
More than a Music Box: Radio Cultures and Communities in a Multi-Media World
Edited by Andrew Crisell

Volume 9
A 'Belle Epoque'? Women in French Society and Culture 1890–1914
Edited by Diana Holmes and Carrie Tarr

Volume 10
Claims to Memory: Beyond Slavery and Emancipation in the French Caribbean
Catherine Reinhardt

Volume 11
The Meanings of Magic: From the Bible to Buffalo Bill
Edited by Amy Wygant

THE MEANINGS OF MAGIC

From the Bible to Buffalo Bill

Edited by

Amy Wygant

Berghahn Books

NEW YORK • OXFORD

First published in 2006 by

Berghahn Books
www.berghahnbooks.com

Library of Congress Cataloging-in-Publication Data

The meanings of magic : from the Bible to Buffalo Bill / edited by Amy Wygant.
p. cm. – (Polygons)
Includes bibliographical references and index.
ISBN 1-84545-178-3 (hardback : alk. paper)
1. Magic. 2. Popular culture. 3. Magic–Religious aspects–Christianity.
I. Wygant, Amy.

BF1621.M43 2006
133.4′3–dc22 2006018469

British Library Cataloguing in Publication Data

A catalogue record for this book is available from the British Library

Printed in the United States on acid-free paper

ISBN 1-84545-178-3 hardback

Contents

Acknowledgements vii

List of Illustrations ix

Introduction: Magic, Glamour, Curses 1
Amy Wygant

PART I: MAGIC AND GOD

1. Magic and the Millennium 33
David S. Katz

2. Showman or Shaman? The Acts of a Biblical Prophet 55
Mark Brummitt

3. Curse Tablets and Binding Spells in the Greco-Roman World 69
John G. Gager

4. Magic, Healing and Early Christianity: Consumption and Competition 89
Justin Meggitt

PART II: MAGIC, CULTURE, SCIENCE

5. All the Devils: Port-Royal and Pedagogy in Seventeenth-Century France 117
Nicholas Hammond

6. The Magic of French Culture: Transforming 'Savages' into French Catholics in Seventeenth-Century France 135
Sara E. Melzer

7. A Magus of the North? Professor John Ferguson and his Library 161
David Weston

8. The Golden Fleece and Harry Potter 179
Amy Wygant

9. Cowboys and Magicians: Buffalo Bill, Houdini and Real Magic 199
Ronald G. Walters

10. The Search for a New Dimension: Surrealism and Magic 221
Alyce Mahon

Notes on Contributors 235

Index 239

Acknowledgements

At this book's core are some of the lectures given as part of the University of Glasgow's Arts and Humanities Research Institute summer term seminar, 2002, and as part of the first postgraduate conference of the Arts and Divinity Graduate School, July, 2002. Thanks go to all who made these intellectual encounters exciting, vital, and indeed possible, including Alison Phipps, Catherine Steel, John Caughie, Noël Peacock, Sandra Peacock, Genevieve Warwick, Sam Cohn, John Barclay, Diana Barclay, the late Meg Stevenson, Bernard Wasserstein, Colin Smethurst, Claudine Smethurst and Simon Newman, as well as to all the contributors for their good cheer and cooperation. The support and encouragement of Lieve Spaas, Kenneth Varty, and Hetty Varty made the work light and I remain grateful for the steady professionalism of Mark Stanton at Berghahn Books. For help of a different kind, I thank Philip Snowdon.

List of Illustrations

Figure 1	'A Good Look.' *Sunday Times, Style,* 15 August 2004. Photo: N. Stylianou.	11
Figure 8.1.	G. Macchietti, 'Medea and Aeson'. Palazzo Vecchio, Florence. © 2005 photo Scala, Florence.	188
Figure 8.2.	'Medea and Pelias' [sic], painted enamel, Victoria and Albert Museum, London.	189
Figure 8.3.	'Medea rejuvenates Aeson'. L. Dolce, *Le Trasformationi,* 1558. Beinecke Rare Book and Manuscript Library, Yale.	190
Figure 8.4.	'Medee rajeunit Eson'. B. Salomon, *La Metamorphose d'Ovide figuree,* 1557. Courtesy of the Department of Special Collections, Glasgow University Library.	191

Introduction: Magic, Glamour, Curses

Amy Wygant

A glance at any dictionary will show that the word 'magic' can be defined. There you will see that it means something approximating 'the attempt to influence events (This, from the more disbelieving of definers. It is 'the art of influencing' for others.) or act upon objects in a way which seems unnatural and counter-intuitive, and which calls upon the aid of superhuman spirits' (*Oxford English Dictionary*, *Chambers*). But, although the unnatural, the counter-intuitive and indeed the superhuman do feature in this volume, the magic with which it is concerned is powerful precisely because it eludes and exceeds definition. This book is about an all-pervasive recourse to the notion of magic which has invaded mass-market media, and which in the late twentieth century was productive of phenomena ranging from the Millennium Bug to the ill-fated engagement to be wed of the most successful of modern magicians, David Copperfield, and supermodel, Claudia Schiffer. Without needing to bother with definitions, indeed while itself becoming a definition of the most unlikely objects and activities, 'magic' became a central paradigm in our speaking, writing and thinking, our representations of ourselves, our souls, our ways of acquiring knowledge, the universe itself and its creation. Magic became a hermeneutic tool and provided, in all of its powerful, hieratic indefinability, a general model of interpretation. In this respect, nothing has changed since. A quick trawl through one recent Sunday broadsheet found 'a central pit where you can watch the chefs prestidigitate' in a restaurant review (Gill 2004: 47), an evidently premature lament for the lost 'magic touch' of multimillionaire composer Andrew Lloyd Webber (Sierz 2004: 6), and a claim that author Cornelia Funke leads 'a life as magical as her children's bestsellers' (Burnside 2004: 10). The travel section will generally include at least one description of a 'magical' mass-market tourism destination (actual fairy sightings optional), and the home interiors pages may well promote 'magical' lighting that you can purchase at B&Q. At the same time, magic comes through the letterbox as an advertising enticement for us all to see a new production of *Macbeth* from Glasgow's theatre**babel**: 'Scotland is a country of menace and black magic. A land where the nation's greatest hero is about to become its greatest enemy' (theatre**babel** 2004). And at one point in the history of British slang a couple of years ago, my undergraduate students actually responded with the single word 'magic', when they wanted to indicate their general assent to some idea or suggestion. Around that time, I felt that I could claim that 'Ours Is a Magical Age' (http://www.sharp.arts.gla.ac.uk/issue1/wygant.html). The chapters in this book seek to pin down a few of the perimeter positions in this general enchantment of the cosmos. They will not define magic, but they will show us some of the contexts and developments which have produced an historical moment at which magic defines us.

While avoiding the fool's errand which would be an attempt to pin 'magic' down, the notoriously difficult and somehow pointless defining of a Zeitgeist, we could certainly ask nevertheless why it is the case that magic seems to be everywhere. As a paradigm for interpretation, it is by no means obvious and is certainly not timeless. The tremendously influential historian of magic, J.G. Frazer, declared that the Age of Magic had long ago been succeeded by the Age of Religion on the way to the Age of Science. Did Jacqueline Lichtenstein not once claim that pre-Enlightenment Europe saw the world through a different hermeneutic: the grammar, power and controversies of painting? (Lichtenstein 1989). And did magic not die a death in the Enlightenment? Our present acquiescence to the magical has a history, and oddly, that history might best be understood not by defining what we might mean by 'magic', but instead by putting some critical pressure on the 'everywhere' that it seems to inhabit. This is the Greek cosmos, and indeed the cosmetic. There is firstly a magic of appearance which has much to do with our nebulous 'everywhere', and there is, secondly, a magic of culture which seeks to ensure that our 'everywhere' will be broadcast to everywhere else.

This cosmos inhabits a semantic field which includes 'glamour', 'charisma' and 'makeup', as well as cosmetics, and whose members always seek to name a paradoxical situation. That is, cosmos is world, but this cosmos is nothing but ornament, cosmetics, the variable arranging of our bodies as a function of changing fashion in order that they might embellish, decorate and inspire desire (Papageorgiou 1986). Our makeup is our character, our constitution, the set of qualities which composes us, and yet it is at the same time the paint which conceals rather than elucidates truth. Charisma is not essentially a political quality, yet no politician can be elected without it, nor may any teacher, the magus, actually teach. As for 'glamour', a closer look at its curious career may help us to understand why magic governs appearance in our 'everywhere'.

A glamour was originally a spell cast by a witch to deceive the eyes. The first meaning of 'glamour' in the *Oxford English Dictionary* is 'magic, enchantment, spell, esp. in the phrase to cast the glamour over one'. In German, its first meaning is still 'der Zauber; das Blendwerk', 'magic; a blinding, dazzling, or deceiving'. The word was originally Scottish, a corrupt form of 'grammar' or 'grammarye' meaning learning in general and occult learning in particular. Its early references come from Robert Burns, who claimed in a 1789 poem that the rotund Francis Grose the antiquarian would out-conjure 'Ye gipsy-gang that deal in glamour,/ And you, deep-read in hell's black grammar/ Warlocks and Witches' (Burns 1990: 230), and from Walter Scott's 1805 'Lay of the Last Minstrel':

> It had much of glamour might,
> Could make a ladye seem a knight;
> The cobwebs on a dungeon wall
> Seem tapestry in lordly hall;
> A nut-shell seem a gilded barge,
> And sheeling seem a palace large,
> And youth seem age, and age seem youth—
> All was delusion, nought was truth (Scott 1878: 24).

When the notorious late fifteenth-century witch-hunting manual, the *Malleus maleficarum*, came to be translated into

English by Montague Summers in 1928, then, 'glamour' suggested itself as a gloss on the original's 'prestigia', defined in part I, question 9, 'Whether Witches may work some Prestidigitatory Illusions so that the Male Organ appears to be entirely removed and separate from the Body':

> A glamour is nothing but a certain delusion of the senses, and especially of the eyes. And for this reason it is also called a prestige, from *prestringo*, since the sight of the eyes is so fettered that things seem to be other than they are. [...] The devil can cast a glamour over the senses of a man. Wherefore there is no difficulty in his concealing the virile member by some prestige or glamour (Kramer and Sprenger 1971: 59–60; Kramer [1497]: 136–38).

The latest scholarly translation of the *Malleus*, which secures the now generally accepted thesis that Kramer was its sole author, is a 2000 translation into German from the original Latin. It struggles with the key terms in this passage, offering 'Blendwerk', for 'prestigium', and a selection of terms for 'prestringo', all requiring careful references in notes to the original (Kramer 2000: 270–71).

'A glamour', then, was a witch's weapon, a way of altering the true appearance of things, ontologically on the side of seeming, the alteration of nature, counterfeiters and cosmetics. There was a rancorous debate in early modern England over women's use of cosmetics, called not 'makeup', which seems to have come into use in the second half of the nineteenth century, but rather 'paint', and the anti-cosmetics treatises aligned face painting with witchcraft and general ungodliness. A 1616 treatise by Thomas Tuke was 'Against Painting and Tincturing of Women. Wherein the abominable sinnes of Murther and Poysening, Pride and Ambition, Adultery and Witchcraft are set foorth & discovered. Whereunto is added the Picture of a Picture, or, the Character of a Painted Woman (Tuke 1616). Face painting, it was argued, lead to prostitution, which was the cause of all of England's ills, including the plague. This was its history-bound danger, one from which we can now feel a happy distance, one at which we can look with a curious eye. But there was another, transhistorical danger of face painting, and this was that it posed the possibility that a woman or man could take identity into her or his own hands, redefine the God-given order of the cosmos, transform and re-fashion the self. The self-transforming face painter blurred the boundary between creature and creator (Dolen 1993). Tuke claims that 'she is a creature, that had need to be twice defined, for though shee bee the creature of God, as she is a woman, yet she is her owne creatrisse, as a picture' (Tuke 1616: 57).

A reference to the witch hunt which resulted from this uneasiness comes from as late as 1916. Richard Le Gallienne, writing in *McClure's Magazine* and referring to 'a friend' who refused to date a woman who used face powder, allowed that

> I suppose that there are other human anachronisms like my friend still existing here and there, survivals from the days of the thumb-screw and the ducking-stool, but they must be very lonely, and I hardly know where they would look for wives. [...] The innocence of the powder-puff has been discovered' (Le Gallienne 1916: 31).

Here, then, and not so long ago, was a certain belated border crossing between the witchcraft of cosmetics and their absolution, their 'innocence'.

In France, women's painting was aligned with painting in general and fell under the same condemnation as did painterly colour in the debate over the use of line and colour which consumed the Royal Academy of Painting and Sculpture in the late seventeenth century. That is, colour was that part of painting which seduced from afar and produced an unstable pleasure which did not last. It was opposed to the primacy of the idea, which was expressed by drawing. Up close, the illusion produced by colour is destroyed and the real existence of the paint is revealed as matter itself. It was this matter, the body of the canvas or the woman, which was mistrusted, part of a general suspicion that condemned everything that appeared unstable, changeable, or transitory (Lichtenstein 1987; Lichtenstein 1989). In the century's earliest dictionary, Cotgrave's 1611 *Dictionarie of the French and English Tongues*, the general suspicion of face painting, said to have been introduced into France in the sixteenth century by the Italian queen, herself popularly assumed to be a witch and poisoner, Catherine de Medicis, was already fully deployed:

> Farder: To paint, colour, disguise, tricke up, set out with false beauties, to polish with a borrowed luster, to use pretences, to deceive the eares, or bleare the eyes with faire but counterfeit matters. *De toute femme qui se farde donne toy soigneusement garde*: Pro. Take heed of any woman that doth paint' (Cotgrave 1968).

Furetière's dictionary, while defining *'cosmetique'* as a matter for medical doctors (*'terme, dont les Medecins se servent en parlant des remedes & des fards qui servent à l'embellissement du visage, & à entretenir le teint frais'*, 'term used by doctors to refer to remedies and paints which serve to enhance the face and maintain a clear complexion'), warns under the entry *'farder'* that *'Les femmes qui se fardent deviennent ridées avant le temps'* 'a woman who paints becomes wrinkled before her time' (Furetière 1727).

So much for this first, archaic, definition of 'glamour': the attempt to deceive the eyes with paint or potions participated in an ancient fear of female power, and reflected the need for the face to reveal true identity and to disclose in an unproblematic way true thought and feeling. Hence the Scott poem's anxiety that the glamour could 'make a ladye seem a knight' and tamper with the aging process, making 'youth seem age and age seem youth'. Clearly, in the *Oxford English Dictionary*'s second definition of 'glamour', 'a magical or fictitious beauty attaching to any person or object', an entire aesthetics, since this is now about beauty and no longer explicitly about the devil, resides in the 'or'. 'Or' is the locus of anxious indecision, as well as an historical pivot or turning point between glamour's witchcraft and its fictions.

The meaning of 'glamour' with which we will be most familiar, 'charm, attractiveness, physical allure, esp. feminine beauty' is documented by the *Oxford English Dictionary* only from the 1930s, and this move from glamour's being something that women do, to being something that women have, coincided with an historic transformation in feminine appearance, and participated in a larger cultural contest over women's identity. In the latter half of the nineteenth century, makeup had begun to move from the stage into everyday life, and the admiration for actresses and professional beauties had begun to provide a standard for female appearance. But the rise of the mass-market cosmetics industry in the 1920s, led by U.S. corporations such as Maybelline and Revlon, as well as, crucially, the consolidation of the Hollywood film industry into large and efficient movie factories, provided a new platform for glamour's invasion of our perceptions.

On the one hand, the golden age of Hollywood cinema purveyed an unexamined notion of the glamorous. One credulous publication, which is mainly about dresses, *Those Glorious Glamour Years. Classic Hollywood Costume Design of the 1930s*, begins breathlessly, 'Of all the words associated with Hollywood, the one most often used to conjure its unique image is the magic term "glamour"' (Bailey 1982: 7), and divides its chapters into 'Evening Glamour', 'Daytime Glamour', 'Glamour at Home', 'Glamour at Play', 'Epic Glamour' and 'Wedding Glamour'. 'In the Thirties glamour was the core adjective to any feminine star's aura', it further observes (Bailey 1982: 7), and, indeed, 'glamour' seems to have been one of the buzz words of the decade (Peiss 1998: 151). But, on the other hand, glamour was a commodity. The big Hollywood studios were 'glamour factories', production-line, profit-making concerns whose product was motion pictures and glamour (Davis 1993). This business-like system made Hollywood into the glamour capital of the world, and an MGM screenwriter was able to observe that 'When Metro did a short with Joan Crawford dragging a fifteen- or twenty-thousand-dollar mink coat along the ground, every woman in the audience thought, "Boy, would I like to do that! That's the way to live." Glamour's what the movies sold, that was their business' (Davis 1993: 368).

On the ground in Hollywood, this quality of glamour seems indeed to have had much to do with attire, dresses and 'dressing up'. But it was also, as the screenwriter observed, a 'way to live'. The social scene was described by Englishwoman Pamela Mason as 'There were parties every night, and everybody dressed up and it was very glamorous' (Davis 1993: 328). But one of the ways in which the women in the audiences for Hollywood films appropriated the quality of glamour for themselves was through the use of makeup. The film stars purveyed a painted look that had formerly been associated with prostitutes, and Hollywood makeup technicians such as Max Factor eventually sold products originally formulated for the film studio employees, such as Pan-Cake makeup, introduced in 1938, nationwide. Magazines for middle-class women, as well as movie and romance magazines aimed at working-class and young women, exploited the links between motion pictures and cosmetics with beauty hints columns and advertising featuring screen stars. A full-page advertisement in *Vogue* in the 1930s suggested that 'The difference between your lips and those of the glamorous cinema star is that you use a blunt lipstick while she uses a lipbrush', and promised that the Cinema Sable lip brush would 'draw real cinema lips on you with all the deftness of a Hollywood make-up man, so that your lips will appear as perfect and as beautiful as those you see on the screen' (Corson 1972: 516). Capping a decade of women's being hammered by this kind of aspirational glamour, *Glamour Magazine* was launched on 7 March 1939.

The self-fashioning of personal identity, trigger for centuries of fulminations, condemnations, and indeed executions, was now glamour's gift and indeed imperative to ordinary women, and makeup promised personal transformation. *Vogue* in 1933 described the scenario: 'Beauty today [...] is no longer left to fate. It is born more often than not in the mind of a homely little girl looking in the mirror at herself for the first time seriously, gritting her teeth, and making up her mind that she is going to launch a thousand ships as well as Helen' (Corson 1972: 508). Crucially, makeup now was a thought process and a moral issue, a matter of courage and determination, the gritting of teeth: *Vogue*'s 'little girl' makes up firstly her mind, and only secondly her face.

By the 1940s, this courage of the ordinary woman to change herself through the use of makeup would become a U.S. national strategic concern, as journalists worried that a 'national glamour shortage would seriously lower national morale' (Furnas 1941: 19). 'The nation can hardly afford to have Johnny come marching home on leave to find his girl friend looking and feeling like somebody in the low phase of manic depression' (Furnas 1941: 19). Lipstick was worn as a badge of courage, and an advertisement in a 1943 *Ladies' Home Journal* claimed that '[Lipstick] symbolizes one of the reasons why we are fighting' (Peiss 1998: 241).

As for the sex wars, advertising in the 1920s and 1930s had advocated the use of makeup as a means of getting and keeping a husband, and so participated in a long-standing cultural attempt to control women's sexuality through the promotion of heterosexual romance and marriage. It was historically ironic, for the acquisition of a husband through the use of the arts of cosmetics and makeup had long been a matter of intense suspicion and indeed of legislation. In the late eighteenth century, the English Parliament passed a law that

> All women, of whatever age, rank, profession or degree, whether virgins, maids, or widows, that shall from and after this act impose upon, seduce or betray into matrimony any of His Majesty's subjects by the use of scents, paints, cosmetics, washes, artificial teeth, false hair, Spanish wool, iron stays, hoops, high-heeled shoes, or bolstered hips, shall incur the penalty of the law now in force against witchcraft and like misdemeanors, and that the marriage, upon conviction, shall stand null and void (Corson 1972: 245).

Further, there is some indication that women themselves, no matter what the advertising media might have been urging upon them, used makeup and cosmetics as part of acts of female sociability, and not as a strategy to inspire male desire. The beauty industry in the U.S. had been founded by women and had been successful in its early days because women sold products to each other through such methods as door-to-door selling, the traditional retail trade having proved hostile to them. As late as the 1990s in the U.K., Anita Roddick, who founded The Body Shop in 1976, claimed that 'we want to spark conversations with our customers, not browbeat them to buy' (Roddick 1991: 25). The retreat from the sex wars into a female language of beauty, however, was appropriated and recuperated for heterosexual norms by an influential Revlon advertising campaign in the early 1950s. 'Glamor' was the name both for the campaign's appeal, and for the prize in a contest in which all the contestants were women.

Revlon's 'Fire and Ice' campaign in 1952 was a spectacular advertising and media success ('It's the Ad' 1952: 69). Its powerful image is of a beautiful black-haired, blue-eyed model, who wears diamond drop earrings, a slinky silver sequined dress, and a billowing puff of a red cape ('Are you made?' 1952: 27). She stares directly out at the reader, and wears lipstick and nail polish meant 'for you who love to flirt with fire, who dare to skate upon thin ice'. The full-page image is accompanied by a 'psychological quiz' asking, 'Are you made for "Fire and Ice?"' and headed by a paragraph which wonders,

> What is the American girl made of? Sugar and spice and everything nice? Not since the days of the Gibson Girl! There's a *new* American beauty. [...] Men find her slightly, delightfully baffling. Sometimes a little maddening. Yet they admit that she's *easily* the most exciting woman in all the world! She's the 1952 American beauty, with a foolproof formula for melting a male!

The quiz included fifteen 'provocative' questions, personally chosen from a list prepared by Revlon's advertising agency by Martin Revson, Revlon's vice-president in charge of sales ('It's the Ad' 1952: 66). 'Have you ever danced with your shoes off?' 'Do you secretly hope that the next man you meet will be a psychiatrist?' 'Would you streak your hair with platinum without consulting your husband?' If the reader could 'honestly' answer at least eight of the questions affirmatively, according to the concluding copy, then she was 'made of "Fire and Ice"', 'a daring projection of your *own* hidden personality!'

The moment defined by this image and text is called by the historian of beauty culture in the U.S. one of 'pure glamour' (Peiss 1998: 251), and, at the time, *Business Week* called this one of the most effective advertising campaigns in cosmetics history, combining 'dignity, class, and glamor' ('It's the Ad' 1952: 63). Moreover, the inspiration behind the campaign had been the Revlon creative team's suspicion that U.S. women were ready for a change, tired not only of the constricting fashions of Dior's New Look, but also of the incursions of 'the "other woman"'. 'In this case, however, the other women were the European glamor girls. Brought to the U.S. by the boatload for movies, plays and nightclubs, they had even begun to usurp the spotlight on the social scene' ('It's the Ad' 1952: 65). This sense that U.S. women were engaged in a battle with Europeans arriving 'by the boatload' laden with glamour explains the ad's otherwise puzzling insistence on U.S. supremacy and its cheerleader-like tone. A postwar war was being fought, not for territory or resources, but rather for glamour, something not 'nice' but rather baffling, maddening, hidden, and fundamentally psychological, 'a daring projection of your *own* hidden personality!'

'Glamour', seemingly, had thus become the name of a general poetics of appearance. 'Pure glamour' was a way of being, no longer a technique, strategy or product. This is a new, we might say democratic, form of its magic, generally broadcast, suffusing appearances, defined anecdotally not systematically, but nevertheless governing its domain just as surely as did the old magic of the witch's glamour. And it continues to do so today, as we can observe in a latter-day 'Fire and Ice' image from the mass-market media (Figure 1).

The model sits in an exotic wicker chair (In fact, the setting is the Abbey Road Pub in London), looking out at the beholder with eyes narrowed to slits ('A Good Look' 2004). Her legs are crossed, signifying what that usually signifies: Ice. She is wearing a red dress and a red necklace; she has red hair and red lips. Her hat is an anti-halo: a round white circle balanced and floating on her mop of curly hair, not secured to her head. It has one erect feather and is shadowed by a non-functional black net veil, remnant of a different aesthetic. This anti-angel wears gold high-heeled shoes and is seated on a gold cushion. She is lit from behind, by means of an intensely bright light that shines out at the beholder from just underneath her seat. She is sitting on the sun: Fire.

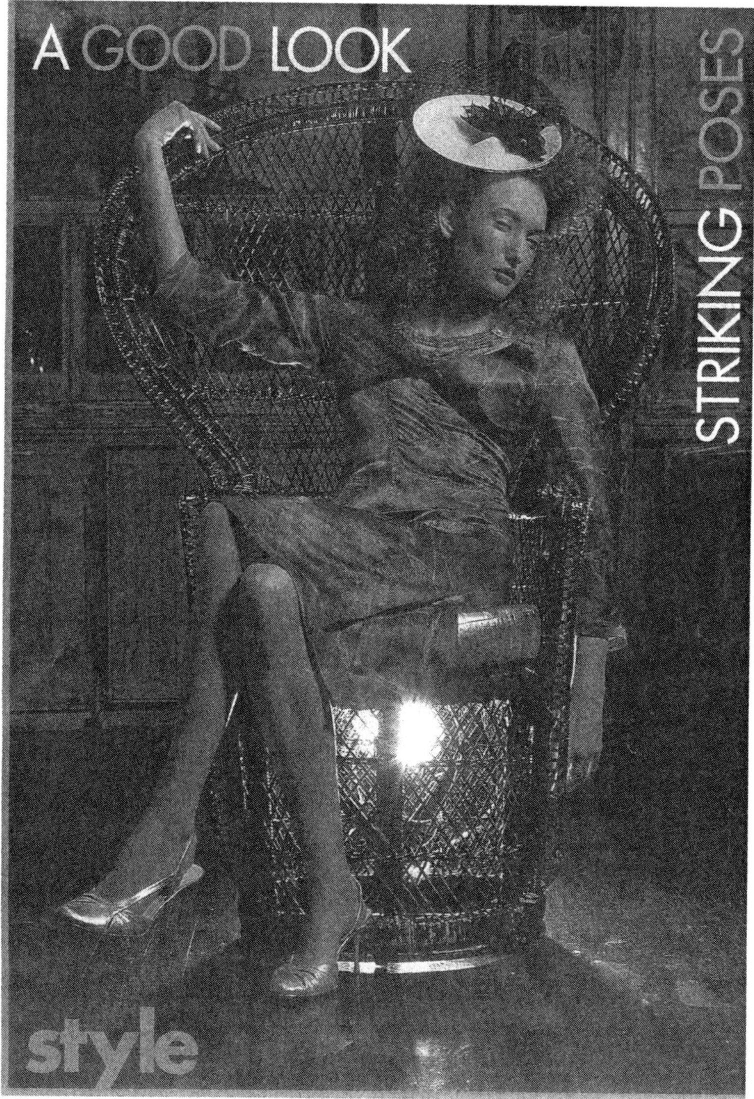
A GOOD LOOK
STRIKING POSES
style
How to do effortless glamour? Deck yourself out in a silk dress, a pair of gold heels and a divine hat. Then sit in a chair in the corner and pretend you haven't noticed that everyone's staring at you

Figure 1 'A Good Look.' *Sunday Times, Style,* 15 August 2004. Photo Nick Stylianou.

The copy accompanying this icon asks, 'How to do effortless glamour?' and then proceeds to describe the effort involved. 'Deck yourself out in a silk dress, a pair of gold heels and a divine hat. Then sit in a chair in the corner and pretend you haven't noticed that everyone's staring at you.' Like the glamour of the early modern witch, then, this is glamour which the woman does, not a quality which she has. That she is 'decked out' means in the first place that she is covered, 'adorned with finery', or, as Cotgrave would have had it, 'tricked up, set out with false beauties'. Also, the woman 'decked out' is a ship under sail, a vessel of hope and dreams vulnerable to reef and weather and so ontologically on the side of changability and fickle fate. She has appropriated sacred signifiers for her own use: her hat is precisely 'divine' and some alchemist has, through dint of sacrifice and virtue, changed her shoes to gold. Acting the part of glamour, she has chosen her setting, 'a chair in the corner', in which she can 'pretend'. This is not magic: her bits and bobs cost a grand total of £987, and the accompanying small print gives numbers that we can phone to acquire them. And it is not effortless. Or is it?

What the woman has done seems greater than the sum of her efforts. That is, like the witch, she has somehow, by some mysterious tele-means not reducible to £987 of attire, exerted power over the eyes: 'everyone's staring at you'. She has transfigured space, changing her seat in 'a corner' into the centre of attention, the object of the collective gaze. As the *Malleus maleficarum* defined it, 'The sight of the eyes is so fettered that things seem to be other than they are'. This is not necessarily about a heterosexual conquest. The woman has fettered the eyes not just of men, but of 'everyone'. 'Don't stare! It's impolite!' She negates the training of civility, and reduces us to children, indeed to brutes. Ruminants, welcome to the cave of Circé, welcome to the land of Medea, welcome to your local pub, where, along with 'everywhere' else, appearance is now fashioned along the lines of a power which is truly and correctly, if indefinably, called 'magical'.

This first model of magic as a general poetics of appearance is closely related to the second model, a magic of culture. As many of the contributions to this volume were being finalised, at the end of March 2002, the world ostensibly heard from Osama bin Laden for the first time since shortly after the 9/11 atrocities. The communication took the form of an email sent from a server in Karachi to the London-based Arabic newspaper *al-Quds*, and it read in part, 'then came the New York military expedition to set afire the homes of today's Hubal, crushing its towers, disgracing its arrogance, *undoing its magic*, stripping all the banners that marched behind it and proclaiming the beginning of its downfall, God willing' (emphasis added) (http://www.channel4.com/news/home/20020328/Story07.htm). This is a tall order: to crush things, burn homes, bring disgrace, and, issuing proclamations, definitively to rain on someone's parade, stripping banners and discouraging marching, and it is worth asking what, or, again, where, the magic which is explicitly evoked here might be.

Again, the movies are instructive. Hollywood films from the first half of the twentieth century inspired desire not just among U.S. women for the lips promised by the Cinema Sable lipbrush, but also among many other audiences for an entire panoply of objects drawn from U.S. material culture. Those in other countries began attempting to imitate the 'way to live' which the images on the screen literally magnified. If certain kitchen appliances, gardening tools or typewriters were shown in a film, 'orders soon began pouring in from Rumania, Bolivia, Tasmania, and from all over the world' (Davis 1993: 6). The objects on the screen were advertising more powerful than advertising itself, and an entire sub-genre of the advertising industry arose, 'product placement'. But the objects were also an advertisement for U.S. economic success and their desireability testified to an undefined power of the commercial imagination, greater than the political.

This power itself, although complicated and open to the same kind of analysis as is that of the glamour of appearance, was nothing new, and an important work of recent scholarship argues that it was operative, for example, in the French formal garden in the seventeenth century. Chandra Mukerji (1997) has pointed out in the precisely titled *Territorial Ambitions and the Gardens of Versailles* that there is nothing necessarily obvious about a nation's being defined by the geographical territory it occupies. Before the early modern period, an empire was known by its linking of centres of power, not its domination of an area. The new territorial state of early modernity was the first to be defined by its boundaries, and it was only then that cartographers were first commissioned to make images of states and estates. The formal garden was a microcosm of this new configuration of earth-based, rather than heaven-based power, a showcase for the manufactured products, engineering and military prowess, habits of dress and social choreography, comportment, and, above all, domination of the land which its periphery encompassed. In this respect, the formal garden was the Hollywood movie of its day: it signalled what others were required to understand about the political unit which had produced it. In the case of 'France', the garden meant to show that 'France' was a location, and also to signal that any ambiguity about its boundaries would be regarded as an excuse to go to war (Mukerji 1997).

The Hollywood movie, however, was not about territorial boundaries but about non-locatable cultural ones whose one goal was to undo and scatter themselves. Easily exportable, aggressively marketed, it held out the scintillating possibility that all 'outsiders' could become 'insiders' if only they could acquire the right props. And its major unexamined assumption was that its audiences would want to become 'insiders' and live within a valence that the French call 'sweetness of life', that the Hollywood script writer called 'the way to live', and that Sara Melzer analyses here for early modern France. The movies believed and traded, that is, in their own cultural magic. Historically, it is no accident that the major cinema-specific resistance to this unexamined magical attractiveness came from the place where cultural magic seems to have been invented and has been most beautifully and tellingly analysed (I think of Roland Barthes), France.

Under these conditions, what constitutes resistance in general, and what is an excuse to go to war if territorial boundaries have ceased to be the point? Some think that cultural magic can and should be undone. Others think that cultural magic, like the magic of appearance, can and should be democratised; and that accusations of cultural witchcraft, like accusations of witchcraft as such, belong to a dark ages of the mind best consigned to the past.

Magic and God

Now the 'Hubal' evoked in the supposed bin Laden email quoted above was the moon god of pre-Islamic Arabia, worshipped at the Kaaba in Mecca, and smashed by the Prophet in order to discourage his tribe from their worship. 'Hubal' is not named in the Koran, but his three daughters are thought by some to be the subject of the Satanic verses (http://encyclopedia.thefreedictionary.com/Hubal). This combative stance towards religions which predate the monotheological ones finds an instructive contrast, and indeed a symmetrical opposite, in the latest version of the Arthurian legends to grace our popular culture, Touchstone's benighted film, *King Arthur*, which filled the seats of the multiplexes in Britain in the summer of 2004. One early scene finds Arthur's knights, insistently characterised as areligious mercenaries, protecting a Christian cleric from attack by 'Woads', non-Christian indigenous people wearing blue makeup and speaking a language which requires subtitles. Their leader is Merlin: 'Some say he is a dark wizard'. In the thick of it, a knight confronts the cross worn by the terrified cleric with the question, 'Do you think this will save you?' and, symmetrically, when Arthur has the band's leader at swordpoint, the camera focuses on the blue sun symbol painted on the Woad's forehead. The cleric dies in the fracas; Arthur spares the Woad. The moral, *Animal Farm*-like, seems to be: Rome, Christianity, empire: bad; Britain, paganism, insurgency (aficionados will appreciate Arthur's later 'freedom' speech to his knights before battle): good. Needless to say, Guinivere is a Woad (she speaks English, though), and Merlin marries the two at the end, Arthur thus reclaiming the Woad identity of his pagan mother.

These two simplistic scenarios may be used to illustrate an important point once made by John Gager, and to explain why there is no section in this book called 'Magic and Religion', which would at first glance seem entirely to be the point both of the bin Laden email and of a certain kind of contemporary concern of mass-market culture indexed by *King Arthur*. Although, as Fritz Graf has pointed out and analysed at length, 'the debate about the distinction between magic and religion has been long and bitter' (Graf 1997: 2), the debate has a severe terminology problem. 'Magic' and 'religion' may be tautological. When Gager asserts that 'magic, as a definable and consistent category of human experience simply does not exist' (Gager 1992: 24), he is not disavowing miracle cures, Houdini-esque events, or the nonrational in general. What he means is that, if we aim to talk about religion, 'the beliefs and practices of "the other" will always be dubbed as "magic", "superstition" and the like' (Gager 1992: 25). One person's priest is another person's wizard; one person's sun-worshipper is another person's Son-worshipper. The task for those who would pin down a few of the perimeter positions in this debate is thus not to distinguish between religion and magic, but rather to ask, as Gager points out, how and why, in what places and at what times, under what conditions and according to whom, magic has seemed an effective category of the sacred.

Accordingly, we have here not 'Magic and Religion', but rather 'Magic and God'. David Katz writes of magical messianic thought over a vast historical sweep of time from the twelfth-century Calabrian abbot Joachim of Fiore to Ronald Reagan. What is the force of prophesy that it can take hold of the imagination and convince us that 'the end is nigh'? Or cause us to head for the Highlands with our stock of survival gear, convinced that the Millennium Bug will make airplanes fall from the skies and end civilization as we know it? Katz points to the conceptual confusion in the midst of the beautiful symmetries, precise dates, and neat scenarios of millenarianism, and begins this volume with the influential J.G. Frazer. Frazer's greatest contribution to the anthropology of religion was his distinction between magic and religion, and it was one which operated beautifully in a scholarly climate in which evolutionism dominated the human sciences. Everywhere, an age of magic had been succeeded by an age of religion, Frazer thought: Man first tries to compel God, and when that fails, he begs. The religious person beseeches supernatural powers; the magician tries to conform these powers to his own will and intentions. It is testimony to the strength of Frazer's thought that scholars were still working to complicate it and indeed to show its limitations in the late twentieth century; Gager's position as stated above is in part a reaction against it and what is now perceived as its Christiano-centric bias. Katz's millenarians stretch Frazer's definition beyond the breaking point. Their magic of numbers and dates produces a frisson of the unexpected for most, which is however precisely expected by the chosen few. To think oneself above or beyond it is to be sadly mistaken. Katz, along with Richard H. Popkin, once pointed to the significance of the date 19 April in the recent history of U.S. millenarian activity (Katz and Popkin 1999: ix). It was the date of the death of the followers of David Koresh in Waco, Texas in 1993; and on 19 April 1995 the Federal Building in Oklahoma City was bombed. Was it not odd that Katz's lecture for the University of Glasgow's Summer Term Seminar, from which the present chapter is drawn, took place on 19 April 2002?

It is worth keeping in mind, as Mark Brummitt reminds us in 'Showman or Shaman' here, that prophesy is powerful because it is believed to come from God. This makes prophesy into a kind of performance on the part of the prophet, and it makes the Yahwist God into the ultimate *metteur en scène*, a deity-director choosing props and setting, and controlling the script and movements of the prophet-ventriloquist. However, Brummitt is interested not in 'domesticating' this kind of easy scenario, but rather in complicating it by imagining the act of prophesy from the point of view of the spectator, by asking the 'to whom?' question suggested by John Gager. And, if prophesy is performance, a thesis little open to question following the days of the tele-evangelists analysed by Katz and Popkin (Katz and Popkin 1999: esp. 'The End of the World and the Nuclear Messiah', 205–48), then its performativity is open to analysis. It can be made not domestic but rather strange, a matter which Bertold Brecht explored at length and which Brummitt here elaborates. Taking three examples from the book of Jeremiah, Brummitt views the prophet's performance as a function of the text's figuring of the audience: the elite audience as one ingredient among several in a recipe for prophesy in Jeremiah 19; the people as the potter's clay in Jeremiah 18 (if the pot collapses, is it the fault of the clay?), and, in the odd matter of the loincloth in Jeremiah 13, the possibility that the events produced by the direction of God may be neither dream nor reality, and that the only audience for this prophesy may be its readers.

This reversal of critical power based upon a decision about what actually can be known, what kind of question has the potential to be answered, is one which informs as well the contributions of Justin Meggitt and John Gager. Gager is interested in curses, Meggitt, in cures. Gager here takes on the promise given by the Matthean Jesus to his followers, and in particular to Simon Peter. To him are promised 'the keys of the kingdom': 'Whatsoever thou shalt bind on earth shall be bound in heaven, and whatsoever thou shalt loose on earth shall be loosed in heaven' (Matthew 17: 19). Gager's interest is neither in the authenticity of the words nor in separating their magical from their religious components. Instead, he aims to determine how Jesus's words would have been understood by a passerby in that time and place. This takes us to one important context of the promise: curse tablets, a repertoire which Gager has called 'a dark little secret of ancient Mediterranean culture' (Gager 1992: 3). Written primarily on lead, and usually containing a verb of binding, they sought to inflict harm or death, defeat in war or athletic competitions, mental suffering, involuntary celibacy, and general lack of success upon whomever was named. They were widespread, probably 'worked' in some sense, cut across all social classes, and were used during a continuous history of more than twelve hundred years. They are related to collections of curse recipes found in books called 'grimoires', a word which belongs to the etymological family of 'glamour', and their conceptual categories of 'binding' and 'loosing' lived on in early modern France as the 'nouements d'aiguillettes' practiced by witches to cause impotence (Gelin 1910), and viewed with notable scepticism by Montaigne.

So, was Jesus a magician? Morton Smith long ago showed that there was some kind of case to be made for his resemblance to common magicians of the first-century Mediterranean world, and he showed as well that the 'magical' elements that remain in the gospels are probably only isolated remnants of what was once a strong tradition (Smith 1978: 81–93). Those elements have notably to do with exorcisms and healing miracles. Justin Meggitt here claims, however, that scholarship on the matter has not given sufficient weight to the character whom Gager calls 'the passerby', and who might become what Meggitt calls 'the patient', that is, the one who believed him- or herself to be exorcised or healed. In doing so here, and in his forthcoming *Christ and the Universe of Disease*, and in thus turning the question around: not, 'Was Jesus a magician?' but instead 'Did the consumers of the results of his healing activities believe him so to be, and, if so, what did that imply?', Meggitt introduces an important refinement in the evident cultural relativism of magic: that is, it is a matter precisely of *cultural* relativism, and a culture's decision to call an event 'magic', rather than to understand it within the structures of some other form of alterity, is significant. Equally significant is what a patient operating within a particular culture would then decide to do about an encounter with an event deemed magical. What if being healed by the historical Jesus did not necessarily imply that the patient should then allow him- or herself to be led to God and become a follower of Jesus? And what if sufferers addressed themselves to Jesus simply because he performed for free services such as exorcisms for which others charged dearly?

Magic, Culture, Science

The magic of culture is, in extreme cases, an excuse to go to war, as well as, more commonly, an excuse to go shopping. But 'magic' is also that without which no teacher is ever truly effective, and a synonym for art. It names the desire for love and the desire for learning, the inseparable pair called the transference by psychoanalysis. Here, Ronald Walters, Nicholas Hammond, Alyce Mahon and Sara Melzer secure some components of culture in terms of the magical: memory, the surreal, performance and representation, and the lure of the transformation of identity. And, producing an argument for the notion that science is never 'pure' but rather forever inbricated with the cultural structures which fund it, regulate it and expect it to produce miracles, David Weston and I try to imagine what the obscure science of alchemy could possibly mean to an eccentric nineteenth-century Glaswegian antiquarian chemist, and to a new generation of twenty-first-century readers, the children agog at Harry Potter.

There is no cultural force more powerful than teaching, and the teacher is always in some sense a magus. 'What have you done with my son?', 'Qu'as-tu fait de mon fils?', is certainly one of the most pointed questions in all of French seventeenth-century theatre, asked in the final act of Jean Racine's *Phèdre* by the king Theseus of his son's teacher, Theramenes. Here, Nicholas Hammond explores the historical context in which the power of the teacher whom Leo Spitzer called variously 'a scholar in philosophy on the stage', 'a humanistic historiographer' and, finally, 'a sage', was formed (Wygant 1994: 693). It was a long historical moment at which the greatest teachers of the age, the Jesuits and the Jansenists, were engaged in a war of mutual demonisation. The stakes of this war were those of memory itself: Hammond writes of 'the almost obsessive need to memorialize' of the Port-Royal Jansenists, and of the courage of a dying nun, herself explicitly demonised and consigned to 'all the devils', emblematic of the historical fate of her house. The most famous pupil of the Jansenists, Jean Racine, was in little doubt that this destruction came about as a result of the quarrel over 'the instruction of the young', and Hammond's analysis of Racine's last tragedies, written precisely to be performed in a school, shows pedagogical theory become art, 'an almost magical prescience of post-dramatic time'. Racine the orphan's final theatrical word is 'father': *Athalie* ends with the reminder, the memory, the promise and prophesy that kings will themselves be judged by a higher power, wronged innocence will find an avenger, and the orphan, a father: 'Et l'orphelin un père' (l. 1816).

We are not far from the powerful magic of acculturation that Sara Melzer elaborates here with respect to the colonising project of early modern France. For France's clients, the 'savages' of the New World, seem somehow to have been paralysed and incapable of resistance when confronted with the statehood and religious institutions of France. Once the Jesuit missionaries had provided the Amerindians with elements of French material culture, French food, clothes and lodging, the seductive magic of that culture took over and they wished automatically to become French. They were transformed, given a French heart, and even babies reportedly felt it. That which was 'savage', that is, that which was wild, shadowy and beyond the borders of the civilised, inhabiting the space of magic as it had been understood from antiquity, was magically brought into the confines of the polis, assimilated, educated, acculturated, and aligned with the moral order of the perfect community.

Or was it? The danger, as Freud knew perfectly well, lies within, and Melzer here analyses one of the most virulent French witchcraft trails of the century, in which the French magistrate Pierre de Lancre went to a border territory, the Basque region, and perhaps unsurprisingly found that more or less all of its 30,000 inhabitants were witches. For witches they had to be, since they were apparently uninterested in becoming French. They did not speak much French, traded mainly with Spain, and both the men and the women had much to do with the devil's space, the New World, although for different reasons. Neither church nor state could protect them from the devil if they refused to share its codes of civility. Seventeenth-century France is thus caught up in a narrative of the struggle between black magic and white magic, and on the side of the angels is French culture itself.

J.G. Frazer considered scientists, the third term in his magic-religion-science triad, to be, conceptually, cleaned up and evolved magicians. If the priest begs God's favour, that is, and the magician attempts to compel it, then the scientist has just become more successful at bending God's will to her or his own. And yet, once again, Frazer's structures require complication. The leading scientist of the early modern period, Isaac Newton, for example, was the exponent of an elaborate millenarian theology, and Katz and Popkin have argued that our image of Newton the scientist should be turned around: science for him was just the means to a more important end, that of demonstrating the truth of religion (Katz and Popkin 1999: esp, 'Measuring the Apocalypse: Isaac Newton and the Messiah', 89–106). Equally, Newton the supposed hero of a modern science was intensely involved in practical alchemy.

As a man of science, he was not alone in this. Practical alchemy, the attempt by the application of heat of various kinds to turn base metals into gold by means of the 'philosophers' stone', which would confer both eternal life and unlimited riches, became evidently ill judged only when fire was finally understood to be a chemical process and not a material substance. This depended upon Joseph Priestley's isolation of that part of air in which fire burned most brightly, which he called 'dephlogisticated air', in 1774. With the great French chemist Lavoisier's subsequent renaming of that part of the air 'oxygen', a conceptual transformation had been accomplished. Fire was no longer a substance which could effect changes which were miraculous, the changing of an animal body into a sacrificial victim worthy of God's notice, for example, or the changing of base metals into gold.

The dream of eternal life died hard, and a belief in a literally rejuvenating effect can be found in cosmetics treatises as late as the early nineteenth century (*Lady's Toilette* 1809: esp. 'Of the possibility of growing young again', 293–310). 'Miracle' face creams and 'magical' moisturisers promising anti-ageing effects fly off the shelves to this day (Feinmann 2005). But subsequently, interest in alchemy itself was mainly confined, on the one hand, to philosophical alchemy, of which Carl Jung was perhaps the greatest twentieth-century exponent, and, on the other, to a certain kind of antiquarianism which combined the collector's spirit with a fascination for all things occult. One such collector's activities are detailed here by David Weston.

In the nineteenth century, the University of Glasgow was a hotbed of scientific enquiry, not, as some might imagine, as the result of some national passion for it, but rather, as the university's historians report, because the teaching term lasted only from late October to early April and chair-holders thus had time to do research (Brown and Moss 1996: 93). The progenitor of modern thermodynamics, William Macquorn Rankine, was professor of civil engineering (1855–73), Joseph Lister was the first professor of surgery (1860–69), William Hooker taught at Glasgow (1820–41) before becoming the first director of the Royal Botanic Garden at Kew, and Lord Kelvin held the chair of natural philosophy for more than half a century (1846–99). In the midst of the business and bustle of this world-class scientific materialism, Glasgow's Regius professor of chemistry from 1874 to 1915 became a book collector and historian of science. John Ferguson, appointed to the Regius professorship at the age of thirty-six, while encouraging his students in the more usual kinds of research activities and fostering their careers in important posts throughout Britain, planned perhaps to write a history of chemistry, and certainly acquired one of the most splendid collections anywhere to be found of early printed books and manuscripts treating witchcraft and demonology, Romany language and culture, cosmetics, herbalism, medicine, conjuring and, most importantly, alchemy. The Ferguson Collection, acquired by Glasgow University Library after his death and since augmented, is one of his enduring monuments, the other being the thousand-odd quarto pages of the *Bibliotheca Chemica* (Ferguson 1906), which remains the starting point for any research in the history of chemistry, alchemy and pharmaceutics.

Who was this man? Weston, Keeper of Special Collections for Glasgow University Library and author of the article on Ferguson in the *New Dictionary of National Biography*, suggests that, in the context of the Second City of Empire, surrounded by men (Ferguson never married) who were industrious, who look steely-eyed out of nineteenth-century photographic portraits, and who were, above all, busy, the model most suited to the stance Ferguson took was 'a magus of the North'. Ferguson would have known all about the magoi, Persian priests responsible for royal sacrifices, funeral rites and the interpretation of dreams (Graf 1997: 20). He would have known as well that, for the Greeks, the magus was lumped together with beggars and seers and marginal itinerant priests who operated in the space of magic, a space which was always conceptually and usually literally outside of the polis (Graf 1997: 25). Perhaps, indeed, that was just where Ferguson wished to be.

But in addition to esoteric antiquarianism, alchemy lodged itself in at least one other place following its demise as an experimental activity, and that is in popular culture. *Harry Potter and the Philosopher's Stone*, when it appeared in 1997, was acclaimed as the book that saved reading for children. It was a commercial crossover success on the adult fiction bestseller lists as well, and, along with its five sequels, it has been Britain's most successful popular culture export since the Beatles. The philosopher's stone has certainly conferred eternal fame, if not life, and practically unlimited wealth on at least one person as a result: its author J.K. Rowling, who is now, among those whose wealth is earned, the wealthiest woman in Britain. But its story, that of a boy in training to become a good alchemist, seems variously warpable ('Scottish boy finds his fortune attending a school of witchcraft', read the original summary in the *New York Times* Bestseller List, for example

[Nel 2002: 262]) and its title can lose its alchemical reference (it famously became the 'Sorcerer's Stone' in the U.S. translation) without any discernable change in its effect. So what difference, I ask in my contribution here, 'The Golden Fleece and Harry Potter', does the alchemical patina on a text make? Oddly, alchemy seems to work with texts in just the same way as it is meant to work with matter: looking at three early modern alchemical tales, including that of the great witch and cosmetician, the infanticidal, regicidal barbarian Medea, I find that alchemical structures conform texts to their own purposes. They work like the philosopher's stone to transform and reconfigure a text according to a process which could be called 'magic' just as well as it could be called by its more usual name, 'reception history'. Titles, plots, all of the elements which for us make a text what it is give way to an alchemical process perhaps best described as an aura. Here, we come as close as this volume is going to come to deciding that magic and literature are the same thing. Enchanting, the text is, quite literally, enchanted.

What, then, is the cultural platform upon which the science of alchemy could lately seem so meaningful to our children? Let us return to the Cinema Sable lipbrush, which promised, sorcerer's apprentice-like, to 'draw real cinema lips on you with all the deftness of a Hollywood make-up man', and ask what exactly the status of the word, 'real', would be in the expression, 'real cinema lips'.

'Audiences understood that [it] was fiction but approved its claims to authenticity. They realized it represented an exaggerated and idealized view [...] but thought they were seeing "the real thing"'. This comment could begin to describe the fettering of the eyes which could be persuaded by 'real cinema lips', but, in fact, the phrase in the ellipsis is 'of frontier life', and this comment is found in an analysis of the cultural power of Buffalo Bill Cody's Wild West Show (Kasson 2000: 221). Both the 'real cinema lips' and Buffalo Bill participate in a kind of artful doubleness which Ronald Walters analyses here as 'real magic'. It includes the 'modern magician' Harry Houdini, as well as the 'Prince of Humbug', P.T. Barnum, and, in an analysis which must necessarily imply that the 'real cinema lips' are a bit of a meta-humbug, Walters points out that the failure of either Houdini or Cody to make a successful transition to film marks a sea change in the pact according to which U.S. audiences allowed themselves to be deceived by the products of the culture industry.

It is true that Cody turned to film to 'recapture his youth' (Kasson 2000: 263), and that audiences simply rejected the grey beard and sagging flesh that did not accord with their image of the brave Indian fighter. Indeed, the Glasgow *Herald*'s regular column 'From the Herald Archives' has recently reprinted an announcement from '100 Years Ago' that 'After an interval of several years, Buffalo Bill's Wild West and Congress of Rough Riders are about to pay another visit to Glasgow' ('From the Herald Archives' 2004). The announcement assures Glaswegian readers, forever at risk of being drenched, that there will be a roof over their heads during the show and mentions that 'at night the grounds will be illuminated by electricity', which Cody had been employing in his performances since 1893. But the photograph which accompanies the announcement is clearly not a current one. In 1904 Cody would have been fifty-eight years old; the image, however, is of a slim man with dark hair and beard, hands on hips drawing back his fringed jacket to reveal an enormous square belt buckle fastened over a flat stomach. In his case, it seems that a film made of his aging body was not magical enough.

In the case of Houdini, on the other hand, no one was sure whether his filmed escapes from chains, locks and closed containers, sometimes underwater, were 'real' or were the products of clever editing. Film, that is, was in this case too magical.

That both Houdini and Cody met their match in that most 'modern' of media of the early twentieth century, film, means for Walters that recent attempts to establish the modernity of their showmanship are problematic and that Buffalo Bill's aging physique was not the only reason that his films flopped. Walters prefers instead to emphasise the aesthetic mode which they brought to an end, and to point to a shift in U.S. popular culture which changed the very terms under which mass audiences consumed both reality and its deceptions. There was a past of performance practice, which included curiosity cabinets, Caliostro and the Feejee Mermaid, and it was ending in a medium which was both too magical and not magical enough for it. That this was indeed backward-looking and not a forward-facing modernity finds an odd confirmation in the latest biography of Harry Houdini, which includes as its very beginning a counter-binding spell from the fourth century: '"Let every bond be loosed, every force fail, let all iron be broken, every rope or every strap, let every knot, every chain be opened, and let no one compel me, for I am" – say the Name' (Silverman 1996: unnumbered page).

Freud had read J.G. Frazer closely and appears to have been convinced by the evolutionary magic-religion-science triad. In the third essay of *Totem and Taboo*, 'Animism, Magic and the Omnipotence of Thoughts', he made his most extensive statement on magic. But the situation is complicated: while Freud placed psychoanalysis firmly within the final term, science, of Frazer's evolutionary scheme, the Surrealists of whom Alyce Mahon writes here considered the Freudian unconscious to be a powerful counterweight to scientific determinism and Cartesian rationalism. It was on the side of magic, and opposed both to science and to religion. Small wonder, perhaps, that Freud looked upon the surrealist project with a jaundiced eye, writing to Stefan Zweig in 1938 that 'Until now I was inclined to regard the Surrealists – who seem to have adopted me as their patron saint – as one hundred per cent fools (or let's rather say, as with alcohol, ninety-five per cent)' (Cowles 1959: 271). The event which changed Freud's estimation was his meeting with Salvador Dalí and his viewing of the painting which Dalí had brought along, his 'Narcissus'. If the surrealists thought that Freud was magical, Freud, in his 'magic' essay returned the compliment and thought that it was art which was magical, understood through his technical definition of magic as the properly effective power of thoughts:

> People speak with justice of the 'magic of art' and compare artists to magicians. But the comparison is perhaps more significant than it claims to be. There can be no doubt that art did not begin as art for art's sake. It worked originally in the service of impulses which are for the most part extinct today. And among them we may suspect the presence of many magical purposes (Freud 1950: 90).

Followed as it is by Freud's footnote on the magical efficacy of 'the primitive artists who left behind the carvings and paintings of animals in the French caves', this observation, on the one hand, can guide us through the Surrealists' engagement with magic as Mahon describes it here: they did indeed style themselves as magicians, mediums, and members of a hermetic society; they emphasised the importance of drives and impulses, favoured the extinct and the exotic; and, most importantly, they believed in the initiatory, effective, transformational power of art, as Mahon here shows in her analysis of the Surrealists' first major postwar exhibition, held in the Galerie Maeght in Paris in 1947. The Surrealists indeed had 'purposes', something which was essential to the Freudian notion of magic.

But, on the other hand, the 'magic' of which Freud writes frequently left its latter-day practitioners, his neurotic patients, paralysed with the fear that their evil thoughts might become reality. A wife forbids her husband to have his razors sharpened, curses must not be uttered in a moment of anger lest they result in death, and the neurotic inhibition upon movement of any kind becomes gradually more complete (Freud 1950: 96). We are not far, then, from Baudelaire's great address to his reader, 'Au Lecteur', in which the learned alchemist, 'Satan Trismégistre', vaporises our willpower: 'Et le riche métal de notre volonté/ Est tout vaporisé par ce savant chimiste' (Baudelaire 1964: 33). This vaporisation operates at night. The matter of magic, alchemy, God, the devil, witches, prophets and spells is also a matter of a pillow for our heads and a gentle rocking: 'Sur l'oreiller du mal c'est Satan Trismégiste/ Qui berce longuement notre esprit enchanté'. I began with the question of why it is that magic seems to be a general paradigm for our perceptions and experiences, and carried on with the notion that the 'what' of magic, its definition, being impossible to specify, is best sidestepped in favour of its 'where'. If we could just find it, or so was my fond hope, then we might be able to circumscribe it, to pin down a few points in its field. And here it is: in the ancient world, in Ronald Reagan's cabinet meetings, at the bedside of a dying nun, amongst Buffalo Bill and His Congress of Rough Riders, in the University of Glasgow Department of Special Collections, in the most successful children's literature of our generation.

But perhaps equal in importance to the 'where' of magic is its 'when', and the time of magic is clearly night time, the time given to us for dreams, the haven and refuge of the 24/7 society, our daily holiday from the Enlightenment. As each of us turns the day's dross into nightly gold (or flies off to Satanic orgies in the New World, as the case might be), magic claims us, with its curses and blessings. This is its everywhere, its everyone.

References

'A Good Look'. 2004. *Sunday Times, Style*, p. 3. 15 August.

'Are you made for "Fire and Ice?"' 1952. *Mademoiselle*, pp. 26–27. November.

Bailey, M.J. 1982. *Those Glorious Glamour Years. Classic Hollywood Costume Design of the 1930s*. London: Columbus.

Baudelaire, C. 1964. *Les Fleurs du mal et autres poèmes*. Paris: Garnier-Flammarion.

Brown, A.L. and M. Moss 1996. *The University of Glasgow 1451–1996*. Edinburgh: Edinburgh University Press.

Burns, R. 1990. 'On the late Captain Gorse's Peregrinations Thro' Scotland, Collecting the Antiquities of That Kingdom'. *The Complete Illustrated Poems, Songs & Ballads of Robert Burns*. London: Lomond Books, pp. 230–32.

Burnside, A. 2004. 'A Life as Magical as Her Children's Bestsellers'. *Sunday Times, Ecosse*, p. 10. 15 August.

Chambers Twentieth-Century Dictionary. 1972. Edinburgh: Chambers

Channel 4. http://www.channel4.com/news/home/20020328/Story07.htm (accessed March 2002).

Corson, R. 1972. *Fashions in Makeup from Ancient to Modern Times*. London: Peter Owen.

Cotgrave, R. 1968. *A Dictionarie of the French and English Tongues* (1611). Menston: Scholar Press.

Cowles, F. 1959. *The Case of Salvador Dali*. Boston and Toronto: Little, Brown.

Davis, R.L. 1993. *The Glamour Factory. Inside Hollywood's Big Studio System*. Dallas: Southern Methodist University Press.

Dolen, F.E. 1993. '"Taking the Pencil out of God's Hand": Art, Nature, and the Face-Painting Debate in Early Modern England'. *PMLA* 108: 224–39.

eSharp. http://www.sharp.arts.gla.ac.uk/issue1/wygant.html (accessed November 2005).

Feinmann, J. 2005. 'War on Wrinkles'. *The Independent*, pp. 40–41. 21 June.

Ferguson, J. 1906. *Bibliotheca chemica: A Catalogue of the Alchemical, Chemical and Pharmaceutical Books in the Collection of the Late James Young of Kelly and Durris*. Glasgow: Maclehose.

Frazer, J.G. 1994. *The Golden Bough* (London, 1890, 1900, 1911–15). Abridged R. Fraser. Oxford: Oxford University Press.

Free Dictionary. http://encyclopedia.thefreedictionary.com/Hubal (accessed August 2004).

Freud, S. 1950. *Totem and Taboo. Some Points of Agreement between the Mental Lives of Savages and Neurotics*, trans. J. Strachey. New York and London: W.W. Norton.

'From the *Herald* Archives'. 2004. *Glasgow Herald*, 16 July.

Furetière, A. 1727. *Dictionnaire universel*. La Haye: Husson et al.

Furnas, J.C. 1941. 'Glamour Goes to War'. *Saturday Evening Post*, p.19. 29 November.

Gager, J.G. ed. 1992. *Curse Tablets and Binding Spells from the Ancient World*. New York and Oxford: Oxford University Press.

Gelin, H. 1910. 'Les Noueries d'aiguillette en Poitu'. *Revue des études rabelaisiennes* 8: 122–33.

Gill, A.A. 2004. 'Table Talk: Roka'. *Sunday Times, Style*, pp. 46–47. 15 August.

Graf, F. 1997. *Magic in the Ancient World*. Cambridge, MA and London: Harvard University Press.

'It's the Ad that Sells Cosmetics'. 1952. *Business Week*, pp. 63–69. 13 December.

Kasson, J.S. 2000. *Buffalo Bill's Wild West: Celebrity, Memory, and Popular History*. New York: Hill and Wang.

Katz, D.S. and R.H. Popkin. 1999. *Messianic Revolution. Radical Religious Politics to the End of the Second Millennium*. New York: Hill and Wang.

Kramer (Institoris), H. 2000. *Der Hexenhammer. Malleus Maleficarum*, trans. W. Behringer, G. Jerouschek, and W. Tschacher, ed. G. Jerouschek and W. Behringer. Munich: Deutscher Taschenbuch Verlag.

———. *Malleus maleficarum*. [1497]. [Paris]: Jean Petit.

Kramer, H. and J. Sprenger [sic]. 1971. *The Malleus maleficarum*, ed. M. Summers. New York: Dover.

Lady's Toilette, containing a critical examination of the nature of beauty, and of the causes by which it is impaired. 1809. London: W.H. Wyatt.

Le Gallienne, R. 1916. September. 'On the Use and Abuse of Complexions'. *McClure's Magazine*, p. 31.

Lichtenstein, J. 1987. 'Making Up Representation: The Risks of Femininity'. *Representations* 20: 77–87.

———.1989. *La couleur éloquente*. Paris: Flammarion.

Mukerji, C. 1997. *Territorial Ambitions and the Gardens of Versailles*. Cambridge: Cambridge University Press.

Nel, P. 2002. 'You Say "Jelly", I Say "Jell-O"? Harry Potter and the Transfiguration of Language'. In *The Ivory Tower and Harry Potter. Perspectives on a Literary Phenomenon*, ed. L. Whited, pp. 261–84. Columbia and London: University of Missouri Press.

Oxford English Dictionary. 1989. 2nd ed. Oxford: Clarendon Press

Papageorgiou, V. 1986. *Euripides' Medea and Cosmetics*. Stockholm: Almqvist & Wiksell.

Peiss, K. 1998. *Hope in a Jar. The Making of America's Beauty Culture*. New York: Metropolitan Books.

Roddick, A. 1991. *Body and Soul. Profits with Principles. The Amazing Success Story of Anita Roddick and The Body Shop*. New York: Crown Trade Paperbacks.

Rowling, J.K. 1997. *Harry Potter and the Philosopher's Stone*. London: Bloomsbury.

Scott, W. 1878. *Poetical Works of Sir Walter Scott*. London: Macmillan.

Sierz, A. 2004. 'Can Lloyd Webber's Ghostly "Woman in White" Banish the Spectre of his recent West End Failures?' *Sunday Times, Culture*, pp. 6–7. 15 August.

Silverman, K. 1996. *Houdini!!!: The Career of Erich Weiss*. New York: HarperCollins.

Smith, M. 1978. *Jesus the Magician*. London: Gollanz.
theatre**babel**. 2004. '*Macbeth*, directed and designed by Graham McLaren'. Advertising flyer for the 10th anniversary production, 22–25 September.
Tuke, T. 1616. Against Painting and Tincturing of Women. Wherein the abominable sinnes of Murther and Poysening, Pride and Ambition, Adultery and Witchcraft are set foorth & discovered. Whereunto is added the Picture of a Picture, or, the Character of a Painted Woman. London: Edward Marchant.
Wygant, A. 1994. 'Leo Spitzer's Racine'. *MLN* 109: 632–49.

PART I

MAGIC AND GOD

CHAPTER 1

MAGIC AND THE MILLENNIUM

David S. Katz

'Roughly speaking, all men in Australia are magicians, but not one is a priest': thus, in characteristic blind self-parody, did the great James George Frazer (1854–1941) illustrate the distinction between magic and religion at the core of his great work, *The Golden Bough*, which appeared in various editions between 1890 and 1915. His reference, of course, was to 'the aborigines of Australia, the rudest savages as to whom we possess accurate information', the primitive inhabitants of the Victorian anthropologist's carefully classified dream world. Frazer shared in the belief that 'recent researches into the early history of man have revealed the essential similarity with which, under many superficial differences, the human mind has elaborated its first crude philosophy of life'. Just as Darwin had proved the evolution of the human body from simpler organisms, the new science of anthropology hoped to learn about the evolution of the human mind from proving that the same 'motives have operated widely, perhaps universally, in human society, producing in varied circumstances a variety of institutions, specifically different but generically alike' (Frazer 1994: 12, 52, 53).

Frazer's background was Free Church of Scotland; he was an undergraduate at Trinity College, Cambridge, and once he entered he never left, although his fellowship had to be renewed three times until it was confirmed for life at the age of forty-five. It was there that Frazer became friends with William Robertson Smith (1846–94), the celebrated and often notorious fellow Scotsman who was trying to apply anthropological methods to the study of Scripture. Robertson Smith was also one of the chief editors of the superb ninth edition of the *Encyclopaedia Britannica*, which was being published in alphabetical order during those years. Smith met Frazer by the time they had reached the letter 'T', a fateful letter in the anthropologist's dictionary. Brushing aside Frazer's objections that he really did not know anything about the subjects, Smith assigned him to write the articles on 'Taboo' and 'Totemism'. The first article would be the embryonic draft of *The Golden Bough*; the second, a draft for his two works on totemism, the last of which would inspire Freud to make his own contribution to the field (Frazer 1887; Frazer 1910).[1]

But of course it was Frazer's *Golden Bough* that had the greatest influence on so many aspects of European intellectual life. Robertson Smith died in 1894, and by then Frazer had rejected his mentor's emphasis on religion as a social institution in which the group was the prime unit. Frazer had come to see religion as more of a philosophical system actually devised by individuals and based on supernatural sanctions. This religious system would endure until it was replaced by a better one, science. Robertson Smith had been content to draw his anthropological data only from the world of the Semites; Frazer cast his net much wider, but everything he said was meant to apply to the biblical peoples as well.

Frazer sharpened up his general thesis for the second edition of *The Golden Bough*, published in 1900. The original subtitle of the book, 'a study in comparative religion', was changed to read, 'a study in magic and religion'. Frazer argued that these terms reflected two very different world views. Magic 'assumes that in nature one event follows another necessarily and invariably without the intervention of any spiritual or personal agency. Thus its fundamental conception is identical with that of modern science; underlying the whole system is a faith, implicit but real and firm, in the order and uniformity of nature'. Frazer called 'magic, the bastard sister of science'. So far, so good, but he was aware that any definition of religion, on the other hand, would be fraught with difficulties. He had a stab at it anyway:

> By religion, then, I understand a propitiation or conciliation of powers superior to man which are believed to direct and control the course of nature and of human life ...Thus in so far as religion assumes the world to be directed by conscious agents who may be turned from their purpose by persuasion, it stands in

> fundamental antagonism to magic as well as to science, both of which take for granted that the course of nature is determined, not by the passions and caprice of personal beings, but by the operation of immutable laws acting mechanically.

The magician-scientist is very unlike the priest: 'He supplicates no higher power: he sues the favour of no fickle and wayward being: he abases himself before no awful deity'. Indeed, 'If he claims a sovereignty over nature, it is a constitutional sovereignty rigorously limited in its scope'. Frazer saw mankind as going through definite stages: 'an Age of Religion has thus everywhere, as I venture to surmise, been preceded by an Age of Magic'. Primitive man first tries to compel nature, and when that fails, he begs. This, in turn, is followed by a more efficient kind of compulsion, called science (Frazer 1994: 45, 46, 48, 55). Frazer's distinction between magic and religion was seminal, and according to his most recent biographer is 'Frazer's single most important contribution to the anthropology of religion' (Ackerman 1987: 167).

As Frazer himself admitted, all this waffling about the golden bough was 'little more than a stalking-horse to carry two heavy pack-loads of facts'. Nevertheless, Frazer had an enormous influence on all historians of religion and biblical scholars. His distinction between religion and magic; his notion of the magician being closer to the scientist than to the priest; his use of anthropological data from a wide variety of sources: all this shows Frazer to have been himself a 'stalking-horse' for much later historical works, especially the studies of religion, magic, witchcraft and the occult which were published in the 1970s.

It is especially telling that Frazer should use the notion of a magician-scientist as a kind of constitutional sovereign, as this is the very same image that Isaac Newton employed two centuries before in speaking of God, when devising his famous and enduring synthesis between religion and science. Newton stressed the image of a Deity with absolute power, a God of Dominion, who nevertheless demonstrated his gracious authority by obeying the very laws that He himself had established. The law of gravity was posited by God and would continue to operate as evidence of his constitutional rulership as long as the earth survived, which, incidentally, would not be forever. Among God's promises, and this in the Book of Revelation, was to create 'a new heaven and a new earth: for the first heaven and the first earth were passed away'. Having been promised, God's word becomes law, capable of being relied upon no less than the gravitation of the earth (Katz 2004: ch.3). The way in which God would accomplish this cosmic destruction and millennial rebuilding was certainly *supernatural*, quite literally. But it was also *magical*, in the 'Harry Potter' sense, including wonderful beasts and aerial battles. The millennium was at the centre of a religion made magical, and stretches Frazer's definition beyond the breaking point. As we shall see, 'magic' and 'millennium' are words that (super)naturally go together.

[I]

Despite the natural modern tendency to consider those who still believe in the imminent coming of the Messiah as in some way deviant from the main line of Christian belief, in a very real sense it is precisely these people who have kept faith with the original message of the New Testament. Indeed, anyone who believes that the Bible is the literal word of God can hardly do otherwise than to accept the millenarian concept: the notion that one day soon Jesus Christ will return and establish on this earth a regime with his saints that will endure for one thousand years. Millenarianism is deeply rooted in the New Testament itself. It forms the core of an entire branch of theology, eschatology, concerned with the 'last things'.

Jesus himself spoke of his Second Coming, and gave a good many hints about the characteristics of the apocalypse, the revelation of Christ. In the twenty-fourth chapter of Matthew, Jesus reveals to his disciples that His return will be preceded by false prophets, wars and rumours of war, nation rising against nation, famine, plague, earthquakes, the darkening of the sun and moon, stars falling from heaven, and an undefined 'sign of the Son of man in heaven'. When this appears, 'they shall see the Son of man coming in the clouds of heaven with power and great glory'. A trumpet will sound, and angels will 'gather together his elect from the four winds, from one end of heaven to the other'. These are promises for the future: the exact time of their occurrence is as yet unknown to mankind. As Jesus puts it, 'But of that day and hour knoweth no *man*, no, not the angels of heaven, but my Father only ...Watch therefore: for ye know not what hour your Lord doth come'.

The Revelation of St John the Divine gives further details. He speaks of a 'beast' who rules over mankind for forty-two months, and is granted 'great authority' by Satan. At a certain point, the kings of the whole world gather at 'a place called in the Hebrew tongue Armageddon', followed by natural disasters and ultimately the appearance of the Messiah on a white horse:

> His eyes *were* as a flame of fire, and on his head *were* many crowns; and he had a name written, that no man knew, but he himself. And he *was* clothed with a vesture dipped in blood: and his name is called The Word of God. And the armies *which were* in heaven followed him upon white horses, clothed in fine linen, white and clean. And out of his mouth goeth a sharp sword, that with it he should smite the nations ... And he hath on *his* vesture and on his thigh a name written, KING OF KINGS, AND LORD OF LORDS. [Rev. 20:12–16]

The beast and the false prophet are defeated in battle, and cast 'alive into a lake of fire burning with brimstone', with Satan thrown into a bottomless pit for a thousand years. It is during this millennium that Christ rules on earth with those 'which had not worshipped the beast, neither his image, neither had received *his* mark upon their foreheads, or in their hands; and they lived and reigned with Christ a thousand years'. This is the basis of the idea of a thousand-year rule by Christ and the saints. The text continues to note that this glorious fate is not promised to everyone, 'But the rest of the dead lived not again until the thousand years were finished. This *is* the first resurrection'. After the end of the thousand years, Satan is released for a final battle, again defeated, this time forever, to join the beast and false prophet in the lake of fire. Jesus only then sets up 'a great white throne' for the Last Judgment of all human beings who ever lived, as 'a new heaven and a new earth' descend from above 'for the first heaven and the first earth were passed away'.

Millenarians also take great note of the seventh chapter of the Book of Daniel in the Old Testament, with its image of 'four great beasts came up from the sea, diverse one from another'. They argue over the symbolism of these creatures: a lion, a bear, a leopard, and a ten-horned monster with 'great iron teeth' on whose head sprouted 'another little horn, before whom there were three of the first horns plucked up by the roots: and, behold, in this horn *were* eyes like the eyes of man, and a mouth speaking great things'. Many people thought these four beasts represented the rise and fall of successive great world empires, perhaps Babylon, the Medes or Persians or

Assyrians, Greece, and finally Rome and the Roman Catholic Church. After the fall of this last beast, a Fifth Monarchy of Saints would arise, which would rule the earth with Christ for a thousand years. By the later medieval period, these obscure phrases in the Old and New Testaments had been woven together into a coherent system. In most respects it remains the same in the theology of modern Fundamentalists.

[II]

Even those who believe that historians always find earlier examples expressing what appear to be modern ideas before their time, must surely recognise the rudiments of modern messianism in the work of Joachim of Fiore (c.1132–1202), a twelfth-century Calabrian abbot. Any history of messianic revolution must take account of Joachim. We know little about his early life, although he seems to have served at the Sicilian court at Palermo. At some point he had a religious experience, travelled to the Holy Land, and on his return dedicated himself to the monastic life, eventually in a new and remote monastery of his own at Fiore in Calabria, and it is by the name of his new institution that he is generally known. Yet Joachim was not a rebel: in his will, written two years before his death, he ordered his followers to submit his uncensored works for papal approval, taking care, of course, to leave 'the originals in safekeeping'.[2]

Joachim's prophetic system is compelling not only by its inner logic, but also because of the way in which it foreshadows later theories. Norman Cohn, in his classic book on medieval millenarianism, describes Joachim's system as 'the most influential one known to Europe until the appearance of Marxism' (Cohn 1970: 108). The key concept in Joachim's system was that there was a secret meaning hidden in the Bible which, if properly decoded, would enable mankind to perceive the pattern of history, and thereby both to understand the past and to predict the future. He argued that 'concords' or 'sequences' could be found throughout the Bible, parallels that linked the scriptural texts and demonstrated their web of divine unity. The number twelve, for instance, was exemplified in the twelve patriarchs, the twelve tribes, the twelve apostles, and the future twelve leaders. Noah sent out a raven and a dove after the Flood, a black and a white bird, symbolising the later religious orders of the Dominicans and Franciscans.

Joachim's Bible was the ultimate hypertext, and could be read in three dimensions.

Joachim divided history into three great periods, or dispensations, each of which commences with a period of incubation. The first is the Age of the Father, characterised by married men, the *ordo conjugatorum*, beginning with Adam and Eve and continuing until the arrival of Jesus. The incubation period of this Age extended from Creation until Abraham, when the Jews were given the Law by which the elect of mankind lived until the end of this Old Testament dispensation. The second period is the Age of the Son, symbolised by priests, the *ordo clericorum*, during which time Christians lived under grace and the New Testament dispensation. The incubation period for the Age of the Son began with Elijah, who foreshadows Christ. Since Matthew wrote that there were forty-two generations between Abraham and Jesus, Joachim, applying his theory of concords, concluded that there would be an equal number of generations of about thirty years each between Jesus and the onset of the third age.

The third age is the most dramatic, being the Age of the Holy Spirit, the *ordo monachorum* or *ordo contemplatium*. If Joachim's calculations were right, it would begin about the year 1260 (forty-two generations multiplied by thirty years per generation), which meant he knew he would no longer be around to see it. It would begin after a transition period of about three and a half years (half of seven) during which time the Antichrist would reign, a secular king who would destroy the Christian church. Indeed, Joachim was even more specific: there would be two Antichrists, one in the transition period and another at the time of the Second Coming. He believed that contemporary events seemed to indicate that human history was drawing to a close, and his own candidate for the first Antichrist was Saladin (1138–93), whose Islamic conquests appeared to threaten the security of Christians in Europe.[3] No wonder Joachim was on the alert for Antichrist at 'all times and all places'.

This flowering of this last age still lay in the future, but Joachim thought he knew the main outlines of what would occur. Two new religious orders would arise to convert the entire world to Christianity, the *viri spirituales*, which would also include a third group of hermits. There would be twelve patriarchs whose task it would be to convince the Jews to accept the inevitable rule of Christ on earth. There would be a *novus dux*, a leader in the last days who would show mankind that it was the life of the spirit that was important, that one should free oneself from fixation on trivial mundane things. (Importantly, he would not be the Last Emperor, part of an entirely different mythical tradition.) A holy pope, the *pastor angelicus* (apparently a different figure from the *novus dux*), would come forth to lead the Church. This would be a time of love and joy, and the understanding and knowledge of God would manifest itself in the hearts of everyone. The incubation period of the third age extended from the beginning of monasticism in western Europe, that is, from the lifetime of Saint Benedict (c.480–c.543) to the present, that is, the thirteenth century.

History would come to an end with the Second Coming, and the final stage was not really an age, but an epilogue, the time of the *Ecclesia Spiritualis*, when the entire world would become one enormous monastery. Everyone around the globe would spend time in prayer and meditation, praising God around the clock. This was the Kingdom of the Saints, which would survive for one thousand years, until the Final Judgment and the destruction of the world.

As is readily seen, Joachim of Fiore's scheme was beautiful in its symmetry. Just as he looked for repeating numbers in the scriptures and in history, his notion of three ages was no accident. The Church expounded a three-fold division of history: the time before the Old Testament law, the period of the Old Testament law, and the period under the grace of the New Testament and Jesus Christ. In a sense, Joachim was compelled to divide his chronology into three parts so as to remain in minimal conformity with accepted views, but his main interest was in the new order of the world to come, and in this he had many students who found his interpretation wholly convincing. Significantly, Joachim's views got a sympathetic hearing despite his direct opposition to the prevailing Augustinian view that the Kingdom of God had begun with the Church itself and that there would never be another millennium on earth apart from the one we were already enjoying under Christ.

Joachim managed to remain an accepted and revered figure within the church hierarchy, in large part because he never argued that the Church in any way impeded the progress of divine history or the implementation of God's plan. He also never set an exact time for the onset of the Second Coming: 'I say openly that the time when these things will happen is near', he wrote, 'but God alone knows the day and the hour. Insofar as I can estimate according to the harmony of the concordance, if peace from these evils is granted up to the year 1200, thereafter I will observe the times and the moments in every way so that these things do not happen unexpectedly'(quoted in McGinn 1979: 316).

Yet his ideas were explosive, and they could hardly be controlled. Shortly after Joachim's death, a group of men arose who believed themselves to be the new spiritual order that he had promised would appear at the end of days, in the years before 1260. These were Spiritual Franciscans, some of whom came to be called 'Fraticelli' ('Little Brothers'), members of that religious order who even before the death of St Francis of Assisi in 1226 opposed those who wanted to moderate and liberalise the original simple way of life that was their order's credo. The Spiritual Franciscans were condemned by the pope. For many of them, Joachim's views suited their self-image, and they saw Francis of Assisi as the angel of the sixth seal of the Apocalypse, who in the Joachim's divine plan was to be the harbinger of the Third Age.

It was natural that interest in Joachim of Fiore and his system became more intense as the deadline year of 1260 approached. Gerard of Borgo San Donnino, a Spiritual Franciscan, edited excerpts from Joachim's works, including other prophecies and meditations on the New Testament, and circulated it as *The Everlasting Gospel* in about 1254. Gerard paid for this indiscretion by being incarcerated for life, but Joachim's prophecies now attracted more widespread attention, especially as the implication was that this new *Everlasting Gospel* was meant in the dawning of the Third Age to supersede both the Old and the New Testaments.

The year 1260 was widely expected to be the last, and it was characterised by a penchant for penitential processions of self-flagellating sinners, a fad which began in Italy and spread north to Germany and to her eastern borders. Whether or not this movement was directly connected to Joachimism is still a subject of debate, but the timing was significant. When Jesus Christ failed to appear in that year, the date was shifted to 1290 and to other possible venues, since the calculation after all was based only on a general conception of the length of a generation. The Spiritual Franciscans were gradually eliminated, but the influence of Joachimite ideas and symbols remained widespread, and continued until modern times.

Joachim's plan is still remembered and called into account. Montaigne wrote in the sixteenth century that he was very keen to see with his own eyes 'the book of Joachim, the Calabrian abbot, which predicted all the future popes, their names and appearances'(quoted in McGinn 1979: 29). But that Joachim never went into such detail was precisely the secret of his success, although the basic plan behind Joachim of Fiore's programme has been repeated many times over. The division of world history into three, the notion of different distinct eras or 'dispensations', the concept of an incubation period the last of which will be characterised by worsening conditions: all this is to be found in its entirety in modern fundamentalist theology, which has so much religious and political influence today.

[III]

A very easy way of illustrating the continuity of magical messianic thought is to look at one of the most influential writings concerning the fulfilment of prophecy in modern times, *The Late Great Planet Earth* by Hal Lindsey (b.1929), first published in 1970, with undefined assistance from Carole C. Carlson. Its author and publisher announce on the jacket that the book has sold nearly twenty million copies, making it by far the best-selling book in the messianic tradition, apart from the Bible itself. Lindsey was born in Houston, Texas, and attended the university there. He then worked as a tug-boat captain on the Mississippi River but gave it up in order to study at the Dallas Theological Seminary, a centre for Fundamentalist dispensationalist thought.[4] Lindsey went on to become a leader in the Campus Crusade for Christ, and today serves a church in the Los Angeles area.

Lindsey's book has been so influential because of his clear exposition of the dispensationalist scheme, and his dynamic description of how the Book of Revelation has come to life before our very eyes, beginning with the establishment of the State of Israel in 1948, when 'the prophetic countdown began!' As human history nears its end, a precise pattern of events unfolds, the most critical of which 'is the Jew returning to the Land of Israel after thousands of years of being dispersed. The Jew is the most important sign to this generation'. The Cold War, so important to contemporary Fundamentalism, is portrayed as the fulfilment of the biblical prophecies concerning what will happen immediately before the final End. In more recent books, Lindsey warns the West against becoming too complacent about the permanent demise of the Evil Empire. The culmination of history will be the Battle of Armageddon, in the Jezreel Valley of northern Israel, at which time the damned will be destroyed, the just will be saved, and Christ will reappear on earth and rule for a thousand years.

In general terms, Lindsey said, the seven years preceding Armageddon and the Second Coming of Christ will be a time of wars, disasters and catastrophes. 'The new State of Israel will be plagued by a certain pattern of events that has been clearly forecasted'. One pattern involves Russia, the northern nation prophesied in Ezekiel 38 and 39, which will arise and oppose Israel. Hebrew texts, Bible commentaries and current events show that the prophet must have been referring to Russia. Indeed, the Hebrew word *rosh* (head), which appears in Ezekiel is likely to be a reference to Russia, which is also the 'Gog' so frighteningly described there. Yet although Russia is arming and equipping her allies in the Middle East, who will attack the restored Jewish state, they are doomed to be defeated 'by an act that Israel will acknowledge as being from their God. This will bring many in Israel to believe in their true Messiah'.

Unfortunately, this Middle Eastern conflict is predestined to escalate into the Third World War. Lindsey notes that the establishment of the State of Israel created a necessary but insoluble problem between Jews and Arabs; a local conflict destined to accelerate into the Apocalypse. The Israelis will make a compact with the Antichrist, at that time to be serving as the leader of the European Union, which will allow them to reinstitute biblical holy sacrifice. They will then rebuild the Temple, at which point the Divine Timepiece will begin marking off the final seven years, the times of tribulation. The Dome of the Rock on the Temple Mount, a place holy to Islam, is an obstacle, Lindsey admits, but 'Obstacle or no obstacle, it is certain that the Temple will be rebuilt. Prophecy demands it'. Perhaps an earthquake will clear the site for construction when the 'most important prophetic sign of Jesus Christ's soon coming is before us'. In any case, not long afterwards the Antichrist will take over the entire world, claiming that he and the European Union can bring peace and security. At exactly the half-way point, this new-modelled Roman Emperor will go to Jerusalem and have himself proclaimed God Incarnate, a warning sign to 'the believers of that day that Armageddon is about to begin'. Israelis who recognise Jesus as the messiah will flee and hide themselves in the mountains and canyons of Petra, across the Jordan River in the Hashemite Kingdom.

Lindsey is privy to information about the exact strategic nature of the imminent war against Israel. He knows that Russia will invade Israel simultaneously with the Arab countries, and a map in his book shows the tactical challenge this will pose. Another map details the course of the war, showing the arrival of Russian and European armies in Israel. Ezekiel 38:19 revealed that 'there shall be a great shaking in the land of Israel', accompanied by 'great hailstones, fire, and brimstone'. Lindsey interprets this biblical text as a reference to nuclear war: 'this could be a direct judgment from God, or God could allow the various countries to launch a nuclear exchange of ballistic missiles on each other'. China will also be involved. Vast numbers of peoples and cities will be destroyed. While all of this is going on, Lindsey predicted, about a third of the Jews in Israel will finally see the light and accept Christ, being rewarded by miraculous preservation. 'As the battle of Armageddon reaches its awful climax and it appears that all life will be destroyed on earth – in this very moment Jesus Christ will return and save man from self-extinction'.

The Cold War is thus part of the divine plan, as described in the Bible, that leads to the Battle of Armageddon and the Second Coming. 'We have seen how current events are fitting together simultaneously into the precise pattern of predicted events'. Indeed, 'It's happening. God is putting it all together' in such a way that it will have 'a greater effect on mankind than anything since Genesis 1'.

Hal Lindsey is a classic dispensationalist, accepting the general timeline as revealed by John Nelson Darby (1800–82), the Protestant Irishman who updated Joachim's prophetical philosophy for Victorian Britain. The most supernatural, even magical, aspect of this view is the 'Rapture', which will allow the faithful to be spared the tribulations of the last seven-year period of woe. 'Rapture', as Lindsey defined it, means that 'Someday, a day that only God knows, Jesus Christ is coming to take away all those who believe in Him'. These true believers will be lifted off the earth and kept in Heaven until the final terrible events have passed. No one knows exactly when this will occur, yet 'we believe that according to all the signs, we are in the general time of His coming'. The faithful are advised to live in a sense of general anticipation for the Second Coming of Christ.

Lindsey's book has a number of obvious sub-texts. One is that true believers should keep fast to the dispensationalist interpretation of events, even if many churches tend to treat it as verging on heretical. They should keep track of events in Israel in order to know when the messianic 'countdown' will begin with the rebuilding of the Temple in Jerusalem. A second implied theme is that the United States will lose its leadership of the Western nations unless it accepts Christ. Failure to do so will propel it into the abyss with the rest of the Western nations, overwhelmed by drugs, satanic witchcraft and oriental religions. Indeed, Lindsey warned, it is very possible that 'Drug addicts will run for high political offices and win through the support of young adults' (Lindsey 1970: 45–55, 60, 69, 135–44, 150, 156, 165–74, and generally, chapters 7–10).

Lindsey's more recent work updated some of his prophecies, but nothing significant altered his original predictions of 1970, and this despite the fact that the fall of the Soviet Union was a blow to his scenario, and the Gulf War and the emergence of radical Islamic movements provided interpretative challenges. But Lindsey still believes that an invasion of Israel will take place, driven among other reasons by the necessity to have access to that country's potash resources. The present period before the Rapture has also given him time to consider the implications of his views for Jewish history. In another book, entitled *The Road to Holocaust* (1989), Lindsey has suggested that anti-semitism began with a misreading of Scripture from Origen and Augustine, Church Fathers who either did not understand millenarianism or rejected it outright, and continued. Lindsey makes Luther a chief villain in excluding the Jews from divine history and in formulating the very perversion of Christianity that helped make Nazism possible. He also cites many books about the Holocaust, especially those by Raul Hilberg. As he sees it, the Jews are the ones who will bring about the fulfilment of God's prophecies at the End of Days. They have been in a sort of limbo for centuries, awaiting the moment. With the establishment of Israel, the Jews once again became critical actors in the world historical drama. Those who tried to destroy the saving remnant of the Jews were acting against God's plan for mankind (Lindsey 1972; 1983; 1989; 1995).

Although Hal Lindsey has remained the most well-known and popular of the millenarian interpreters of the Bible and current events, unlike many others, however, he has never tried to create an organised movement around himself or his ideas. He promotes his message not only in inexpensive paperbacks but also in video-tape presentations and prophetic newsletters which help adjust his basic plot-line to the latest news. He has also led tours to Israel, so that believers can see the actual places where the great events will shortly take place. His views, meanwhile, have been taken up by many others, such as Randy Weaver, whose wife and son were killed by FBI agents in the well-publicised stand-off at Ruby Ridge in 1992 (fictionalised in the Hollywood film, 'Arlington Road'). We know that Weaver and his wife were inspired by *The Late Great Planet Earth* to join the survivalist movement and to await the Time of Tribulation in the isolated shelter in Idaho where their tragedy was enacted.

[IV]

Another of Hal Lindsey's admirers is former President Ronald Reagan. Many Christian Fundamentalist views have become so mainstream, that it is not surprising that Reagan took them on board. As Gore Vidal put it, Reagan 'has come among us to dispense not only good news for the usual purposes of election, but Good News. Reagan is nothing so mundane as an American president. Rather, he is here to prepare us for the coming war between the Christ and the Antichrist. A war, to be specific, between the United States and Russia, to take place in Israel'.[5]

When Reagan was hospitalised in the 1960s, he was visited by the Rev. Donn Moomaw, his pastor from Bel Air, California, and by Billy Graham, the famous evangelist. According to Reagan himself,

> We got into a conversation about how many of the prophecies concerning the Second Coming seemed to be having their fulfilment at this particular time. Graham told me how world leaders who are students of the Bible and others who have studied it have come to the same conclusion – that apparently never in history have so many of the prophecies come true in such a relatively short time. After the conversation I asked Donn to send me some more material on prophecy so I could check them out in the Bible for myself.[6]

In 1971, when governor of California, Reagan asked Graham to deliver a spiritual 'State of the State' address to the California legislature, during which he preached to the politicians that the only alternative to Communism was the dispensationalist biblical plan. Reagan asked Graham if Jesus would be here soon. Graham, giving his standard reply, assured him that 'Jesus Christ is at the very door' and could be here any moment ... or not. Reagan also read Lindsey's book *The Late Great Planet Earth* in 1971, and was soon discussing it with many people and recommending that they study it. When Reagan became president, he had Hal Lindsey give a talk to the chief planners in the Pentagon about 'theological' strategies for nuclear war (Halsell 1986: 43, 47).

But the most interesting account of Reagan's views during those years comes from James Mills, at that time president pro tem of the California state senate, and who published a report of their discussion in the *San Diego Magazine* only in August 1985. According to Mills, 'Each and every conversation I've ever had with Ronald Reagan finally became so stirring that recalling it revives in me a degree of internal unrest. This is particularly true of our dialogue about Armageddon'. Mills was seated next to Governor Reagan at a banquet, when a fiery dessert, cherries jubilee, was served. Reagan suddenly began talking about the biblical prophecies, especially those in Ezekiel 38–39, which he thought had best 'foreseen the carnage that would destroy our age'. He insisted that Libya's becoming a Communist state is 'a sign that the day of Armageddon isn't far off'. He also noted that Ezekiel foretold that Israel would come under attack from the ungodly nations, Libya among them. Mills, who had been raised as a Fundamentalist, reminded Reagan that this passage in Ezekiel 38:5 also said that Ethiopia would become an evil power, but Haile Selassie had not become a Communist or joined forces against the Chosen People. (The third country mentioned by Ezekiel is Persia.) Reagan agreed, but insisted that 'there is only one thing left that has to happen. The Reds have to take over Ethiopia'. When Mills expressed his doubts, the President pressed his point, insisting that 'it's inevitable. It is necessary to fulfil the prophecy'. (Mills noted in 1985 that Haile Selassie was indeed deposed by the Communists three years after their conversation.) Reagan was sure that the End of the World was on the horizon, and assured Mills that

> All of the prophecies that had to be fulfilled before Armageddon have come to pass. In the thirty-eighth chapter of Ezekiel it says God will take the children of Israel from among the heathen, where they'd been scattered and will gather them again in the promised land. That has finally come about after 2000 years. For the first time ever, everything is in place for the battle of Armageddon and the Second Coming of Christ.

When Mills replied that, according to Scripture, no man can know when this will happen, Reagan virtually quoted Hal Lindsey in insisting that 'Everything is falling into place. It can't be too long now. Ezekiel says that fire and brimstone will be rained upon the enemies of God's people. That must mean that they'll be destroyed by nuclear weapons. They exist now, and they never did in the past'.

Reagan followed up these general views by giving Mills a strategic picture of the Third World War, based on Lindsey and his book. Gog from the north would lead all the powers of darkness against Israel. Bible scholars have been saying that Gog must be Russia, since there is no other powerful nation north of Israel. The prophecy made no sense before the Russian Revolution, when Russia was a Christian country, but now that Russia is both Communist and atheistic and has set itself against God, 'it fits the description of Gog perfectly'.

Mills was so shaken by what Reagan had told him that he immediately made extensive notes of what had been said, on the basis of which he wrote up his magazine article published in 1985 as a warning to the nation. Mills knew President Reagan fairly well, although he himself was a Democrat, and was convinced that Reagan's foreign and military policies stemmed from his apocalyptic views. Mills even believed that Reagan's fiscal plans were 'in harmony with a literal interpretation of Biblical prophecies. There is no reason to get wrought up about the national debt if God is soon going to foreclose on the whole world'. Mills argued that President Reagan's entire worldview was based on the conception that the end of the United States and Planet Earth was imminent. 'It is only by keeping such considerations in mind that we can appreciate where our President may be coming from and where he possibly may be taking us' (Mills 1985).

Ronald Reagan made no secret of his belief in the coming Apocalypse. Speaking in 1980 on Jim Bakker's 'Praise the Lord' television show, he suggested that 'We may be the generation that sees Armageddon'. He told the televangelist Jerry Falwell that 'I sometimes believe we're heading very fast for Armageddon'. When Reagan became president in 1981, he had Falwell attend a National Security Council meeting and speak about the relevance of the Bible for nuclear war. Falwell apparently also had some influence in drafting the Republican Party planks against abortion and the Equal Rights Amendment. Reagan went into some detail with Thomas Dine, head of the American Israel Public Affairs Committee (AIPAC), a pro-Israel lobby: 'You know, I turn back to your ancient prophets in the Old Testament and the signs foretelling Armageddon, and I find myself wondering if – if we're the generation that's going to see that come about. I don't know if you've noted any of those prophecies lately, but believe me, they certainly describe the times we're going through'.[7]

Reagan's views about the Apocalypse very nearly became an issue in his campaign for re-election in 1984. During the presidential debates with Walter Mondale, the Democratic challenger, Reagan was asked a very pointed question by Marvin Kalb of NBC:

> You've been quoted as saying that you believe deep down that we are heading for some kind of biblical Armageddon. Your Pentagon and your Secretary of Defence have plans for the United States to fight and prevail in a nuclear war. Do you feel that we are now heading, perhaps, for some kind of nuclear Armageddon? And do you feel that this country and the world could survive that kind of calamity?

According to *Time Magazine*, Nancy Reagan gasped, 'Oh, no!' But the President himself answered judiciously that he had talked with various people about the biblical prophecies 'of what would portend the coming of Armageddon', and he knew that a number of contemporary theologians believe that the prophecies are being fulfilled. Nevertheless, he said, 'no one knows whether those prophecies mean that Armageddon is a thousand years away or the day after tomorrow. So I have never seriously warned and said we must plan according to Armageddon'.[8] On national television, Reagan adhered to Billy Graham's party line about the End of the World (Graham 1981).

It is not inconceivable, however, that Reagan's flirtation with the notion of a divinely inspired nuclear holocaust may have been a factor in influencing Gorbachev to call the Iceland summit in October 1986 at very short notice, the purpose of which was to offer complete mutual disarmament. Ironically, perhaps one result of Hal Lindsey's prophecy of a nuclear apocalypse was the end of the Cold War and the consequent elimination of one of the theoretical underpinnings of the dispensationalist Armageddon.

[V]

J.G. Frazer died at the beginning of the Second World War, when Fundamentalism was already thirty years old, if you count from the appearance of twelve pamphlets between 1910 and 1915 under the general heading of *The Fundamentals*, which gave the new movement its name. But the great flowering of American Fundamentalism and its accompanying belief in dispensationalist millenarianism occurred only after the War, as part of the general recovery of religion in the 1950s. We can only guess what Frazer would have made of Hal Lindsey's 'Countdown to Armageddon'.

Frazer had learned from his exhaustive global studies that 'in the most backward state of human society now known to us we find magic thus conspicuously present and religion conspicuously absent'. He thought that one 'of the great achievements of the nineteenth century was to run shafts down into this low mental stratum in many parts of the world, and thus to discover its substantial identity everywhere'. Indeed, he warned,

> We seem to move on a thin crust which may at any moment be rent by the subterranean forces slumbering below. From time to time a hollow murmur underground or a sudden spurt of flame into the air tells of what is going on beneath our feet. Now and then the polite world is startled by a paragraph in a newspaper which tells how in Scotland an image has been found stuck full of pins for the purpose of killing an obnoxious laird or minister, how a woman has been slowly roasted to death as a witch in Ireland, or how a girl has been murdered and chopped up in Russia to make those candles of human tallow by whose light thieves hope to pursue their midnight trade unseen.

Frazer took hope in the fact that the 'shrewder intelligences must in time have come to perceive that magical ceremonies and incantations did not really effect the results which they were designed to produce'. Such people realised that they 'had been pulling at strings to which nothing was attached'. These 'deeper minds may be conceived to have made the great transition from magic to religion':

> Thus religion, beginning as a slight and partial acknowledgment of powers superior to man, tends with the growth of knowledge to deepen into a confession of man's entire and absolute dependence on the divine; his old free bearing is exchanged for an attitude of lowliest prostration before the mysterious powers of the unseen, and his highest virtue is to submit his will to theirs.

Enlightened man finally understood that he was in the thrall of 'a force stronger than any that he could wield, and in obedience to a destiny which he was powerless to control'. The Age of Magic was thus superseded by the Age of Religion (Frazer 1994: 54–56).

Frazer thought that the key moment here was when 'men for the first time recognised their inability to manipulate at pleasure certain natural forces which hitherto they had believed to be completely within their control' (55). But knowledge itself is also a kind of power, of control, and prophecy a particularly powerful kind of supernatural knowledge. The ability to predict the future can turn mortal men into magicians, into prophets, as Frazer's line between magic and religion is hopelessly blurred.

The distance between Joachim of Fiore in the twelfth century and Hal Lindsey eight hundred years later can be measured in many different ways: by language, geography, nationality, religious affiliation, and indeed by almost any criterion known to sociological man. But in at least one very fundamental way, as it were, they are very similar, in that both were driven to comb the Bible in search of divine clues about the course of history and the time of its prophetic conclusion. Both Joachim and Lindsey thought Christ would return in their own lifetimes, or shortly thereafter. They both even like to express themselves in diagrams, which make their millenarian vision easier to grasp.

Another tie which binds Joachim and Lindsey is that both men are primarily theoreticians of messianism, who point the way to the End of the World without feeling the need to take any practical steps to help bring that day closer. Yet despite this caution, both Joachim and Lindsey inspired others to prepare the way for the enthronement of King Jesus. Joachim was responsible for the emergence of the Spiritual Franciscans and the heretical groups that expected Jesus to return about 1260. Hal Lindsey's followers included Randy Weaver, whose survivalism was meant to protect him from the Tribulation, but instead led to the fatal shooting of his wife and teenage son by the FBI.

We need to see people like Joachim of Fiore and Hal Lindsey on the same level plane, and to recognise the persistent existence of a tradition of messianic revolution in the West, stretching from the Middle Ages until our own time. The followers of David Koresh killed at Waco on 19 April 1993, or the conspirators who murdered so many people at Oklahoma City on 19 April 1995 have a clear place on the time line of messianic revolution, in the company of many other groups before them who transformed into practical and violent action the belief that Jesus would soon return in power and in glory. People like Koresh preach a kind of magical millenarian religion, for as Fraser said of the magician-scientists,

> They lure the weary enquirer, the footsore seeker, on through the wilderness of disappointment in the present by their endless promises of the future; they take him up to the top of an exceedingly high mountain and show him, beyond the dark clouds and rolling mists at his feet, a vision of the celestial city, far off, it may be, but radiant with unearthly splendour, bathed in the light of dreams.[9]

Notes

1. Cf. Freud 1913. For Frazer's biography, see Ackerman 1987.
2. On Joachim generally, see Reeves 1969; Reeves 1976; McGinn 1985. Joachim's will is printed in McGinn 1979: 140–41.
3. For Islam and Joachim, see Daniel 1969; Reeves 1974.
4. The term 'Evangelicalism' is sometimes merely a code word for 'Fundamentalism', adopted after the Second World War by those adherents who wished to distance themselves from the ridicule that had been attached to the movement since the Scopes 'monkey trial' of 1925. On Fundamentalism generally, see Cole 1931; Gasper 1963; Sandeen 1970; Barr 1977 Marsden 1980. Generally, see Katz and Popkin 1999.
5. Vidal 1988. Cf. Jones 1985; Linder and Pierard 1991.
6. *Christian Life*, May 1968, quoted in Halsell 1986: 42. The second edition of Halsell is subtitled *The Secret Alliance between Israel and the U.S. Christian Right* (Halsell 1989).
7. Halsell 1986: 46–47. See also Dugger 1984; Pierard 1985; Stockton 1987.
8. Ostling 1984; cf. Raines 1984; Stockton 1987: 242.
9. This wonderful passage has been omitted from Robert Fraser's 'Oxford World's Classics' edition of *The Golden Bough* (Frazer 1994), along with many other gobbets of J.G. Frazer's characteristic purple prose. Robert Fraser's justification for producing a new abridgement of the multi-volume original is that the 'hastily undertaken abridgement of 1922' went 'to extreme lengths not to offend', and left out passages which were 'risky', 'deliciously irreverent' or mere 'speculations', and in any case, most of the actual editing was carried out by Lady Frazer on rather idiosyncratic principles (Frazer 1994: xl–xli). While readers will be grateful, for

example, to have J.G. Frazer's idiotic discussion of the crucifixion back in place, they will dearly miss Frazerian writing at its worst. For the passage quoted above, see Frazer 1922: 64.

References

Ackerman, R. 1987. *J.G. Frazer: His Life and Work*. Cambridge: Cambridge University Press.

Barr, J. 1977. *Fundamentalism*. London: S.C.M. Press.

Cohn, N. 1970. *The Pursuit of the Millennium*, 2nd edn. Oxford: Maurice Temple Smith.

Cole, S.G. 1931. *The History of Fundamentalism*. New York: R.R. Smith.

Daniel, E.R. 1969. 'Apocalyptic Conversion: the Joachite Alternative to the Crusades'. *Traditio* 25: 127–54.

Dugger, R. 1984. 'Reagan's Apocalypse Now'. *Manchester Guardian Weekly*. 6 May (orig. pub. *Washington Post*).

Frazer, J.G. 1887. *Totemism*. Edinburgh: Adam & Charles Black.

———. 1910. *Totemism and Exogamy: A Treatise on Certain Early Forms of Superstition and Society*. London: Macmillan.

———. 1922. *The Golden Bough*. London: Macmillan.

———. 1994. *The Golden Bough* (London, 1890, 1900, 1911–15). Abridged R. Fraser. Oxford: Oxford University Press.

Freud, S. 1913. *Totem und Tabu*. Leipzig and Vienna: Heller.

Gasper, L. 1963. *The Fundamentalist Movement*. The Hague: Mouton.

Graham, B. 1981. *Till Armageddon. A Perspective on Suffering*. Waco, TX: Word Books.

Halsell, G. 1986. *Prophecy and Politics: Militant Evangelists on the Road to Nuclear War*. Westport, CT: Lawrence Hill.

———. 1989. *Prophesy and Politics: The Secret Alliance between Israel and the U.S. Christian Right*, 2nd edn. Westport, CT: Lawrence Hill.

Jones, L. 1985. 'Reagan's Religion'. *Journal of American Culture* 8: 59–70.

Katz, D.S. 2004. *God's Last Words: Reading the English Bible from the Reformation to Fundamentalism*. London and New Haven: Yale University Press.

Katz, D.S. and R.H. Popkin. 1999. *Messianic Revolution. Radical Religious Politics to the End of the Second Millennium*. New York: Hill and Wang.

Linder, R.D. and R.V. Pierard. 1991. 'Ronald Reagan, Civil Religions and the New Religious Right in America'. *Fides et Historia* 23: 57–73.

Lindsey, H. 1970. *The Late Great Planet Earth*. Grand Rapids: Zondervan.

———. 1972. *Satan is Alive and Well on Planet Earth*. Grand Rapids: Zondervan.

———. 1983. *Israel and the Last Days*. Eugene, OR: Harvest House.
———. 1989. *The Road to Holocaust*. New York: Bantam.
———. 1995. *The Final Battle*. Palos Verdes, CA: Western Front.
Marsden, G.M. 1980. *Fundamentalism and American Culture*. Oxford: Oxford University Press.
McGinn, B. 1979. *Visions of the End: Apocalyptic Traditions in the Middle Ages*. New York: Columbia University Press.
———. 1985. *The Calabrian Abbot. Joachim of Fiore in the History of Western Thought*. New York: Macmillan.
Mills, J. 1985. *San Diego Magazine*. August: 140–41.
Ostling, R.N. 1984. 'Armageddon and the End Times'. *Time*. 5 November: 73.
Pierard, R.V. 1985. 'Religion and the 1984 Election Campaign'. *Review of Religious Research* 27: 98–114.
Raines, H. 1984. 'Reagan and Mondale Clash on Arms Control and C.I.A. in Debate on Foreign Policy'. *New York Times*. 22 October, A24.
Reeves, M.E. 1969. *The Influence of Prophecy in the Later Middle Ages. A Study in Joachimism*. Oxford: Clarendon Press.
———. 1974. 'History and Prophecy in Medieval Thought'. *Mediaevalia et Humanistica*, n.s., 5: 51–75.
———. 1976. *Joachim of Fiore and the Prophetic Future*. London: S.P.C.K.
Sandeen, E.R. 1970. *The Roots of Fundamentalism: British and American Millenarianism, 1800–1930*. Chicago: University of Chicago Press.
Stockton, R.R. 1987. 'Christian Zionism: Prophecy and Public Opinion'. *Middle East Journal* 41: 234–53.
Vidal, G. 1988. 'Armageddon'. In *At Home: Essays 1982–1988*. New York: Random House, 98–104.

CHAPTER 2

SHOWMAN OR SHAMAN? THE ACTS OF A BIBLICAL PROPHET

Mark Brummitt

The biblical prophets are exceptional figures who engage in a range of extraordinary activities. Although they are popularly understood to be foretellers, prediction, which is indeed part of their repertoire (1 Samuel 2.27–34 and 4.11), is only one of their many miraculous feats. A thumb through the narrative books of the Bible[1] – Joshua to Kings – will introduce the reader to an anonymous 'man of God' who withered the arm of King Jeroboam with a word (1 Kings 13.4–5), the prophet Elijah who called down fire from the sky (2 Kings 1.9–12), his successor Elisha who purified water with a single throw of salt (2 Kings 2.19–12), and whose bones retained power even after burial (2 Kings 13.20–21). Stories of this kind whilst theologically oriented,[2] remind us that 'miracle-working is part of the essence of the phenomenon [of biblical prophecy]' (Sawyer 1993: 14).[3]

However, the prophets are primarily understood to be spokesmen[4] not wonder-workers: *forth*-tellers rather than *fore*-tellers[5] for their God, 'Yahweh'.[6] Many of their eccentric activities, which are often linked to oracles and sermons, appear to have some communicative function. So it is that Zedekiah dons iron horns and in the presence of the king of Judah declares, 'With these you will gore the Syrians and make an end of them' (1 Kings 22:11), a message which proves to be false; Ahijah tears his cloak into twelve pieces, giving ten to

King Jeroboam with the words, 'Thus says the Lord, the God of Israel, "See, I am about to tear the kingdom from the hand of Solomon and will give you ten tribes"' (1 Kings 11: 29–31); and Elisha instructs King Joash to shoot an arrow, whilst placing his hands on the king and declaring, 'The Lord's arrow of victory, the arrow of victory over Aram! For you shall fight the Arameans in Aphek until you have made an end of them' (2 Kings 13.15–17).

Evidence from other ancient cultures suggests that mimetic practices of this kind were believed to have effect power, altering or influencing the events they signified. This phenomenon, dubbed 'sympathetic magic',[7] was believed by James Frazer to result from 'mistaken conception of the association of ideas' (1994: 32).[8] Biblical scholars prefer to explain the link between prophetic act and coming event in terms of the personal will of Yahweh; thus if the biblical prophecies were at all effective, 'their results were not attained through mysterious impersonal forces alone, but through prayer and personal intercession' (Lindblom 1962: 54). This provides exegetes with a useful rule by which they may distinguish between 'magic' and 'religion', theologically weighted by Wheeler Robinson's aphorism, 'Magic constrains the unseen; religion means surrender to it' (cited in Stacey 1990: 234).[9]

Separated from the practice of magic, the function of prophetic performances, or 'symbolic actions' as they are often called, is explained theologically: although they are comparable in form to magic, they are in fact no more than emphatic or symbolic modes of communication,[10] akin in style to street theatre (Carroll 1986: 297). The prophets themselves are performers, not practitioners, and so submit to the will of a deity-director – 'Yahweh Himself stood behind the prophets and worked through them' (Lindblom 1962: 54) – whose influence is absolute to the point of ventriloquism.

This model, replacing the magical with the theatrical, presumes the existence of knowable, pre-constituted 'will of Yahweh' waiting to be mediated by the messenger-prophet. The following three dramas, all taken from the book of Jeremiah, problematise the simplicity of this paradigm. Superficially, they offer an explanation for the destruction of Jerusalem – the earthly 'seat' of Yahweh, its patron god – in 586 BCE: that the residents of Judah and Jerusalem received ample warning about the consequences of their apostasies through these and other communications. But performance is a complex art in which gesture can either uphold or subvert text or script – a phenomenon explored, if not exploited, by twentieth-century dramatists such as Bertolt Brecht – and such ideas of a simple univocality prove inadequate for the narratives as they now stand.[11]

Breaking the Mould: Jeremiah 19

The formal similarities between a prophetic jar-breaking narrated in Jeremiah 19, and a mainstream theatrical performance, can lead to an easy 'domestication' of the event. The New Revised Standard Version of the Bible (NRSV 1995) reads, 'Thus says the Lord: Go and buy a potter's earthenware jug. Take with you some of the elders of the people and some of the senior priests, and go out to the valley of the son of Hinnom at the entry of the Potsherd Gate, and proclaim there the words that I tell you' (19.1).[12] Then, following 'a rather wordy harangue' (Bright 1965: 133) detailing the wickedness of the inhabitants of Judah, which apparently ranges from apostasy to the burning of children (19.3–9), 'the Lord' continues, 'Then you shall break the jug in the sight of those who go with you, and you shall say to them: Thus says the Lord of hosts; So I will break this people and this city' (19.10–11).

We can readily identify a playwright-director (Yahweh, 'the Lord'), a stage ('the Potsherd Gate' with the Valley of Hinnom, a local tip, as a backcloth), a performer (the addressee, an unnamed prophet, presumably Jeremiah), a theatrical 'prop' (the 'earthenware jug'), and an audience (the 'elders of the people' and 'senior priests', representatives of Jerusalem's ruling classes). The minimalism and stark symbolism suggest that it borders on the experimental, but the clear demarcation between performer (with production team) and spectator, means that it actually challenges few formal expectations of the genre, and would have made little impression upon a Jerusalem avant-garde, had one been around at the time; as an example of theatre, it is reassuringly familiar.

The majority of scholarly interpretations conform to this 'theatricalised' articulation of events, regarding the use of drama as adding nothing but emphasis and urgency to the message. Thus Brueggemann describes the jug-breaking as 'hyperbolic' and 'necessary to penetrate the complacent self-assurance of Judah that "it can't happen here"' (1998: 176), and Lundbom, as a message 'made more vivid by the decanter in Jeremiah's hands' (1999: 842).

This is a simple, one-directional model of communication with the performer active as sender, and the spectator passive as receiver. It is a model that, in the words of theatre theorist Keir Elam, results in one of 'the weakest forms of bourgeois spectacle' (1980: 34). But even though 'many a West End or Broadway comedy has operated successfully on this principle' (Elam 1980: 34), there is good reason to consider more closely the reality of the audience's presumed passivity and to suggest that, in actual fact, the audience is unavoidably involved in the performance. It is, of course, the audience who by laughing at comedy brings about its success, or by keeping silent during tragedy, confirms its gravity. But at a more basic level, it is the audience who buys a ticket and so initiates the whole event.

It is the exchange of money for goods which implies that the passive spectator is nevertheless the exploiter rather than exploited.[13] And it is this aspect of the theatrical 'contract' that the writer-director Bertolt Brecht, aware that the 'commodification' of entertainment demands commercial success, blames for inhibiting innovation (Brecht 1964). Noting a reciprocal relationship, he comments, 'this apparatus (a term he uses to denote all the means of theatrical production: the technological, the promotional, and the entity that owns all these) is conditioned by the society of the day and only accepts what can keep it going in that society', and concludes, 'an innovation will pass if it is calculated to rejuvenate existing society, but not if it is going to change it' (cited in Mueller 1994: 80). This in turn, has a rebound effect, then, with the status quo in the arts, both reflecting and perpetuating a status quo in society. Thus even in the most familiar, so-called 'bourgeois' theatre, the audience, by its very passivity, profoundly implicates itself in the onstage activities.[14]

Although Jeremiah's audience-by-invitation has not paid for the pleasure, and is presumably not expecting to see a crowd-pleasing, door-slamming farce, it is nevertheless interesting to examine its relation to the production, and the nature of its purported passivity. We must immediately recognise that, if we understand the audience to be the recipients of a specially prepared message, the audience has in some way 'initiated' the event insofar as it has been brought about with the audience in mind. Unlike modern commercial theatre, however, which is brought about to please its audience and to edify rather than challenge, the jar-breaking is designed to call the audience's very existence, formed as it is from representatives of the people and clerics of Jerusalem, into question. Thus the spectators might be indicted by the radical message, 'thus I will break this people and this city', preceded by the list of accusations, but as recipients of a message, albeit tailored for them, since we are still working with a basically 'bourgeois' model, they are not fully implicated or involved in the performance.

Little change then has been made to the reading of this narrative in terms of form: as the unidirectional delivery of a message. But the message of 'this people' and 'this city' addressed amid its representatives already blurs the distinction between witnesses and participants. Called to be present at a dramatised destruction of their own existence as a 'people' and 'a city' amid the earthenware shards surrounding the Potsherds Gate, the spectators already seem to be less observers than participants in a microcosmic enactment. If this seems a little forced, it should be pointed out that the NRSV translation cited earlier provides separate verbs in the opening command, 'Thus says the Lord: ... *buy* a potter's earthenware jug. *Take* with you some of the elders of the people and some of the senior priests', (my emphasis) and in doing so adds to the Hebrew text, which has only one verb and reads, literally: 'Go and buy/ get [the Hebrew word *qnh* can mean either] a potter's earthenware jug and some elders of the people and some senior priests ...' The instructions now appear as a list of ingredients for disaster: 'you will need one jug, brown, clay; one score of chief priests; an ounce of elders ...', thus making explicit the integral and representational aspect of the ruling class's presence at this performance. The event begins to look less like a last minute preachment than an inaugural ritual, confirming, if not instigating the coming destruction: an execration, a curse.[15]

Moulding a Message: Jeremiah 18

Jeremiah's pot breaking is preceded by a more familiar narrative in Chapter 18: 'The word that came to Jeremiah from the Lord: "Come, go down to the potter's house, and there I will let you hear my words." So I went ... and there he was working at his wheel. The vessel he was making was spoiled in the potter's hand, and he re-worked it into another vessel, as seemed good to him' (18.1–4). Favoured by evangelicals, it is a narrative which has made its way into songs about the personal miracle of spiritual maturation, '... break me, melt me, mould me, fill me ... ' (*Songs of Fellowship* 1991: 510), despite its communal message and the violent destruction it portends – 'Can I not do with you, O house of Israel, just as the potter has done?'[16]

The pattern of command, 'Come, go down to the potter's house', followed by confirmation, 'So I went down to the potter's house', resembles the recognised form of a symbolic action narrative.[17] On this particular occasion, however, the story riffs upon the genre by positing the prophet as spectator-commentator, rather than as actor-messenger. In effect, the presumed 'theatrical' model of communication is obscured, resulting in its frequent exclusion from the lists of prophetic dramas.[18]

For Brecht, a definition of theatre should be able to withstand the loss of the primacy of the performer, or a qualitative change in the spectator: from passive consumer to active commentator. In fact, motivated by his ambition to break the cycle in which art both reflects and perpetuates the cultural and political status quo, Brecht sought out what would now be called the 'interactive' potential of theatre.[19] Between 1929 and 1932, he collaborated in a series of performances known collectively as the *Lehrstücke*, best translated as 'Learning Plays'. Not only did these plays attempt to challenge the prevailing political system, turning on the tension between the good of the individual with the good of the collective, they also interrogated the prevailing form and production of theatre which, as we have seen, he believed both confirmed and continued the greater system. By exploiting a gap between the 'intentions' inscribed in a performance, and the audience's acceptance of those intentions, Brecht hoped to avoid a 'shallow harmony' between spectator and stage, whilst engineering a form of engagement in which no single point of view could be accepted without testing.

Brecht's first play to earn the title '*Lehrstück*' from the outset was *The Decision* (1930), taking as its theme the 'rational self-sacrifice of an underground agitator' (Brecht 1997: xiv). *The Decision* was not written to be performed for an audience 'outside' the event; rather, it was intended 'exclusively for the instruction of the performers' (Brecht 1997: 347), taking the form of a court of inquiry in which four agitators make their case to the Party, played by a mass chorus. The agitators explain that, while conducting Communist propaganda in China, they were compelled to shoot the youngest comrade. As they justify their deed, they each take it in turn to play the

Young Comrade in a variety of political situations, always grouping 'as three confronting one' (Brecht 1997: 63). Thus, throughout, the line between performer and spectator is in continual motion.

The Decision is sometimes criticised for being little more than an apology for Stalin's purge trials,[20] and a crude call for a literal self-sacrifice to the impersonal needs of the revolution. However, Mueller argues that the theoretical tenets it proposes regarding such matters as the effective cessation of labour, and the use of 'underground' agitation 'are not meant to dominate the play as eternal truths' (1994: 90) and that Brecht, aware of their faulty, time-bound nature, opens them up for discussion. In 'Tips for the rehearsal of *The Decision*', its composer, Hanns Eisler, suggests that, 'it is very important that the singers should not treat the text as self-evident, but should discuss it during rehearsals. Each singer has to be quite clear about the political content of what he is singing, and should criticise it' (Brecht 1997: 346). To confirm the sincerity of these egalitarian intentions, all participants were expected to fill in a questionnaire asking whether they thought the piece was 'politically instructive'.[21] Theatre has become a training ground, or laboratory even, for the new society Brecht believes is about to come into being. And it is the form, not the content, which he considers to be of the greatest significance: the continual breaking and realigning of roles of performer and spectator, the openness to resistance and reinterpretation.

It has been usual for Jeremiah to play king, to be 'Yahweh', but in Chapter 18 he must concede that role and become a spectator. The consequent separation of the prophet from his preferred posture, his mime of the divine, whilst remaining the official 'voice' of the deity, brings about a number of disjunctions that confound 'active' and 'passive' articulations of the event. For example, cut adrift from the *enacted* 'message', the *spoken* message no longer remains part of a simple, unidirectional presentation, but is situated outside the action and so must be configured as a reading of it. The traditionally passive position of the spectator is now taken by the unmistakably active place of the interpreter. Conversely, the traditionally active role of the performer is now fulfilled by the wholly unsuspecting passivity of a potter. But this formal reconfiguration of roles gives rise to a still more profound rift in the figure of Yahweh, resulting in an emerging gap between the words and deeds of the deity.

Initially converging to suggest a simple active-passive hierarchy, word and deed, act and comment, agree that the potter represents Yahweh as 'doer', and the clay, a malleable, 'done to' Israel: 'Can I not do with you, O house of Israel, just as this potter has done, says the Lord?' (18.6). But left unqualified, script and gesture put the deity in a position of irresistible privilege, with no motivation other than whim.[22] However, the descent into a theology of caprice is avoided by the provision of a rationale based on Israel's tendency to rebel, here caricatured by a national confession: 'We will follow out our plans, and each of us will act according to the stubbornness of our evil will' (18.12). Thus Israel's apostasy is cited as licence for Yahweh's crushing and remoulding intervention.

Common wisdom suggests, however, that when a pot in progress spoils or turns out misshapen it is generally the fault of the potter, not the clay. Clay may range from wet to dry, rough to smooth, but never does it ever fight back; it can only respond to the craftsman's skill. Thus this attempt to steer theologically clear from creating a God of caprice suggests, however unintentionally, the dangerous possibility that Yahweh, represented by a not so infallible potter, might be not quite so absolute, lacking the necessary skills of his trade as patron of a city and people.

No longer adequately understood as a simple, 'rhetorical' device, the drama is unable to provide a comforting theodicy for the catastrophic collapse of Jerusalem. It is a place for trying out, a court of enquiry in which key figures implicated in the events of 587 BC can take on different roles, active-passive, representative-interrogative, in an attempt to understand and survive the disaster.

Sartorial Semantics: Jeremiah 13

The drama of Jeremiah 18 is narrated in the first person and from the point of view of the spectator-interpreter. Similarly, Jeremiah 13 tells its story in the first person: 'Thus says the Lord to me' (13.1). Yet the command that follows, '"Go and buy yourself a linen loincloth"', indicates that the prophet is not now the spectator, but once again the actor. In this new role he is directed to '"... put [the linen loincloth] on your loins, but do not dip it in water"' (13.1), an odd request perhaps,[23] but not particularly implausible. However, as they go on, the instructions do begin to stretch credulity, requiring the prophet to, '"take the loincloth that you bought and are wearing, and go now to the Euphrates, and hide it there in the cleft of a rock"' (13.4), then '"after many days"', to '"go now to the Euphrates, and take from there the loincloth that I commanded you to hide there"' (13.6); the whole performance ending with the unremarkable discovery, 'But the loincloth was ruined; it was good for nothing' (13.7*b*).

What seems unlikely about this narrative is the fact that the river Euphrates is about four hundred miles from Jerusalem, a distance, which according to Ezra 7.7–9 takes four months to complete. Jeremiah's two return journeys then would occupy him for more than a year.[24] These logistics alone make the performance seem improbable, but they render it ineffective as a performance, too. How are the citizens to know about the events enacted at the Euphrates? If by report, then the drama is redundant: the prophet could have stayed home and simply told a story. And if it is unlikely that the prophet made the journey himself, it seems even more unlikely that he took an audience with him.

To overcome these problems commentators have suggested that Jeremiah 13 records either a dream, or a vision.[25] The narrative, however, has none of the usual markers to support these suggestions. Instead, it is punctuated throughout by confirmations that the instructions were indeed followed: 'So I bought a loincloth, according to the word of Yhwh and put it on my loins' (13.2), through to, 'So I went to the Euphrates, and dug, and I took the loincloth' (13.7*a*).

An alternative and now preferred suggestion is that the Euphrates would itself have been designated symbolically, either by a river neighbouring Jerusalem,[26] or a marker in its streets (Carroll 1986). Although this makes the presence of spectators entirely plausible, it should be noted that there is in Jeremiah 13, in contrast to Jeremiah 19, no reference of any kind, anywhere, to an audience. Of course, one may simply argue that the narrative infers, requires even, an audience to make sense. But as it stands in this first person account, the actor alone is the spectator of his own drama. The effect of this solipsistic stance, apart from turning the performance into something suspiciously like a private ritual, is a reinforcement of the textuality of the performance: without wanting to retreat from the argument so far, there is one other audience discernable within Jeremiah 13: the reader.

Brecht's better known 'epic theatre', his term for the plays *Mother Courage, The Caucasian Chalk Circle* and so on, was designed to bring about a change in the attitude of the spectator, from passivity to critical productivity, by 'defamiliarising'[27] the norms of social behaviour and exposing them as contingent and historical. The *Lehrstücke* differ by radicalising this stance. Not interested in representing the structures of capitalism, the 'Learning Plays' attempt rather to erase them, breaking down the central contradiction between producer and the means of production in theatre itself by rejecting both a fixed text and an actor-spectator separation.[28] They are practical exercises in which the principles and strategies of a new kind of society are practiced. Jameson likens the form, with its exclusion of the public and rotation of parts, to 'a master class, but one which does not necessarily have a master director present either' (1998: 63), and 'an infinite rehearsal' in which every alternative can be tried out and debated: the text and its performance blur into an 'enlarged discussion' (1998: 64) in which theory and practice are united in performance.

Not including the prophet as his own spectator, the audience of Jeremiah 13 is the reader. As if to acknowledge this, the 'readings' of more than one actively engaged spectator are already embedded in the text. Interpretation begins in 13.9, but rather than a close-fitting, point-for-point account of the event, there follow three rather impressionistic, though not mutually exclusive, commentaries. The first, in 13.9, suggests that the ruined loincloth signifies Yahweh's intended humbling of his people, whereas in 13.10, it represents Judah's self-induced decay, 'This evil people who refuse to hear my words, who stubbornly follow their own will ... shall be like this loincloth, which is good for nothing'; then finally in 3.11, it symbolises the intimacy of the people's relationship with their god, 'For as the loincloth clings to one's loins, so I made the whole house of Judah cling to me'.

Now gathered into the text, the interpretations become part of an event to which subsequent readers are the audience. Since none exhausts the significance of all the elements – no reference is made to the river Euphrates, or the 'after many days', or the burial – and none fits quite perfectly, subsequent readers are goaded into offering their own interpretations. Origen read Jeremiah 13 as an allegory of supersessionism, the loincloth-Israel set aside by God in favour of the Gentile Church (Lundbom 1999: 671); Calvin, as the record of a vision based preachment (Holladay 1986: 396). Moving ahead, twentieth-century commentators, eager to solve its riddles, offer their own 'final' explanations: it is a real event from the career of Jeremiah presenting Yahweh's answer to Judah's pride (Holladay 1986: 398); a 'symbolic gesture' in the Jeremiah tradition forming a replication of the entire national history of Judah (Brueggemann 1998: 127); or most probably a post-exilic parable 'of a prophetic insight of the historical Jeremiah' (McKane 1986: 292). And Jeremiah and his loin-cloth no longer appear as a polished and completed performance with a single, direct message, or a theological ventriloquist act, the prophet perched on the divine right arm, but 'an infinite rehearsal in which every alternative [historical and fictional] can be tried out and debated': a blurring of act and text in never ending discussion.

Conclusion

Prophetic symbolic action narratives are not so easily tamed by the subordination of the magical. Though domesticated by the more rational 'magic of theatre' paradigm, they nevertheless continue to defy theological reduction, always retaining something of the pre-rational and ritualistic, always interrogating as much as delivering theological truisms.

Notes

1. Throughout this chapter, 'Bible' will refer specifically to the Old Testament/ Hebrew Bible, excluding the New Testament.
2. Read as witnesses to the power of God, the rationale given to Moses' miracle of turning his staff into a snake, 'so that they may believe that the Lord ... has appeared to you' (Exodus 4.4–5), is thought to apply here also. This said, Stacey notes, 'The element of caprice that exists in some cases suggests that the actions ought to be disowned as instrumental magic' – one thinks of 2 Kings 2.23–24, for example – but, he continues, 'the fame of the agents ensures that they are accepted as part of the authentic Hebrew tradition' (Stacey 1990: 249).
3. Sawyer continues that this is also true of the 'Writing Prophets', Isaiah, Jeremiah, Ezekiel and so on, in which emphasis is placed upon the prophets' words. The many visions and predictions of these figures indicate that a distinction between the narrative and 'Writing' prophets is 'one of degree, not of kind' (1993: 16).
4. And spokes*women*. Though few have made it into the canon, there were indeed female prophets. Deborah (Judges 4.4) and Huldah (2 Kings 22.14) are among the best known.

5. A now clichéd distinction set out by Lindblom (1962: 1). Blenkinsopp observes some of the difficulties in clearly identifying the work and role of the prophet (1996: 26–30).
6. The divine name, conventionally translated 'the Lord'.
7. A term made popular though not coined by James Frazer to describe a worldview which recognises a sympathy between like things – the 'Law of Similarity' – or things which have been in contact – the 'Law of Contact' (Frazer 1994: 26).
8. Frazer traces an evolution of this 'association of ideas' from magic, 'a spurious system of natural law' (Frazer 1994: 26), through religion, to science. For discussions of Frazer's influence in the study of Old Testament, see Stacey 1990, and Jeffers 1996.
9. This whole approach depends upon a rather crude understanding of magic and a distinction between magic and religion that was assumed predominately in the West. Carroll defies Frazer's evolutionary magic-religion distinction and argues that magic lies at the heartland of all religion. At the same time, Carroll manages to re-inscribe something of Frazer's evolutionism by suggesting that later Yahwist writers transformed the 'primitive magic of early prophecy into the account of the rational activity of the prophet as spokesman of Yahweh' (1979: 59). It is perhaps better to consider texts such as Deuteronomy 18.9–14, the Bible's most explicit ban of magical practices, as less a later denial of earlier, 'primitive' practices, than, an 'ideological consensus to edit out magic and divination as theologically unsound' (Jeffers 1996: xiii). This 'editing out' seems to be a treating-as-foreign, rather than a treating-as-primitive (Jeffers 1996: 259).
10. This still predominant view is summarised by Stacey: 'Prophets normally declaimed oracles, but sometimes, in order to make their message more impressive, they performed dramatic actions to accompany the oracle. The oracles and the dramatic actions pointed to future events, and, once the word had been spoken and the action performed, the fulfilment must inevitably come to pass. The idea of actions inevitably bringing about fulfilment suggests a magical procedure and indeed prophetic drama does have the appearance of magic, but the theology is Yahwist. The prophet is not coercing the deity but submitting to his will' (Stacey 1990: 4).
11. Though the narratives are set before the fall of Jerusalem, the texts were formed by a complex process greatly influenced by the events that followed the disaster.
12. All biblical citations are from the NRSV (1995), unless obviously reconfigured to make a particular point.
13. A characteristic of passive consumption noted by Walter Benjamin (Mueller 1994: 80).
14. With this comforting reciprocity in place, expected and so anticipated by both parties, any disruption can have dire consequences, as witnessed by the several stories of audiences storming

stages and theatres being closed down, events which accompanied the opening of Ibsen's *Ghosts* (1881) for example.

15. There is plenty of evidence of pot breaking as recognised method of execration. See Pritchard 1955: 328, and for a more general discussion on curse tablets, Graff 1997.
16. It is often suggested that the act of remoulding in Jeremiah 18 makes for a more hopeful representation than the pot-breaking in Jeremiah 19.
17. A genre recognised to have a loose form (Fohrer 1965; Stacey 1990). Confirmation is a recognised element that is not always present. It is, for example, absent from the otherwise exemplary Jeremiah 19.
18. Fohrer (1965), who delineated the form, remains unpersuaded by the fact that the narrative otherwise fits his template.
19. Instead of 'sharing an experience' (Brecht 1964: 39), he argues, the spectator must come to grips with things. He hoped to challenge the ideological function of theatre with a radically new kind of play, which would in turn impact upon the economic base of theatre, and as part of a 'knock-on' effect, the whole social order. The direction of this evolutionary push, from ideological superstructure to the economic base, runs counter to the Marxist idea of the primacy of economic forces and relations as it is usually understood, and it now seems naïve to believe that the capitalist system could be brought down by cabaret. But these were optimistic days for German Marxists: Communist choirs were a growing force, relations with the USSR were good, and it would have been easy to believe that a new society was just around the corner.
20. And to be fair, the purge trials had not, at this time, begun.
21. Question three, for example, asks, 'To which lessons embodied in *The Decision* do you object politically?' (Brecht 1997: 346).
22. Or maybe the sensual pleasure of clay between divine fingers?
23. Less odd, however, than the command in Jeremiah 27.2: 'Make yourself a yoke of straps and bars, and put them on your neck'.
24. Placing this performance in competition with the protracted 'epics' of Ezekiel.
25. So thought Calvin (Holladay 1986: 396).
26. The usual suggestion being that there was a Palestinian river or place called Perath a few miles north of Jerusalem (Bright 1965: 96).
27. The function of the *Verfremdungseffekt*, often translated 'the alienation effect'.
28. Brecht recognises that the audience's role as passive consumer is that of exploiter. However, he also recognises that the audience is exploited by the system of bourgeois theatre, the 'helper' of that society.

References

Blenkinsopp, J. 1996. *A History of Prophecy in Israel.* Louisville: Westminster John Knox Press.

Brecht, B. 1964. *Brecht on Theatre: The Development of and Aesthetic,* ed. and trans. J. Willett. London: Methuen.

———. 1997. *Collected Plays: Three,* ed. J. Willett. London: Methuen.

Bright, J. 1965. *Jeremiah.* New York: Doubleday.

Brueggemann, W. 1998. *A Commentary on Jeremiah: Exile and Homecoming.* Grand Rapids: Eerdmans.

Carroll, R.P. 1979. *When Prophecy Failed.* London: SCM.

———. 1986. *Jeremiah.* London: SCM.

Elam, K. 1980. *The Semiotics of Theatre and Drama.* London: Routledge.

Fohrer, G. 1965. *Introduction to the Old Testament,* trans. David Green (1968). London: SPCK.

Frazer, J.G. 1994. *The Golden Bough: A New Abridgement.* Oxford: Oxford University Press.

Graff, F. 1997. *Magic in the Ancient World,* trans. F. Philip. Cambridge: Harvard University Press.

Holladay, W.L. 1986. *Jeremiah 1.* Philadelphia: Fortress Press.

Jameson, F. 1998. *Brecht and Method.* London: Verso.

Jeffers, A. 1996. *Magic and Divination in Ancient Palestine and Syria.* Leiden: Brill.

Lindblom, J. 1962. *Prophecy in Ancient Israel.* Oxford: Blackwell.

Lundbom, J.R. 1999. *Jeremiah 1–20.* New York: Doubleday.

McKane, W. 1986. *Jeremiah I–XXV.* Edinburgh: T&T Clark.

Mueller, R. 1994. 'Learning for a New Society: the *Lehrstücke*'. In *The Cambridge Companion to Brecht,* eds. P. Thompson and G. Sacks, pp. 79–95. Cambridge: Cambridge University Press.

New Revised Standard Version of the Bible, NRSV. 1995. Oxford: Oxford University Press.

Pritchard, J.B. 1955. *Ancient Near Eastern Texts Relating to the Old Testament.* Princeton: Princeton University Press.

Robinson, H.W. 1927. 'Prophetic Symbolism'. In *Old Testament Essays,* ed. D.C. Simpson. London: Charles Griffin.

Sawyer, J.F.A. 1993. *Prophecy and the Biblical Prophets.* Oxford: Oxford University Press.

Songs of Fellowship, SOF. 1991. Eastbourne: Kingsway Music.

Stacey, W.D. 1990. *Prophetic Drama in the Old Testament.* London: Epworth Press.

CHAPTER 3

CURSE TABLETS AND BINDING SPELLS IN THE GRECO-ROMAN WORLD

John G. Gager

Imagine this. You are walking the dusty pathways of an ancient Galilean village. As you pass through a narrow alley you chance to overhear a charismatic figure addressing a small band of his followers. 'Whatever you bind (dêsês) on earth will be bound in heaven and whatever you loose (lusês) on earth will be loosed in heaven'.

These words appear twice in the gospel attributed to Matthew (16.19 and 18.18), and only in Matthew. The 'speaker' is Jesus of Nazareth. I have no interest here in seeking to determine whether Jesus ever spoke these words. My sole concern is with an altogether different matter: How would a reasonably well-travelled person in the eastern Mediterranean, overhearing this promise of special power, have understood these words? What cultural patterns would have come to mind as our passer-by sought to interpret the key terms: binding (dein) and loosing (luein), heaven (ouranos) and earth (gê)?

Scholars of the New Testament have offered numerous answers to these questions. In his 1985 article, Richard Hiers surveyed these results. They include a range of options: the authority to absolve individuals from vows, to determine forbidden and permitted actions, to exclude persons from religious communities, and to grant or withhold forgiveness of sins. But as Hiers and others have pointed out, most of these solutions rely on much later evidence, most of it drawn from Rabbinic Judaism. And while later church authorities did claim the power to ban individuals and to forgive sins, based on these passages, there is little to point in this direction during earlier stages of the Jesus movement. Far more interesting, and convincing, is Hiers's own take on these issues. As he puts it, 'It is surprising that none of these interpretations attends to passages where terms for binding and loosing appear in intertestamental Jewish sources or elsewhere in the NT'. Based on his own survey of Jewish intertestamental texts (e.g., 1 Enoch, Jubilees and the Testaments of the 12 Patriarchs), Hiers concludes that the terms 'binding' and 'loosing' refer predominantly 'to the binding of Satan or satanic beings (e.g., demons) and the loosing of such beings or their erstwhile victims' (1985: 235). And while he is reluctant to attribute the sayings of Matthew 16 and 18 to Jesus, he does situate them within a specific and well-known sphere of activity characteristic of the early Jesus movement, namely, the exorcism of demons. Matthew may have reinterpreted them in the direction of providing 'plenary authority for the church's leaders to resolve whatever problems or issues might arise' (Hiers 1985: 250), but in their earlier, pre-Matthean settings, they guaranteed to members of the Jesus movement the power to bind and loose demons.

Building on and extending Hiers's analysis, this chapter draws attention to another body of ancient texts, many of them not only contemporaneous with the early Jesus movement but even more widely distributed than Jewish intertestamental literature. These texts, not mentioned by Hiers and largely ignored by students of religions in the Greco-Roman world, are known under the general rubric of 'curse tablets' and 'binding spells'.[1] More precisely, they are commonly referred to, even in ancient texts, as *katadesmoi* (Greek), and *defixiones* (Latin). The thesis of this chapter thus runs as follows: An ordinary passer-by, overhearing this promise of power, would have located the language of 'binding' and 'loosing' in the familiar realm of *katadesmoi* and *defixiones*.

But first, some basic data on these ancient metal tablets. More than 1600 have been recovered from a variety of sites, some from carefully excavated archaeological sites and many more from museums and private collectors. For the most part, the tablets consist of flat, thin sheets of lead alloy. All are inscribed with various kinds of writing: standard ancient languages; crude sketches of human, animal and other forms;

special designs in the shape of triangles, narrow columns and wing-shapes, usually formed by letters of the Greek or Latin alphabets; *charakteres* or non-standard letter-shapes, mostly derived from the Greek alphabet; garbled versions of terms and proper names originating ultimately from other ancient languages (e.g., Hebrew, Persian, Egyptian); reverse or scrambled proper names; and unrecognisable 'words' commonly referred to as *voces magicae*.[2] One striking feature of these various forms of speech is their remarkable persistence over time and space. In short, many of these terms and figures show up in places as geographically diverse as Syria, Egypt, Carthage (North Africa), Rome, Greece, Spain and Britain.

The destination of these tablets, once inscribed and paid for, was two-fold: first, they were rolled up or folded and frequently pierced with a nail; and second, they were deposited in a variety of special, and recurrent locations – springs, wells, cemeteries, sanctuaries, stadiums and the residence of the intended target or victim. Some sites appear to have been heavily favoured and have yielded large numbers of tablets: two hundred or more from a burial site at Amathous on Cyprus; some 130 from the spring dedicated to Sulis Minerva at Bath (England); and a large number from the Agora in Athens. What these large caches reveal immediately is the public character and wide popularity of the practice.

The extraordinary popularity of these innocent looking tablets receives further confirmation, if needed, once again, in their remarkable geographical, chronological and cultural distribution. They range throughout the entire Mediterranean region, from Egypt and Palestine through Asia Minor, Greece and southern Russia, extending to Germany, Gaul, Britain and Spain, and reaching across the full breadth of North Africa. As to languages, they use Coptic, Demotic, Greek, Hebrew, Aramaic, Latin and, of course, the non-standard languages mentioned above. In other words, this linguistic versatility attests to the profound multilingualism of the ancient Mediterranean. Culturally, or perhaps, religiously, the vast majority belongs to the amorphous category of 'paganism'. More precisely, they invoke a wide range of deities and lesser spirits from various cultural zones of the time. On the other hand, there are numerous tablets of an unmistakably Jewish origin and a few that are Christian. But even in the so-called pagan tablets, one finds quite regular invocations derived from Judaism, e.g., IAO, Adonai, Moses and others. And among the later tablets, names like Jesus and Mary begin to appear.

Indeed, if one were to define and describe a truly pan-Mediterranean cultural form, *defixiones* and *katadesmoi* would rank at the very top of the list, right along with public baths and hippodromes.

Dates

The earliest surviving tablets date from around five hundred BC and the very latest, probably a Christian text, can be placed almost a thousand years later, around five hundred AD. While there can be no doubt that ritual forms of cursing and binding existed long before our earliest tablets, their disappearance after five hundred AD remains something of a mystery. In any case, the cumulative evidence points to one inescapable conclusion: curse tablets and binding spells present us with a universal feature of Mediterranean culture in antiquity. We may even call it the ancient world's 'dirty little secret', for the reason that until recent times, they have received so little attention.

The Literary Evidence

Apart from the 1600 or so surviving tablets, our knowledge of ancient *defixiones* derives from two additional sources: numerous references to them in literary texts and handbooks, and collections of recipes ('grimoires') used by professionals in preparing tablets for their paying customers. A number of these handbooks have survived, some as mere fragments, others as virtually complete documents on papyrus (Betz 1986). Beyond these Greek papyri, there exist translations of similar handbooks into Syriac and Arabic, the most notable of which is the *Picatrix* (known in Arabic as the *Ghayat al-Hakim*).[3] Along with recipes for various spells and charms, these collections contain prescriptions for curse tablets and binding spells. What is more, as we shall see presently, a number of actual tablets stem from these recipes.

It has now become quite clear that these handbooks travelled widely in the Mediterranean world, no doubt in the luggage of professionals who themselves circulated freely, especially during the period of the Roman empire. This wide circulation surely explains the remarkably similar forms and language of spells across wide stretches of time and space.

Beyond this, the numerous literary references require the conclusion that these tablets, and their purveyors, marked a common feature of the cultural landscape. Thus there is no reason whatsoever to doubt the word of the younger Pliny (70s of the first century AD), himself no fan of magic: 'There is no one who does not fear to be spellbound by curse tablets' (Pliny, *Natural History* 28.4.19).

Like all other aspects of culture, magic has a history. Thus it would be a serious mistake to assume that these tablets failed to undergo changes throughout their thousand year history or that local variations were lacking. Tablets of Jewish provenance regularly include citations from the Hebrew scriptures. The earliest examples from Greece and Cyprus are extraordinarily simple: many list only the names of those placed under the curse, with no verb and no names of deities or spirits. Others move to a slightly more elaborate form and read 'I bind so and so' or 'I bind so and so to Hermes' (or some other subterranean deity). But these early forms, unlike those from later periods contain no designs or special languages (e.g., *charakteres*), no lengthy invocations and no specification of the occasion or immediate purpose. In the case of these early examples, it is difficult to avoid the assumption that the deposition of the tablets must have been accompanied by spoken formulas of one kind or another. Indeed, at a more general level, it seems wise to suppose that these earliest tablets represent not so much a radical innovation in the very idea of cursing but rather a moment in time of cultural history characterised by a transition from oral to written forms.

Overall, these earliest tablets, when it is possible to discern their purposes, appear to focus on disputes between power groups (military, political, theatrical) and judicial matters. Often they involve persons fully documented by other means, especially public documents and inscriptions. At a late date, love/sex spells, some for attraction, others for separation, will become ubiquitous. Here, in line with our earlier observation about the tendency of the tablets to move from oral to written forms, the inscriptions become increasingly, sometimes even wildly complex. The elements include elaborate invocations of deities, *daimones*, and spirits of the dead; lengthy lists of body parts to be bound (Gordon 1999b); highly intricate designs; *voces magicae* of every sort; and so on. The overall tone of these later tablets moves towards what we might call a universal syncretism, with Greek, Egyptian, Jewish and other Near Eastern terms generously intermingled. Not uncommonly, the tablet will be deposited with other items, among them a strand of hair from the intended target and, especially in the case of erotic spells, wax and ceramic figurines representing the target of the spell and sometimes even the client. All of these features point not just to the extraordinary internationalisation of the *defixio* industry, but also to its growing professionalisation, with the attendant consequences of complexity and wide dissemination. Whereas we may assume that the early specialists were local figures, many of them women, in the later period, particularly from the second century AD onward, the predominant types were learned men who travelled widely in the cosmopolitan atmosphere of the later Roman empire.

The Occasions

Faraone (1991) has made the case that clients resorted to *defixiones* in agonistic settings involving intense competition and uncertain outcomes. In such circumstances, participants regularly sought special advantages in an effort to increase their chances of success. But it would be a serious error, though one often committed, to suppose that these spells constituted the only means of dealing with the inevitable anxieties of competition and unpredictable outcomes. Just as modern athletes regularly dress in a rigidly fixed manner, eat the same pre-match meal and utter fixed phrases, they also train regularly, polish their techniques and seek guidance from their coaches. From the athletes' perspective, all of these preparations are necessary and none is dispensable; taken together their aim is to guarantee success in competition. So in antiquity, the commissioning of a binding spell was but one among other precautions taken to gain the prize.

Public Competitions

Defixiones have surfaced in a wide variety of settings involving public competitions, including professional wrestling, footraces and charioteering. They were used by rival actors and choruses who were required to contend against each other for roles in theatrical productions. One tablet, from Greece and probably dating to the fourth or third centuries BC, reads as follows: 'All the choral directors and assistant choral directors with Theagenes, both the directors and the assistant directors' (Gager 1992: 49, no. 1).[4]

Like other early tablets (fifth to first centuries AD), this one mentions no verb of binding and makes no mention of any deity, daimon or spirit, though it does cite one person by name. By contrast, a tablet from the hippodrome of Apamea in Syria, dating to the sixth century AD, illustrates the dramatic changes that had taken place in the *defixio* industry, starting in the first century and accelerating toward the sixth. The spell begins with two full and two partial lines of *charakteres*:

> ....
>
> ....
>
> Most holy Lord, *charakteres*, tie up, bind the feet, the hands, the sinews, the eyes, the knees, the courage, the leaps, the whip (?), the victory and the crowning of Porphuras and Hapsicrates, who are in middle left (lane), as well as his co-drivers of the Blue colours in the stable of Eugenios. From this very hour, from today, may they not eat or drink or sleep; instead, from the (starting) gates may they see daimones (of those) who have died prematurely, spirits (of those) who have died violently and the fire of Hephaestus ... In the hippodrome at the moment they are about to compete may they not squeeze over, may they not collide, may they not extend (their lead?), may they not force (us?) out, may they not overtake, may they not break off, for the entire day when they are about to race. May they be broken, may they be dragged, may they be destroyed. By Topos[5] and by Zablas[6]. Now, now, quickly, quickly.[7]

Such spells from hippodromes throughout the Mediterranean region became extremely popular in the early centuries of the Roman empire. Most share characteristic features of the Apamean tablet: the use of lists ('the feet, the hands...'); the naming of specific persons, in this case the rival charioteers, Porphuras and Hapsicrates; the mention of the team or faction (here the Blues) to which the targeted individuals belonged; the invocation of spirits of dead persons as agents of the spell, especially those who had died prematurely or by violence; the use of technical vocabulary, in this case terms associated with the world of professional racing; and the use of 'mysterious' terms, here Topos and Zablas. Just how widespread, and how potent, such curses were in the hippodrome is illustrated by a report concerning a famous charioteer of the fifth century AD, 'Thomas' by name, whose jealous rivals accused him of garnering his victories through magic and witchcraft (no doubt meaning binding spells) rather than by skill alone (Hodgkin 1886: 226).

Lawsuits

Studies of ancient lawsuits and trials expand at great length on the various steps taken in preparing to defend oneself in court: gathering evidence, producing witnesses, hiring a gifted speech-writer, bribing judges/jurors and so on. Yet not one of these studies even hints at what must have been another standard step in the process: the commissioning of a binding spell against one's accusers. While this practice appears to have been especially common in the law courts of Athens, there is ample evidence of its use throughout the Mediterranean world as early as the sixth century BC. Literary sources reinforce the picture. Cicero records the case of a Roman lawyer who lost track of which case he was pleading in mid-speech, and blamed his memory lapse on spells and curses (*Brutus* 217). Later, in the second century AD, the physician-philosopher Galen, while indicating his own disdain for the power of spells, reports that others made the following claim: 'I will bind my opponents so that they will be incapable of saying anything during the trial' ('On the Power of All Drugs', Galen 1965: XII, 251).

One especially poignant example of these judicial spells consists of two tablets from Aquitaine in Gaul (modern France):

> I denounce the persons written below, Lentinus and Tasgillus, in order that they may depart from here for Pluto and Persephone. Just as this puppy harmed no one, so (may they harm no one) and may they not be able to win this suit. Just as the mother of this puppy cannot defend it, so may their lawyers be unable to defend them…

In other cases, especially the earlier ones (fourth to second centuries BC), the tablets simply list the names of those to be bound, often scrambling the spelling of the names in various ways. Later examples, in line with the general trend for all spells and curses, become much more elaborate, invoking a wide range of deities, spirits and daimones. But overall, the goal of these litigious spells remains constant: to render one's accusers incapable of speaking against the defendant, i.e., the client, in court. Quite literally, the client aimed to render the accuser 'tongue-tied'. As one tablet from Greece, dating to the fourth century BC, states, 'And just as this lead is worthless and cold, so let that man (Pherenikos) and his property be worthless and cold and those who are with him who have spoken and counselled concerning me' (Gager 1992: 127f. no. 40).[8]

Before leaving the category of judicial spells, it is worth noting similar curses directed at the other group of famous public speakers, the rhetors. Here, too, we find that rival rhetors sought to undermine each others' performances through binding spells. One such incident concerns the famous fourth century rhetor, Libanius. When migraine headaches rendered him literally speechless and doctors proved unable to effect a cure, Libanius finally received word in a dream that he had been targeted by a curse ritual. In the end, his students discovered a dead chameleon in the lecture hall, with one leg covering its mouth. At that point the illness disappeared and his career resumed. But in a fit of pique, the professor chided his students for not taking reports of curses seriously:

> When you believe that a charioteer or a horse has been hobbled in this manner [i.e., by a spell], everything is in an uproar. But I am treated with indifference when the same thing happens to me (*Oration* 1.36).

Business Rivalries

Competition in antiquity was not limited, any more than it is today, to the hippodrome or the lecture hall. Small businesses frequently scrambled against each other for clients in the public marketplace. Hesiod offers the following portrait in his *Works and Days* (ll. 20–25):

> Rivalry stirs even the shiftless to toil ... This sort of competition is useful for mortals – one potter is envious of another, one craftsman of another, one beggar of another, one singer of another.

Much later, Pliny the Elder (d. 79 AD), in his *Natural History* (28.4.19) reports that 'many people [probably rival potters] believe that the products of potters' shops can be crushed by these means [i.e., curse spells]'. Curse tablets of this sort cover a wide variety of businesses and their owners: pubs, brothels, wood shops, doctors, metal workers and, of course, charioteers.

In this category, I cite but one example, from Nomentum (Italy), dating to the first century BC or AD. While the tablet mentions Malcius's trade and income, and thus belongs to the category of business spells, its particular interest lies in the extensive list of body parts associated with, or rather embodying, the two targets, Malcius (male) and Rufa (female):

> Malcius (the son or servant) of Nicona: (his) eyes, hands, fingers, arms, nails, hair, head, feet, thigh, belly, buttocks, navel, chest,

> nipples, neck, mouth, cheeks, teeth, lips, chin, eyes, forehead, eyebrows, shoulder-blades, shoulders, sinews, bones ... belly ... penis, shin: in these tablets I bind (his) business profits and health ... (Gager 1992: 172, no. 80).[9]

Richard Gordon (1996b) has written extensively on this tablet, as well as on the broader question of lists, a common feature in numerous tablets. While observing that the deployment of lists was widespread in other aspects of ancient Mediterranean culture (law courts, the military, primary and advanced education, fiscal administration and athletic contests among others), Gordon holds that lists are displayed in harmful spells for quite specific reasons. First, 'the list belongs to the fabric of things' (Gordon 1999b: 246). And it does so in a two-fold manner: as a culturally familiar form of speech, now transferred into a socially illegitimate zone, and as an embodiment of the designated target. By naming the parts of their bodies, the client seeks to connect with the target. And by listing specific body parts, and aligning them in a particular sequence, the intended victim is reduced to a symbolically effective minimum. Malcius *is* his eyes; Rufa, her genitals.

Love/Sex

In his hilarious send-up of popular beliefs about the effectiveness of spells, Lucian of Samosata recites the following tale:

> Finally, the Hyperborean moulded a little Cupid of clay and said to it, 'Go fetch Chrysis'. Off flew the figure and a few seconds later Chrysis appeared knocking at the door (Lucian, *Lover of Lies*, 14).

Surely among all human conditions, matters of sex and love must rank at the very top of any scale that would measure uncertainty, risk and anxiety. Not surprisingly, binding spells on tablets emerge as a prominent feature in Greco-Roman culture. Nonetheless, few actual examples survive from the earlier period (sixth to first centuries BC); only in the time of the Roman empire do they become common.[10]

Before turning to one striking example, it may prove helpful to draw attention to important studies of love/sex spells in the Greco-Roman world. The first is an essay by the late John Winkler, 'The Constraints of Eros' (Winkler 1991). Winkler proposes two conclusions that merit attention. One holds that the explicit goal sought by most attraction spells (agogai) is that the (mostly) female targets should be overcome with insomnia and unquenchable burning, with the result that, like Chrysis above, they will be brought to the ardent suitor's bed. Here, Winkler notes, love (eros) is represented as a powerful illness. But the real burning, he insists, lies not in the target/victim but rather in the client/suitor: '[T]he intended victim is in all likelihood sleeping peacefully, blissfully ignorant of what the love-stricken lunatic is doing on his roof ... suffering in that unfortunate state known as eros' (ibid.: 225). His other conclusion is that these attraction spells open an unanticipated window onto a hidden dimension of ancient culture. 'Agogai, viewed from this angle, are a backhanded tribute to the potential power of female sexuality...' (ibid.: 233).

In his recent essay, 'Agents and Victim. Constructions of Gender and Desire in Ancient Greek Love Magic', Christopher Faraone distinguishes between two key Greek terms for love, *philia* and *eros*, and observes that *philia* is reserved for spells 'generally used by women to maintain or increase affection in men', and that 'describe a reciprocal relationship based on mutual affection' (Faraone 2002: 401). *Eros*, on the other hand, appears primarily in spells deployed by men 'to begin a new relationship by forcing the victim (usually but not always a woman) from their homes and into the arms of the people who perform the spell' (ibid.: 404). In short, the terms chosen and the overall character of the two types of spells follow characteristic gender distinctions in Greek culture generally. In line with this observation, but against a long line of modern scholarship, where females are seen as 'naturally wild and promiscuous', the evidence of love spells themselves suggests a quite different model, one in which it is the women who must be made to burn because they 'are by nature self-controlled and sedate ...' (ibid.: 416). Men, by contrast, are the ones who are 'naturally wild, passionate and difficult to control' (ibid.: 416).

One text reads as follows:[11]

> I entrust this binding spell (*katadesmos*) to you, gods of the underworld, Pluto and Kore Persephone Ereschigal and Adonis and BARBARITHA and Hermes of the underworld and Thooth PHOKENSEPSEU EREKTATHOU MISONTAIK and to mighty Anubis PSERIPHTHA who holds the keys, to infernal gods, to men and women who have died untimely deaths, to youths and maidens, from year to year, month to month, day to day, hour to hour, night to night. I conjure all spirits in this place to stand as assistants to this spirit, Antinoos. And arouse yourself

> for me and go to every place and into every quarter and to every house and bind Ptolemais, to whom Aias gave birth, the daughter of Origenes, in order that she may not be had in a promiscuous way; let her not be had anally, or let her do anything for pleasure with another man, but with me alone, Sarapammon, to whom Area gave birth, and do not let her drink or eat, that she not show affection, nor go out, nor find sleep without me, Sarapammon, to whom Area gave birth. I conjure you, spirit of this dead man, Antinoos, by the name that causes fear and trembling, the name at whose sound the earth opens, the name at whose terrifying sound the spirits are terrified, the name at whose sound rivers and rocks burst asunder ... Drag her by the hair and her heart until she no longer stands aloof from me, Sarapammon, to whom Area gave birth, and I hold Ptolemais herself, to whom Aias gave birth, the daughter of Origenes, obedient for all the time of my life, filled with love for me, desiring me, speaking to me all the things she has on her mind. If you accomplish this for me, I will set you free.

One special feature of this tablet derives from the fact that we possess the template or recipe on which it is based, labelled as 'a marvellous binding spell' in PGM IV, lines 335–384 (*Papyri Magicae Graecae* 2001). In fact, we now possess five separate tablets based on this recipe, discovered at various places in Egypt. The recipe and its 'off prints' contain numerous elements distinctive of 'late Roman' spells and curses. In its simplest terms, our spell represents an attempt by a named client, Sarapammon, to attract a named woman, Ptolemais, so that she will be filled with love for him and have sex with no one but him. Beyond this, the tablet takes shape around the following characteristic forms:

The gods invoked offer a mix of Greek, Near Eastern and Egyptian deities. In addition, the deity whose awesome name is said to cause fear and trembling may be Adonai or IAO, the god of the Jews. In this regard, the spell exemplifies the international, multicultural environment of all late Roman spells and curses. The tablet also displays a full array of *voces magicae*, many no doubt to be understood as the secret, hidden names of the gods addressed in the spell. Other tablets based on the same recipe include the ubiquitous *charakteres*, lengthy palindromes, geometric patterns formed by vowels and extended passages of Greek verse (usually dactylic hexameters or iambic trimeters).

The invocation of local spirits of the dead completes the hierarchy of invisible agents. In this case, the local spirits were to serve as assistants of the higher gods in carrying out the desired task. As in many similar spells, this one involves especially those who have died an untimely death. Finally, the spell invokes one dead man by name, Antinoos, in whose grave the spell must have been deposited.

Uncharacteristically, with respect to curse tablets in general, our spell mentions both the client and the target by name, as well as their respective mothers and, in the case of the target, her maternal grandfather as well. Such identifications by maternal descent are exceedingly rare in the broader culture of the time.

As to Sarapammon's ultimate intentions, this much is clear: He seeks a sexual monopoly over Ptolemais. He is also fearful that she may submit sexually to other men and does not hesitate to employ explicit language regarding the sexual acts he wishes to avert. Toward the end of the spell, we read, 'for all the time of my life, filled with love for me, desiring me ...'. Here the language suggests something more than a one-night stand. At the same time, we must recognise that the language of the spell is highly formulaic, dictated by the recipe, thus making it difficult to assess anyone's real intentions or actions.

Finally, we cannot ignore the explicit and implicit violence of the spell, e.g., 'drag her by the hair', and most of all the figurine pierced with thirteen needles. How are we to deal with these disturbing facts? A number of considerations come to mind. First, violent language and sentiments belong to the genre of cursing/binding in all of its forms. Second, here it seems clear that our client was seeking to attract the target, against her will, and not to do her harm. In this context, it is crucial to imagine that the spell is but one stage or phase in Sarapammon's efforts to win (back?) the affections of Ptolemais. We may allow ourselves to reconstruct earlier efforts to approach her directly and indirectly through friends or relatives. In this sense, the spell may represent an approach of last resort. Third, it seems likely that Ptolemais's imagined sexual adventures embody in no small part a projection of typical male fantasies. If so, it is Sarapammon himself who is not sleeping or eating, and it is his own distraught condition that requires constraint by needles.

Pleas for Justice and Revenge

A large number of tablets, including at least 130 from a spring in Bath (England), seek recovery of lost or stolen property and satisfaction for wounded pride. Others aim at protecting private property, in particular grave-sites. Still others seek restitution, ranging from petty cash to missing slaves.

> Whether pagan or Christian, whether man or woman, whether boy or girl, whether slave or free, whoever has stolen from me, Annianus (son of) Maturina, six silver coins from my purse, you Lady Goddess, are to exact (them) from him ... Postumianus, Pisso, Locinna, Alauna, Materna, Gunsula, Candidina. Euticius ... (Tomlin 1988: 232–34, no. 98; Gager 1992: 195, no. 96).[12]

> Aurelios Phrougianos, son of Menekritos, and Aurelia Juliana, (his) wife to/for Makaria (his) mother and Alexandria (their) sweetest daughter, constructed (this) as a tomb, while still living. If anyone after their burial should bury another corpse or do harm on the pretext of (having made a) purchase, there shall be upon him the curses written in Deuteronomy (Ramsey 1915: 358–61; Gager 1992: 190f., no. 90).[13]

> To the god Nodens. Silvanus has lost a ring. He has given half of it (i.e., its value) to Nodens. Among those whose name is Senecianus, do not permit health until he brings it to the temple of Nodens (Goodchild 1953: 100–02; Gager 1992: 196f., no. 99).

One striking aspect of the final spell, dedicated to the god Nodens, an aspect that goes to the heart of the issue of how widespread was the belief in their effectiveness, appears in a set of the so-called 'confession inscriptions' from Asia Minor. In these tablets, individuals who suspected – or better, who had learned – that they had been targeted plead for justice and revenge, and regularly set up their own tablets, either proclaiming their innocence or, if guilty, announcing publicly that they had returned the property, and that they would henceforth praise the deity responsible for tracking down the culprit (Lane 1976: 17–38; Versnel 1991: 72–74; Ogden 1999: 44f.). While it is true that these pleas for justice and revenge differ in some respects from other *defixiones*, they are particularly precious for the light they shed on how curses and binding spells worked. In particular, they reveal that such transactions were never an entirely private or hidden affair. The public display of the confessional tablets suggests that their power resided not so much in the fantasy world of gods and spirits but rather in the more immediate, Durkheimian realm of local communities, in a word, of social pressure.

Amulets

It would be seriously misleading if we were to leave off this account of curse tablets and binding spells without acknowledging that there existed, alongside or even against them, a full panoply of countermeasures and protective devices. Some of the elite tried to convince themselves and their followers that such harmful spells were entirely impotent. The very same Pliny who argued that 'all our wisest men reject belief in them' (i.e., incantations), proceeds immediately to assert that 'as a body the public at all times believes in them unconsciously' (Pliny: 28.10). And in the same book of the *Natural History*, after proclaiming that 'the power of omens is really in our own control', he goes on to report that 'there is no one who does not fear to be spell-bound by imprecations' (28.17) . Thus amulets were omnipresent at the time and, like the curse tablets they were designed to defeat, they crossed every linguistic and cultural boundary. A Jewish text of the first century BC (2 Maccabees) reports the following incident in the aftermath of a battle between the Maccabees and their Greek enemies:

> On the next day, as by that time it had become necessary, Judas (Maccabeus) and his men went to take up the bodies of the fallen and to bring them back to lie with their kinsmen in the sepulchres of their fathers. Then under the tunic of every one of the dead they found sacred tokens (i.e., amulets) of the idols of Jamnia, which the law forbids the Jews to wear ... (2 Macc. 12.39f.).[14]

Most of these amulets were inscribed on thin metal sheets, often of materials more precious than lead (e.g., silver) and were carried directly on the body of the owner. An especially intriguing subset of amulets appears in the numerous 'demon bowls', a large number of which (more than six hundred) are being published by the Israeli scholar, Shaul Shaked. One bowl, from Mesopotamia, reads as follows; the inscription is written in spiral form on the inside of the bowl:

> I deposit and sink down this bowl and I perform the praxis and it is in the ... (name?) of Rabbi Joshua the son of Perahia.[15] I am writing divorces for them, for all the liliths which appear to them – in this house of Barbanos the son of Qayomta and of

> Saradust the daughter of Sirin, his wife – in dream by night and in sleep by day ... Oh, demons, black-arts, devils and no-good ones, liliths. Perish by them from the world. At this juncture, I have come up against them with authority and I have caused the destroyer to go against you to destroy them and to bring you forth from their house, from their dwelling place, from their threshold and from all ... the place of the bedroom of Baboons the son of Qayomta ... And again you will not appear to them in dream by night or in sleep by days ... I am dismissing you ... and a letter of dismissal ... (Isbell 1975: 52f.).

And on the outside of the bowl appears the following: 'I have acted for your name: YHWH, Elohim, Sebaoth, Gabriel, Michael and Raphael. Your seal is on this sealing and on this threshold. Amen. Amen'.

The following all-inclusive recipe for an amulet appears in a treatise on the special properties of stones:

> For it is the stone of Hermes. It works even on dreams and it drives away apparitions by virtue of its repellent power. And it is a powerful phylactery against the anger of one's master once the image of Hekate or of the Gorgon is carved into it. Anyone who wears it will never succumb to spells, thunder, or lightning nor be wounded by evil demons. It makes its wearer invulnerable to suffering and it also releases from all forms of pollution and curses ... and it works to ward off all life-threatening spells and to release (the wearer) from all forms of pollution and curses, like an antidote. [16]

Conclusion

At the end we return to the Jesus-sayings in the gospel of Matthew. I have no interest here in deciding the authenticity of the sayings or in settling the vexed question of whether Jesus himself may have been a magician. But we do now have a clear answer to the question that does concern us here: How would a casual passer-by have understood these sayings? What sense would they have made in any sociocultural setting of Greco-Roman antiquity? The answer must be that they would surely have been understood as promises of fail-safe formulas for the production of potent curse tablets and binding spells.

Notes

1. For general treatments of these tablets see Jordan 1985, Faraone and Obbink 1991, especially the essays by Faraone, Strubbe, Versnel, Kotansky and Winkler, Gager 1992, and Ogden 1999.
2. For stimulating discussions of these distinctive linguistic features see Stewart 1978, Miller 1986, Gordon 1987 and Gordon 1999a.
3. Numerous Latin translations (*Picatrix*) of the Arabic collection, itself certainly translated from Greek, perhaps via Syriac, have survived. See in particular Pingree 1986.
4. The tablet was first published in *Inscriptiones Graecae*, vol. 3, part 3 Appendix: *Defixionum Tabellae* (1897).
5. The Greek word for 'place'. Behind the expression we may see a reference to the god of the Jews, often referred to in Hebrew as *maqom*/place.
6. A rare term, it appears only once apart from our text, in a Coptic amulet from around 600 AD, where it appears to name an angel (Gager 1992: 58, note 54).
7. Gager 1992: 56–58, no. 6; first published in van Rengen 1984: 192.
8. First published in *Defixionum Tabellae*, no. 107.
9. First published in Borsari 1901: 205–10.
10. This is not to say that love/sex spells were uncommon in the earlier period; see for example *Idyll* 2 of Theocritus (ca 240 BC).
11. I quote from P. Mich 757 (Martinez 1991). The original recipe for this lead tablet has been preserved in the famous Paris manuscript (P. Bibl. Nat. Suppl. gr. no. 574), dating from the fourth century AD. From this original recipe, or one virtually identical to it, four additional copies have survived, each inscribed on a lead tablet.
12. From the finds at Bath (England). The full list contains eighteen names, probably those whom Annianus suspected of the theft; the names are a mix of Greek, Roman and Celtic.
13. This stone inscription stems from Acmonia, in the province of Phrygia in ancient Asia Minor (modern Turkey) and dates to 248/249 AD. On the opposite side of the stone, Aurelios lists his important civic offices. He and his family were almost certainly Jewish.
14. The ban implied here extended no doubt to the wearing of 'pagan' amulets rather than to amulets as such.
15. A Rabbi frequently referred to in Jewish spells; he was thought to have issued a divorce-ban affecting human couples. The ban is used here to send away troubling female spirits (i.e., liliths).
16. *Lithika Kerygmata* 20.14–18; see Abel 1881. The treatise is attributed to the legendary figure of Orpheus.

References

Abel, E., ed. 1881. *Orphei Lithica*. Berlin: S. Calvary et Socios.

Betz, H.D., ed. 1986. *The Greek Magical Papyri in Translation Including the Demotic Spells*. Chicago and London: University of Chicago Press.

Borsari, L. 1901. 'Mentana – Tombe Romane scoperte presso l'abitato', *Notizie degli scavi di antichità*, pp. 205–10.

Faraone, C.A. 1991. 'The Agonistic Context of Early Greek Binding Spells'. In *Magika Hiera. Ancient Greek Magic and Religion*, eds. C.A. Faraone and D. Obbink, pp. 3–32. New York and Oxford: Oxford University Press.

———. 2002. 'Agents and Victim. Constructions of Gender and Desire in Ancient Greek Love Magic'. In *The Sleep of Reason. Erotic Experience and Sexual Ethics in Ancient Greece and Rome*, eds. M. Nussbaum and J. Sihvola, pp. 400–26. Chicago: University of Chicago Press.

Faraone, C.A. and D. Obbink, eds. 1991. *Magika Hiera. Ancient Greek Magic and Religion*. New York and Oxford: Oxford University Press.

Gager, J.G., ed. 1992. *Curse Tablets and Binding Spells from the Ancient World*. New York and Oxford: Oxford University Press.

Galen. 1965. *Opera omnia*, ed. C.G. Kuhn. Hildeshiem: Georg Olms.

Goodchild, R.G. 1953. 'The Curse and the Ring'. *Antiquity* 27 (1953): 100–02.

Gordon, R. 1987. 'Aelian's Peony: the Location of Magic in Graeco-Roman Tradition'. *Comparative Criticism* 9: 59–95.

———. 1999a. 'Imagining Greek and Roman Magic'. In *Witchcraft and Magic in Europe: Ancient Greece and Rome*, eds. B. Ankerloo and S. Clark, pp. 161–269. London: Athlone Press.

———. 1999b. '"What's in a list?" Listing in Greek and Graeco-Roman Malign Magical Texts'. In *The World of Ancient Magic: Papers from the First International Samson Eitrem Seminar at the Norwegian Institute at Athens, 4–8 May 1997*, eds. D.R. Jordan, H. Montgomery, and E. Thomassen, pp. 239–77. Bergen: Norwegian Institute at Athens.

Hiers, R.H. 1985. '"Binding" and "Loosing": The Matthean Authorizations'. *Journal of Biblical Literature* 104: 233–50.

Hodgkin, T., ed. 1886. *The Letters of Cassiodorus*. London: H. Frowde.

Isbell, C.D. 1975. *Corpus of the Aramaic Incantation Bowls*. Missoula, Mont.: Society of Biblical Literature.

Jordan, D.R. 1985. 'A Survey of *Defixiones* not Included in the Special Corpora'. *Greek, Roman and Byzantine Studies* 26: 151–97.

Lane, E.N. 1976. *Corpus Monumentorum Religionis Dei Menis*, vol. 3. Leiden: Brill.

Martinez, D.G., ed. 1991. *Michigan Papyri XVI: A Greek Love Charm from Egypt (P. Mich. 757)*. Atlanta, GA: Scholars Press.

Miller, P.C. 1986. 'In Praise of Nonsense'. In *Classical Mediterranean Spirituality: Egyptian, Greek, Roman*, ed. A.H. Armstron, pp. 481–505. London: Routledge & Kegan Paul.

Ogden, D. 1999. 'Binding Spells: Curse Tablets and Voodoo Dolls in the Greek and Roman Worlds'. In *Witchcraft and Magic in Europe: Ancient Greece and Rome*, eds. B. Ankerloo and S. Clark, pp. 3–90. London: Athlone Press.

Papyri Magicae Graecae. 2001. Ed. A. Henrichs. Leipzig: B.G. Teubner

Pingree, D. 1986. *Picatrix: The Latin Version of the Ghayat al-Hakim*. London: Warburg Institute.

Ramsey, W.M. 1915. *The Bearing of Recent Discovery on the Trustworthiness of the New Testament*. London: Hodder and Stoughton.

Stewart, S. 1978. *Nonsense. Aspects of Intertextuality in Folklore and Literature*. Baltimore: Johns Hopkins University Press.

Tomlin, R.S.O. 1988. 'The Curse Tablets'. In *The Temple of Sulis Minerva at Bath*, vol. 2: *The Finds from the Sacred Spring*, eds. B. Conliffe and P. Davenport. Oxford: Oxford University Committee for Archaeology.

van Rengen, W. 1984. 'Deux défixions contre les bleus à Apamée ...'. In *Apamée de Syrie: bilan des recherches archéologiques, 1973–1979: aspects de l'architecture domestique d'Apamée: actes du colloque tenu à Bruxelles les 29, 30 et 31 mai 1980*, ed. J. Balty, pp. 213–34. Brussels: Centre belge de recherches archéologiques à Apamée de Syrie.

Versnel, H. 1991. 'Beyond Cursing'. In *Magika Hiera. Ancient Greek Magic and Religion*, eds. C.A. Farone and D. Obbink, pp. 60–106. New York and Oxford: Oxford University Press.

Winkler, J. 1991. 'The Constraints of Eros'. In *Magika Hiera. Ancient Greek Magic and Religion*, eds. C.A. Farone and D. Obbink, pp. 214–43. New York and Oxford: Oxford University Press.

Chapter 4

Magic, Healing and Early Christianity: Consumption and Competition

Justin Meggitt

> So ends the old year ... I bless God that I have never been in so good plight as to my health in so very cold weather as this is, nor indeed in any hot weather these ten years, as I am in this day and have been this four or five months. But I am at a great loss to know whether it be my Hare's foote, or taking a pill of Turpentine, or my having left off wearing a gowne. (Samuel Pepys, 31 December 1664 in Latham and Matthews 1970–83: 5:359)

The relationship between early Christianity and magic is often characterised as one of conflict between two irreconcilable phenomena. The New Testament appears to take such a view. Confrontation between the spreading faith and magical practitioners is, for example, a prominent theme in Acts of the Apostles (Garrett 1989; Klauck 2000). A cursory reading of that book reveals a number of incidents in which magicians are converted or defeated and their arts shown to be inferior: most notably, Simon Magus (8: 4–24), Bar Jesus (13: 4–12), and the Seven Sons of Sceva (19: 8–20). The last incident, which resulted in both Jews and Greeks burning their magical books, is intended by the author to be especially significant as it took place in Ephesus, a city associated with magic in the minds of many in the first century, not least because of the so-called *ephesia grammata*, special words endowed with magical power that were famous throughout the empire (Clement of Alexandria, *Stromata* 8.45.2). For Acts of the Apostles, the proclamation of Christianity broke the power of magic. Although the theme is not as pronounced elsewhere, it is possible to read some other early Christian writings as saying much the same thing. Matthew's depiction of the adoration of Jesus by the Magi (2:11) can be interpreted as demonstrating the subjugation of magicians to the new faith (Justin Martyr, *Dialogue with Trypho* 78.9; Ignatius, *Ephesians* 19:3; Augustine, *Sermons* 20.3–4; Powell 2000).

Of course, the differences between Christianity and magic may not be quite as clear as the New Testament maintains. The concern to present the two in clear opposition may result from an awareness that, for those outside, and even for those inside, magic and Christianity could look much the same (Smith 1980; Benko 1980, 1985). Despite being conservative editors of Mark, both Matthew and Luke omit two miracles in which the Markan Jesus is depicted as using spittle to heal: Mark 7:31–37 (the healing of the deaf and mute man) and 8:22–26 (the healing of the blind man at Bethsaida; cf. also John 9:1–7). The use of spittle was a practice that, to a hostile interpreter of the time, could be taken as evidence of magic (Although it need not be: Pliny [*Natural History* 28.37] recommended it although he was an ardent critic of magic, 'the most fraudulent of arts' [*Natural History* 30:1]; even the influential physician Galen could praise its therapeutic use [*On the Natural Faculties* 3.7]). Indeed, the New Testament preserves a tradition, often considered by critics to be extremely early, that Jesus's opponents claimed that he carried out his exorcisms by the power of Beelzebul, the prince of demons, rather than God (Mark 3:22; Matthew 12:24; Luke 11:15). It is unsurprising that pagan and Jewish critics of Christianity were quick to label Jesus a magician (for example, see Justin *Dialogue with Tryho* 69; Origen *Contra Celsum* 1.28, 68), or that his reputation as such became so great that within a few decades of his death his name is found being used on magical inscriptions and his crucified form depicted on amulets (Eitrem 1966: 14; Smith 1978: 161).

Interesting though the subject is, and important as magic was within the first-century empire, I do not wish to spend much time examining the conflict (and congruence) between early Christianity and magic. Others have done this elsewhere (Hull 1974; Smith 1978; Aune 1980; Kee 1986; Garrett 1989; Choi 1997; Klauck 2000). Nor do I wish to answer the related question of whether it is appropriate or not to label the historical Jesus a 'magician'. There is sufficient evidence to make a case of some sort, as Morton Smith has most famously done (1978; though see Aune 1980: 1539). But, as is so often true of such accusations in antiquity, the evidence is ambiguous and it depends upon one's definition of the term 'magic' itself. It is significant, however, that the designation 'magician' was not one that either Jesus or his followers wished to claim for him, although it was something they could have done, if they had so wished.

Nor do I intend to spend much time discussing the correct definition of 'magic'. There are a myriad of worthy discussions of the subject available to those interested, including some found in recent studies of magic in antiquity (Lloyd 1979; Faraone and Obbink 1991; Graf 1997; Faraone 1999; Dickie 2001; Janowitz 2001). It is a complex issue and may well be as problematic as defining 'vulgarity' or 'deviance', as Garrett has observed (1989: 4). The most useful definition probably lies somewhere between the extremes of traditional substantivist and socio-rhetorical conceptualisations. As Jonathan Z. Smith notes, 'magic is *just one possibility* in any given culture's rich vocabulary of alterity' (1995: 19) but the decision to employ *it*, in preference to something *else*, is significant and capable of being ascertained (as can be seen in the *Apologia* of Apuleius of Madaura, a first-hand account of a trial for witchcraft in the second century). 'Magic' is an *evaluative* term. Even though the substantivists are mostly wrong, and their generalisations are largely mistaken (Goode 1949), there is a discernible substance to 'magic', albeit one that is culturally specific, historically variegated, and, often as not, contestable.

Rather, in what follows I would like to focus attention on a different issue: the healing miracles and exorcisms of the historical Jesus. Magic will play a part in the analysis but its role will be peripheral. I am sorry if the title of this chapter is misleading to some but I do not feel I have to apologise too much: after all, to talk about healings and exorcisms in the modern world is for many akin to talking about 'magic'. Nor do I need to feel too guilty, as I believe that the healings and exorcisms of Jesus are worthy of study because on the one hand, they must be central to any historical interpretation of this figure; and secondly, and most importantly, despite the proliferation of studies dealing with this subject in recent years (Alexander 1980; Theissen 1983; Kee 1986; Twelftree 1993, 1999; Blackburn 1994; Trunk 1994; Remus 1997; Eve 2002; Sorensen 2002) there is, I believe, a flaw in all of them that needs addressing: they have failed to take sufficient account of the perspective of those who believed themselves to be healed and exorcised. It is time we re-examined the healings and exorcisms from, in a manner of speaking, the 'patient's view' and attended to what I would like to call the *consumption* of these acts. If taken seriously such a focus opens up fresh new ways of understanding not only the healings and exorcisms themselves but also the genesis of early Christianity.

Healings, Exorcisms and History

However, before we look in more detail at the issue of consumption, let me first detail the reasons why the healings and exorcisms of Jesus should be taken seriously as a subject of historical enquiry at all. Firstly, there is a relatively broad agreement amongst most current scholars of the historical Jesus that during his lifetime he was perceived to have carried out healings and exorcisms. For individuals as diverse in their ideological perspectives as Geza Vermes (1973), E.P. Sanders (1985, 1993), John Dominic Crossan (1991), John P. Meier (1991, 1994, 2001), Gerd Theissen (1992, 1998), E.S. Fiorenza (1995a, 1995b), N.T. Wright (1996), Luke T. Johnson (1997), Dale Allison (1998), David Flusser (1998), Robert Funk and the Jesus Seminar (1998), Paula Fredricksen (2000), Graham Stanton (2002), and J.D.G. Dunn (2003), the healings and exorcisms are considered one of the bedrocks of our knowledge of the historical Jesus. But when one realises the enormous diversity of opinion between scholars on other issues, such as Jesus's perception of his own identity or the reasons for his death, this agreement is worthy of serious note. Indeed, the significance of these traditions for anyone who wishes to examine the historical Jesus cannot be underestimated. As Meier observes in *A Marginal Jew*: *Rethinking the Historical Jesus*: 'Put dramatically, but with not too much exaggeration: if the miracle tradition from Jesus' public ministry were to be rejected *in toto* as unhistorical, so should every other Gospel tradition about him' (Meier 1991: 630).

There are a number of reasons for this unusual agreement. The healings and exorcisms are attested in the major sources that we possess for Jesus's life, and are found in most of the forms of the traditions that we have (Blackburn 1994). Indeed, the healing miracles seem to have been central to earliest preaching about the figure of Jesus (see, for example, Acts 10:38). And whilst it might be legitimate to dismiss many of the specific accounts of healings and exorcisms as retrospective pious fabrications created by those who venerated the memory of Jesus, some individual traditions about the miracles have good reason to be accepted as credible evidence of perceptions of Jesus's activity during his lifetime. There are various reasons for this but perhaps the most persuasive it that it is hard to imagine what benefit the early churches could have gained from inventing some of this data. For example, it is hard to see why the tradition that Jesus was accused by his opponents of carrying out his exorcisms by the power of Beelzebul, rather than God, would have been created by his followers. This datum is all the more credible because it appears to be multiply attested in a range of early sources. It is found not only in Mark and Mark-dependent material (Matthew 9:32–34; Mark 3:22–27; Luke 11:14–16) but also in material independent of Mark and common to both Matthew and Luke (Matthew 12:22–30; Luke 11:17–23) – which most New Testament scholars believe indicates that it is from an early, independent source, referred to as 'Q' – as well as in material unique to Matthew (10:25).

Two specific traditions are usually taken as particularly strong evidence that the historical Jesus was a healer and exorcist (indeed, they are often taken as indicating that the healings and exorcisms were central to his self-perception). The first is John the Baptist's question about Jesus's identity to which Jesus responds by citing the evidence of his healings (Matthew 11:5ff , Luke 7:18ff). This is an awkward tradition that disrupts the narratives of Matthew and Luke and is therefore, most likely to be primitive: John the Baptist has his disciples pose this question *after* John had apparently already recognised Jesus's identity at his baptism. The second tradition takes the form of a saying in which Jesus is recorded as linking his exorcisms to the presence of the Kingdom of God (Matthew 12:28, Luke 11:20), the proclamation of which appears to have been key to his preaching (e.g., Mark 1:15, Matthew 3:2). Davies and Allison can call the authenticity of this saying 'one of the assured results of modern criticism' (1991: 339) not least because of its eschatological intensity (Bultmann 1968: 162), something rather awkward for the later church.

Non-Christian sources, both Jewish and pagan, also corroborate the picture of Jesus the healer and exorcist found in the gospels. The tradition that Jesus carried out miraculous healings is found in the critiques of Trypho and Celsus recorded by Justin and Origen respectively. It may also be alluded to by Josephus in the *Testimonium Flavianum* (found in *Antiquities* 18.63–64) although this is a very contentious passage, certain features of which, including the somewhat neutral reference to Jesus's wonder-working, have long been disputed (Carleton Paget 2001). These sources, with the possible exception of Josephus, are hostile in their estimations of Jesus, questioning the means by which Jesus achieved his miracles, and labelling Jesus a magician of some kind, but none actually doubts that he carried out such acts (though it is obvious from the fragment of the earliest Christian apologists Quadratus, preserved in Eusebius's *History of the Church* [4.3], that at least a few critics doubted the permanence of Jesus's healings). Indeed, it is fair to say that if Jesus was famous for anything amongst his contemporaries, it was for his healing miracles and exorcisms: the unidentified exorcists who are recorded as using Jesus's name in Mark 9:38 and Luke 9:49, and the tradition in Acts 19:13 that the seven sons of Sceva did something similar, point to the antiquity of this estimation.

Before we move on to examine what can be gained by analysing the consumption of the healings and exorcisms, it is important to make it clear that in assuming Jesus was perceived to have carried out healings and exorcisms in his lifetime, I am not, historically speaking, treating him as a special case or engaging in any special pleading. Other figures were thought to be able to do similar things while they were alive, such as Elezear (Josephus *Antiquities* 8.46), the Jewish exorcist who carried out an exorcism in front of Vespasian, or the Syrian exorcist and the Chaldean healer mentioned in Lucian's *Lover of Lies* (16, 11), or the marketplace magicians who 'drive away demons, conquer diseases of all kinds and make the dead heroes of the past appear', referred to by Celsus (*Contra Celsum* 1.68) or, possibly, the pious Jew Hanina Ben Dosa (m. Berakhot 5.5). The belief that individuals could effect miraculous healings was not uncommon and could be taken seriously. For example, when Apuleius was charged with practicing magic part of the case against him included the claim that he had successfully healed an epileptic boy (*Apologia* 44) and a woman with an ear disorder (*Apologia* 48). Even Roman law assumed that many believed supernatural healings were possible: the jurist Ulpian maintained that whilst exorcists and those who practiced incantations should not be considered doctors, nonetheless he had to concede that there were many who forcefully asserted that they had been cured by them (*Digest* 50.13.c.1.3). A large number of those who inhabited the first-century world, Jew and gentile, lived in a world full of miracles. Indeed, Jesus is presented as believing that others had such powers: 'If I cast out demons by Beelzebul, by whom do your sons cast them out?' (Matthew 12:27, Luke 11:19 and Mark 13:22; Matthew 24:24), a fact of which his critics were well aware (*Contra Celsum* 2.49).

Consuming Miracles

For the most part, the perspective and experience of those seeking healing from the historical Jesus has been of little interest to New Testament scholars. In this respect Morton Smith's insightful observation that '… their needs, *not* the later Christian communities, were the earliest matrices of gospel stories' (1978: 9) is extremely unusual and it is a great pity that it was not developed (or substantiated) by either Smith or E.P. Sanders, who subsequently recognised the value of this remark (1985: 164). Such attention to the healed and exorcised is rare. More specifically, New Testament scholars have ignored the first-century 'universe of disease' (a phrase coined by Katharine Park [1992: 60] to express the central, all-pervasive role disease played in shaping the experience and preoccupations of inhabitants of pre-modern Europe) within which the healing and exorcisms took place. For those scholars who have bothered to think about this issue, the context is often only roughly sketched and the 'evidence' used to corroborate their picture is often little more than, as in the case of Smith, anecdotal (Smith begins his book by attempting to evoke the context of disease within which Jesus performed his healings and exorcisms by recounting an encounter he once had with a man he terms a 'lunatic' in the Old City of Jerusalem in 1940 [1978: 9]). For most, the only attention paid to the specific context of the healed and exorcised tends to consist of repeating *ad nauseam* that *lepra* was almost certainly not the disease we know as leprosy today, Hansen's disease (Hulse 1975).

But the failings of current scholarship aside, what, more specifically, did these healings and exorcisms 'mean' to their recipients and how can we go about attempting to describe such meaning? In one important respect it is important to recognise that we do not need to reinvent the wheel. In trying to focus upon the perspective of the healed and exorcised, of analysing, as it were 'the patient's view', we are trying something analogous to the work already undertaken by some medical historians, such as Roy Porter (1985) who have tried to correct dominant approaches that ignore or trivialise the experiences and therapeutic choices of sufferers themselves.

Now 'meaning' is obviously not self-evident and requires some clarification. The meanings I am concerned with here are not the traditional concerns of those that study the healing narratives. I am not concerned with the role the healings and exorcisms played in the themes of the law, the faithfulness of Israel, sin, the arrival of the Messiah or the Kingdom of God, as these are understood in early Christian writings or even the convictions of the historical Jesus. These are the usual 'meanings' that are assumed to be the appropriate concern of New Testament scholarship (Blomberg 1992: 299–307). The gospel narratives are preoccupied with such things so it seems perfectly reasonable that they have absorbed so much attention. Rather, I am interested in the 'meanings' created by the miracle events for those that are healed; I want to look at the *consumption* of the healing events. I use that term *consumption* primarily in the sense in which it is employed in the British Cultural Studies tradition, which pioneered, through the empirical study of reception, the notion that the consumption of a text (which in this context means a cultural artefact of any kind, including a practice or performance, such as a healing) is never a passive thing (Gledhill 1988: 68).

Although such ideas are familiar to many in the humanities, the following quote from the work of the American scholar Lawrence Grossberg may help clarify what is meant:

> No text is able to guarantee what its effects will be. People are constantly struggling, not merely to figure out what a text means, but to make it mean something that connects to their own lives, experiences, needs and desires. The same text will mean different things to different people, depending on how it is interpreted. And different people have different interpretative resources, just as they have different needs. A text can only mean something in the context of the experience and situation of its particular audience. Equally important, texts do not define ahead of time how they are to be used or what functions they can serve. They can have different uses for different people in different contexts ... How a specific text is used, how it is interpreted, how it functions for its audience – all of these are inseparably connected through the audience's constant struggle to make sense of itself and its world (Grossberg 1992: 52–53).

This should come as no surprise to someone studying the historical Jesus. In a crude sense, in recording the Beelzebul accusation, the New Testament itself indicates the diversity of interpretations that could accompany Jesus's healings and exorcisms. Similar differences of interpretation are found, for example, in the response of the inhabitants of Gerasene, who did not respond favourably when confronted with Jesus's miracle working, perhaps on account of the demise of so many of their pigs (Mark 5:1–20, Matthew 8:28–34, Luke 8:26–39), and, rather notoriously, the inhabitants of his home town Nazareth, who seem to have been unimpressed by his reputation as a healer (Mark 6:6; Matthew 13:58).

In order to understand the variegated process of consumption more fully, it is helpful to turn to anthropology of medicine, something employed, with varying degrees of rigour by New Testament scholars such as Hector Avalos (1999), John J. Pilch (2000) and Eric Eve (2002). Anthropology in itself is a particularly valuable discipline for our purposes: it is important to the interrogation of the falsely obvious, that which goes without saying. It assists us in avoiding the interpretative error of confusing nature and history (Barthes [1957] 1973: 11) and advances the processes of defamiliarisation and refamiliarisation so necessary for scrutinising past cultures (Burke 1990: 270). But medical anthropology is especially useful. It is concerned with examining 'how people in different cultures and social groups explain the causes of ill health, the types of treatment they believe in, and to whom they turn if they do get ill' (Helman 2000: 1). To illustrate how varied human cultures are in this respect it is worth reflecting for a moment on our own cultural assumptions about sickness and healthcare (assumptions that, I believe, impede our analysis of first-century culture). Modern Western society is heavily dominated by the biomedical model of sickness in which the body is seen primarily as a machine, disease is seen as a breakdown of the machine, and the doctor's task is repair of the machine. From this it follows that the expectation is that sickness is temporary, episodic and organic. As the work of Ivan Illich (1976) and others has shown, Western social life is increasingly medicalised and natural life processes are frequently pathologised. For example, pregnancy, the menopause and old age are regularly seen as pathological conditions (Oakley 1984, Doyal 1995). Disability is commonly construed as something fundamentally medical, and hence treatable or curable, self-evidently requiring the intervention of medical rehabilitation

(Oliver 1996). Even death is now perceived to be abnormal and a consequence of a particular pathological condition (natural causes are no longer accepted on a death certificate). Of course, conventional medical practitioners are increasingly criticised, particularly in the United Kingdom where there has been a shift in health provision from one that was characterised by paternalism to one characterised by consumerism (Klein 1989). But nonetheless, the following satirical exchange from the *Importance of Being Earnest* following Lady Bracknell's enquiry as to the cause of the sudden demise of the (fictional) Mr Bunbury, is still indicative of the dominance of biomedical power over Western individuals and societies:

> Algernon: The Doctors found out that Bunbury could not live – so Bunbury died.
>
> Lady Bracknell: He seems to have had great confidence in the opinion of his physicians. I am glad however, that he made up his mind at the last to some definite course of action, and acted under proper medical advice.

This is all a long way away from the first-century context and our assumptions are not those of ancient sufferers, as we will see. (It should be added that jokes at the expense of doctors were not uncommon in the empire, as the *Philogelos* testifies, although they were decidedly less funny.)

Although the anthropology of medicine should provide a scholar of the New Testament with an array of helpful analytical resources, I would like to draw attention to one in particular that is especially relevant to the subject of our study: Arthur Kleinman's 'Explanatory Model' (EM), made famous in his seminal work *Patients and Healers in the Context of Culture* (1980). Kleinman's EMs are 'the notions about an episode of sickness and its treatment that are employed by all those who are engaged in the clinical process' (the sick person, family, friends, village healers, doctors, religious authorities, etc.). They are designed to help us understand the processes by which sickness is patterned, interpreted and treated (Kleinman 1980: 104–18). They are partly conscious and partly outside of awareness, dynamic in character, and capable of revision in the light of subsequent events. It is important to note that EMs are not necessarily articulated, and that their value for us does not lie in our ability to describe any particular model but in making us more sensitive to the range of possible elements that might constitute the recipient's model and the range of ways that these elements could be understood to interrelate. For example, the encounter with the historical Jesus, however dramatic its consequences may have been, would be just one episode within an individual's experience of a particular sickness. Even if the outcome was successful, the 'miracle' might not have been understood as definitive from the perspective of the person healed. Kleinman's EMs should alert us to the fact that the 'meanings' of the healing for the recipient could be quite diverse and are dependant upon the prior and subsequent experiences and their interpretation. They are also valuable because they remind us of the agency of individuals, something too readily dismissed by some New Testament scholars who have mistakenly assumed that recognising that the modern Western ideology of individualism was not present in antiquity, and that assumptions based upon its existence are ethnocentric and anachronistic, should lead an exegete to deny the existence of autonomous individuals (Malina and Neyrey 1996: 13). This is a dangerous, erroneous inference (Cohen 1993).

The Sufferers' Experience

So how should we go about examining the experience of the sufferer? How can we describe the ways in which Jesus's healings and exorcisms were 'consumed'? At the very least it is important to be systematic about this and in what follows I will assume that there are three constituent parts of the sufferer's experience: the experience of disease, the experience of illness and therapeutics.

In differentiating between disease and illness, by which I mean, respectively, the physical and social experience of affliction, I am following something of a convention which has been made familiar to New Testament studies through, for example, the work of Theissen and Merz (1998) though it has been a staple of anthropological and sociological studies for some decades (see, for example, Parsons 1951). On one level the dichotomy is false. It is only intended to be heuristic as I would contend that while a disease does have some reference to complex empirical reality it is not equivalent to that reality as it is, at least to a limited degree, socially constructed. Of course, for most of us, there is little in life quite as real as disease but time, however, makes it easier to see the constructed nature of named pathologies that others have taken for granted (and perhaps the unconscious, ideological forces involved in their construction). To give an example, 'wandering womb' was a particularly unpleasant ailment afflicting women in the ancient Mediterranean, which features regularly in the Hippocratic corpus, and other key medical texts such as Galen and Soranus (Solomon 1993, Demand 1994). It had particularly unpleasant symptoms affecting the whole body as the womb allegedly wandered freely around. It was a difficult condition to treat and the only sure way to keep it at bay was to keep that particular organ occupied, so the leading male physicians thought.

Disease

Any analysis must take seriously the physical difference between then and now, particularly the relatively recent decline in the significance of many acute (particularly infectious) diseases; the changes that have resulted from the elimination in much of the world of such killers are smallpox, diphtheria, polio, tetanus and measles, that have dominated disease experience for most people in most epochs of human existence. We are now experiencing a rather unusual period of what Tenner calls the 'Revenge of the Chronic' (1997: 26–70) in which chronic disorders such as diabetes, hypertension, arthritis, Parkinson's disease and cancers have become central, as we undergo enormous alterations in patterns of morbidity and mortality. These advances have created a radically different universe of disease for moderns than for inhabitants of the first-century eastern Mediterranean.

There are difficult methodological and evidential problems inherent in trying to sketch this first-century disease context, in particular, the problems of moving from answering questions about the *occurrence* of diseases in antiquity to determining their *virulence* and *prevalence*, of constructing a plausible disease ecology; these are familiar problems of palaeopathology. The variable and erratic nature of osteoarchaeological data for the first century makes this undertaking particularly difficult, although this period is far from unique in this respect (see, for example, Roberts and Manchester 1997: 9–11). There is not space here to demonstrate that, despite the difficulties, describing the disease context within which Jesus's healings and exorcisms were encountered is something that can be done. It certainly *must* be done. The physicality of disease experience is crucial and too easily neglected. It will not do, as Pilch has recently done (2000: 15) to label the work of Mirko Grmek and others who have made a comprehensive effort to describe disease experience in the ancient world as something that is a concern of the history of medicine and not of someone analysing early Christian sources. Lynn Meskell (1999) is surely correct in her observation that the study of the past is detrimentally affected by the neglect of the materiality of embodiment.

Illness

If we are to understand the perspective of the sufferer it is also important that we reconstruct the social experience of suffering. New Testament scholarship and cognate disciplines have produced some work relevant to this undertaking (e.g., Horne 1999), although the relevant analyses are often by-products of the examination of other issues, considered to be of more pressing interest, such as the question of Jesus's understanding of purity, or Jesus's attitude towards women. As a consequence, our knowledge of the experience of the sufferers is somewhat piecemeal. We have some helpful work on the social experience of individuals suffering from specific ailments but no attempt to engage with the illness experience *in toto* (my concern here) and even these are not without their problems. For example, there have been contextually sensitive interpretations of the social predicament of the woman with the flow of blood (Mark 5:25–34, Matthew 9:20–22, Luke 8:42–48); however, the contextual attention here has often turned out to be less than helpful. It is regularly maintained that Jesus's healing of the woman (although it is more accurate to say that in the Markan and Lukan accounts she heals herself) was not just a physical healing of a distressing ailment but also, because of Jewish purity laws, a profoundly social healing, allowing the woman to be reintegrated into the society from which her state of impurity would have excluded her (e.g., Selvidge 1990, Hooker 1991: 148, Evans 1997: 367). This interpretation is usually substantiated by reference to the regulations in Leviticus 15:25–28 and their elaboration and intensification in the Mishnah, particularly m. Zabim 5.1 (and also m. Niddah and m. Tohorot 5.8). Yet such a reading is implausible for a number of reasons (Levine 1996a, 1996b, Fonrobert 1997, D'Angelo 1999) and not least because the assumption 'that Levitical law had such an exclusionary effect on women ... is not supported by sources either ancient or modern' (Levine 1996a: 311).

In trying to understand the experience of illness in the first century we are also, as in our attempts to examine the experience of disease, hampered by the lack of comprehensive works of synthesis and problems with the primary evidence. If anything the situation is more problematic because of the enormous difficulties raised in trying to distinguish actual practices and perceptions from idealised ones reflected in the unrepresentative literary records of one kind or another. Although there have been a few attempts to present a generalised picture of the social experience of illness in the empire, such as Robert Garland's *The Eye of the Beholder: Deformity and Disability in the Graeco-Roman World* (1995), these studies are rare and do not take much cognisance of Jewish behaviour and attitudes (although Preuss 1978 and Rosner 1995 have done some significant work on the worlds of the Mishnah and Talmud). Most also concentrate on specific and often sensational illnesses and then not for their own sake, but for the part they play in defining the discourses of the period (see, for example, Barton 1993).

Despite the lack of a comprehensive study of illness in the first-century world, nonetheless we can make a few observations. There appear to have been a bewildering diversity of responses to the same ailment both *between* cultures, and indeed, *within* them. For example, there were very different responses to abnormal births between Greek and Roman populations of the time: whereas Greeks tended to treat unusual births, such as those of intersexuals, as aberrations in the natural order but not indicative of anything much and not bringing any particular opprobrium on the parents, Romans interpreted them as eminently suggestive of divine displeasure, at a personal or national level (Garland 1995: 72). Within first-century Judaism it is often thought that those suffering from 'leprosy' would uniformly suffer social isolation because of the biblical command, assumed to be normative, to expel them from society (Levitcus 13:46; see also Josephus *War* 6.426; Numbers 5.6, 12:1–12 etc.). However, it seems as though, at a popular level, many people with leprosy were integrated into some Jewish communities, even attending synagogues (Davies and Allison 1991: 11; see also Papyrus Egerton 2).

Any study of illness in this period should also recognise the diversity of aetiologies that were current, as ideas about the cause of one's sickness have significant implications for how a sufferer is treated by wider society and perceives of her- or himself (Sontag 1978). And here it is easy to be led astray by common assumptions. The malevolent action of demons, for example, is not by any means the main aetiology in the New Testament, *contra*, for example, Seybold and Mueller, who erroneously assert that 'the dominant view in the New Testament is that demons are the causes of sickness' (1981: 100). Although there are clear distinctions between the gospels in the degree to which this is true, as Thomas (1998) has recently shown, Amundsen and Ferngren are right to observe that 'in most of the healings performed by Jesus, not only is there no mention of demonic involvement, but the symptoms are clearly distinguished from those of demon possession' (1995: 2950).

Indeed, there appears to have been considerable room for naturalistic explanations of a person's predicament. For a considerable proportion of afflictions mentioned in the New Testament no particular explanation is given or sought (this is also born out in some popular literature of the period, such as Artemidorus's *Oneirocritica*). As Amundsen and Ferngren note: 'Unless one's conclusions are simply the final articulation of one's presuppositions, one cannot, without violence to the texts in question, infer either any demonic involvement or an immediate divine causality' (1991: 2951).

Likewise, even where demons are actually present in an account we must be careful not to make unwarranted deductions from this that might lead to mistaken judgments about the social treatment of the sufferer. Even in this area there was significant diversity. Belief in demonic causation does not necessarily presuppose belief in a cosmic conflict as, for example, Wendy Cotter has recently demonstrated (1997). Although some New Testament texts seem to encourage us to view Jesus's exorcisms in terms of inaugurating an end time conflict, it is not clear that the original incidents were conceived of in that way by either him or those receiving healing. Nor, indeed, does the presence of demons necessarily presuppose belief in the complex demonology that we find, for example, in some of the Greek magical papyri or the *Testament of Solomon*. The New Testament itself indicates as much. Few demons are named in the gospels (just 'Beelzebul' and 'Legion'), and rarely is a distinction made between types of demon (the only example is found in Mark 9:29). Demons could exist more or less independently of any particular cosmology as we can see, for example in the exorcisms carried out by Apollonius of Tyana (*Life of Apollonius of Tyana* 3:38–39, 4:20) or that of Eleazar the Jewish exorcist (Josephus *Antiquities* 8:42–49), or the Syrian exorcist in Lucian's *Lover of Lies* (16).

Therapeutics

The study of therapeutic strategies open to the afflicted who sought healing from Jesus has usually begun and ended with the pejorative remarks made about doctors in the New Testament, a few references to Apollonius of Tyana or some other miracle worker of the period, and perhaps the famous Asklepios inscriptions at Epidaurus. It has hardly been rigorous. Even Kee (1986), who at least attempted to be rather more systematic and engaged with a broader range of sources, produced a very whiggish analysis of the subject, dedicating significant space to summaries of secondary medical literature on Galen, Soranus and Rufus of Ephesus, hardly a representative collection of individuals (Galen was Marcus Aurelius's physician – so just as Marcus Aurelius was not a typical patient, so Galen was not a typical doctor), and pejoratively characterising more popular forms of medicine as quackery that preyed on the 'gullible' (Kee 1986: 64). This is a strangely insensitive choice of language which effectively stigmatises non-professional healers, whose practices were often thought to be therapeutically valuable, and who, in a variety of different guises, have been the major providers of health care for the great mass of humanity throughout history, including antiquity (Jones 1957; Jackson 1988; Nutton 1991, 1992).

The therapeutic strategies available in the first-century world seem to have been wide-ranging and constantly evolving, although this has rarely been acknowledged as many of the options have been prejudicially dismissed as absurd (Gordon 1995). Indeed, even within apparently conservative traditions, new therapeutic strategies could be fashioned. For example, according to Josephus some Jews of the period tried to obtain healing by shaving their heads and abstaining from wine for thirty days before giving sacrifice in the Temple (*War* 2.313; see also *Antiquities* 3:236; Kottek 1994). Although aspects of this behaviour resemble that officially sanctioned within the biblical text (most obviously the Nazirite vow of Numbers

6:1–21; see also m. Nazir), nonetheless, there is no obvious justification from within normative Jewish traditions for undertaking such a vow to achieve healing. (It may, by the way, cast light on Paul's unusual action recorded in Acts 18:18 [2 Corinthians 12:7–10; although see also Juvenal *Satires* 12:81f.].)

People also appear to have employed therapeutic strategies that were, at least theoretically, incompatible. Of course, for some, this resulted from frustration and desperation, and was a consequence of the perceived failure of one or other course of treatment (Mark 5:26; Plutarch *On the Face on the Moon* 920b), but for others this superficially irrational pluralism seems to have been motivated by a rational desire to increase the chances of a positive outcome: if they could live, they were happy to live with the inconsistency and, like Pepys in the opening quote, not feel the need to make any judgments on the efficacy of one or another therapy. Soranus, for example, remarked that many women liked to use amulets in addition to doctors and midwives during labour (*Gynecology* 3.42), although he personally considered them worthless, except for their psychological effect. Given the high death rate of mothers during childbirth one can hardly blame them for hedging their bets. Similarly, in Aristides's *Sacred Tales* the author recorded oscillating between employing doctors and the unmediated intervention of the god Asclepius; the sick man in Lucian's *Lover of Lies* seems open to a mass of different therapies; even Marcus Aurelius could employ Galen *and* his arch opponent Statilius Attalus, men with fundamentally different convictions about the causes and treatments of sickness. And, as Kleinman's (1980) work indicates, the success of one therapeutic strategy did not *necessarily* lead an individual to reject those that have been tried previously but found to be wanting. Even an apparently miraculous healing need not have been perceived as demonstrating the failure of all previous attempts at healing but could have been integrated into the recipients' narratives of their own suffering (Muela et al. 1998).

One other aspect of therapeutics in the first century is important to highlight: the use of a particular therapeutic strategy was not necessarily accompanied by assent to its implied worldview nor by any particular estimation of its practitioner. The Jewish exorcist Eleazar could carry out an exorcism in front of Vespasian (*Antiquities* 8.42–49), according to Josephus, but there is no indication that anyone was expected to become Jewish as a consequence, nor that they did.

Concluding Remarks

I would like to finish by making a few observations. I hope they will give readers an indication of the benefits of examining the consumption of the healings and exorcisms for scholars of the historical Jesus and the earliest churches. There is much more that I think can be gleaned by such a focus, as I will detail in the future.

Firstly, a couple of observations about the earliest churches and their first adherents. It is now assumed that the healings and exorcisms of the historical Jesus should be understood in the context of first-century Palestinian Judaism. Most commentators believe that there are only a few examples in the gospels where non-Jews are depicted as receiving healing, notably those two occasions on which individuals who are probably pagans are healed, the Syrophoenician/Canaanite woman's daughter (Mark 7:24–30, Matthew 15:21–28), and the centurion's servant (Luke 7:1–10, Matthew 8:5–13, John 4:45–54); and the one occasion where a Samaritan with leprosy is cured (Luke 17:16). However, whilst the primary context for understanding Jesus's healings and exorcisms should be that of first-century Palestinian Judaism, we need to revise our assumptions. The near-universal desire for healing seems to have caused a great deal of cultural interaction between what we often think of, and which in many other respects no doubt were, quite distinct communities. For example, as we have noted, Eleazar was employed by non-Jews and not only were Jewish miracle workers used by non-Jews but Jewish magical practices can be seen in the Greek Magical Papyri and elsewhere (Alexander 1999: 1073–8); John Chrysostom could even complain some centuries later that it was better for Christians to die than to be healed by Jewish 'charms, incantations and amulets' (*Adversus Iudaeos* 8.6), an interesting acknowledgement of both their use by his co-religionists and widespread belief in their efficacy. Consequently, the presence of non-Jews amongst recipients of healing from Jesus is no surprise and may, indeed, be far greater than is often thought. Indeed, if we try to rid ourselves of the assumption that people whose religious identities are not given or implied are Jesus's co-religionists, if we take seriously the alleged locations of the healings and the alleged origins of the crowds that came for healing (see, for example, Matthew 4:23–25; Mark 3:7–8; Luke 6:17–18), the picture might well look very different indeed. Although we must be careful not to exaggerate the degree of diversity within Galilee, the key region within which the historical Jesus operated (Meyers 1997), it was not isolated, road networks allowed for far more cultural interchange than is often assumed (Strange 1997), and a significant presence of non-Jews seems quite likely. Perhaps Jesus's programmatic sermon in Nazareth (Luke 4:16–30), which emphasises his mission to non-Jews, is not so anachronistic as it sometimes seems.

Indeed, the healing and exorcism narratives should be seen as the true genesis of gentile involvement in the new religion – not, I believe the activity of Paul or the unnamed Christians who preached to gentiles in Antioch (Acts 11:20). Although the kind of involvement at this stage might well be considered rather unsatisfactory by the later church, as it need not have been exclusive, and could have been akin to identifying oneself with a celebrity, a category of person legion in antiquity and often credited with healing powers or the ability to bring some other good fortune to their fans (Sande 1999). And even positing this level of commitment may be going too far for most of those healed or exorcised. Kleinman's EMs should lead commentators to recognise that the healings and exorcisms need not, in their original forms, have necessarily led the healed or exorcised person to hold any distinctive or lasting estimation of the figure of historical Jesus beyond the fact that he had healed or exorcised them, or to align themselves in any way with his particular worldview or message (whatever that might be), though obviously a few seem to have done so (for example, the women mentioned in Luke 8:2). For most of those healed, the episode could be integrated into their pre-existing narratives of their sickness and their employment of other therapeutic strategies.

The desire for healing could also lead to interactions between different economic and social groups. We know, for example, that all social classes could employ magical healers of various kinds: it certainly was not solely the preserve of the poor despite polemical assertion to the contrary in early sources (see, for example, *Contra Celsum* 6.41). As Lucian's *Lover of Lies* indicates, a diversity of people, some even quite wealthy, could make use of the power of a Syrian exorcist from Palestine. It is no surprise therefore that those seeking healing, either for themselves or on behalf of others, appear to have come from a range of backgrounds in the New Testament, from the daughter of a ruler of a synagogue (Mark 5:21–43, Matthew 9:18–26, Luke 8:40–55) to a blind beggar (Mark 10:46–52,

Matthew 20:29–34, Luke 18:35–43; see also Luke 8:2). However, this should not overshadow another feature of early Christian healing. Some therapeutic strategies could exclude those who were not wealthy. A good *medicus* (or *iatros*) did not come cheap and some forms of magic seem to have required significant sums of money. Christianity appears to have distinguished itself by offering healing for free (Matthew 14:1–2, Mark 6:7–12, Luke 9:1–6; Matthew 9:37–38, 10:7–16, Luke 10:1–12; Acts 3:6, 20:33, 35; *Acts of Thomas* 20), a point emphasised in the Markan version of the story of the woman with the flow of blood, who is recorded as spending all her money on physicians and becoming worse, rather than better, for it (Mark 5:26; Acts 8:18).

When we take seriously the possible worldview of the sufferers, perhaps some of our cherished Christological assumptions about the meanings of key texts might also need some rethinking. For example, given the significance of Solomon in popular healing traditions of the period (*Antiquities* 8:42–49), and the fascinating but limited evidence that we possess for Jewish expectation of a therapeutic messiah (the recently published Qumran fragment 4Q521 is our only evidence for such a belief in Judaism before the birth of Christianity), perhaps we should think again about some of the uses of the title 'Son of David' in the gospels, particularly when it occurs in the context of a healing, such as on the lips of the blind Bartimaeus (Mark 10:46–52, Matthew 20:29–34, Luke 18:35–43). Possibly the title was originally intended to be a reference to Solomon, (who was, of course, literally 'the son of David') and not necessarily messianic at all in its origins even if this is how the early church developed the title (Berger 1973, 1974; Duling 1975; Smith 1978: 79; Aune 1980: 1526; Charlesworth 1995). Indeed, given the reputation that Solomon had amongst gentiles of this period as an exorcist (Duling 1985, Alexander 1999), Matthew's unusual addition of 'Son of David' to the imploration of the Canaanite woman (Matthew 15:22) may well have been rather less 'surprising' (Davies and Allison 1991: 548) to its first readers than it is often thought to be. It is quite plausible that a gentile might have used such a title for a Jewish exorcist such as Jesus.

There is far more that can be said but it is important to conclude this brief examination of the implications of studying the consumption of the historical Jesus's healings and exorcisms by restating the basic argument of this chapter: New Testament scholarship has largely failed to take seriously the physical and social experiences of affliction, and the various therapeutic strategies open to the afflicted, particularly the poor. By so doing scholars have worked with the assumption that disease and illness are more or less universal and ahistorical and have, where it has been considered a subject of study, promoted a very narrow view of ancient therapeutic strategies and choices, and the intervention of the historical Jesus as necessarily definitive. This is a pity. There is nothing self-evident about suffering. To put it crudely, people did not suffer in the same way in the first century as they do today, and the meaning and significance of the healings and exorcisms, in their original contexts, are not as accessible or uniform as is often assumed.

References

Alexander, P. 1999. 'Jewish Elements in Gnosticism and Magic c. CE 70-c. CE 270'. In *The Cambridge History of Judaism Volume Three: The Early Roman Period*, eds. W. Horbury, W.D. Davies and J. Sturdy, pp. 1052–78. Cambridge: Cambridge University Press.

Alexander, W.M. 1980. *Demonic Possession in the New Testament: Its Historical, Medical, and Theological Aspects*. Grand Rapids: Baker Book House.

Allison, D.C. 1998. *Jesus of Nazareth: Millenarian Prophet*. Minneapolis: Fortress Press.

Amundsen, D. and C. Ferngren. 1995. 'The Perception of Disease Causality in the New Testament'. *Aufstieg und Niedergang der römischen Welt* II.37.3: 2934–56.

Aune, D.E. 1980. 'Magic in Early Christianity'. *Aufstieg und Niedergang der römischen Welt* II.23.2: 1507–57.

Avalos, H. 1999. *Health Care and the Rise of Christianity*. Peabody: Hendrickson.

Barthes, R. (1957) 1973. *Mythologies*, trans. A. Lavers. London: Paladin.

Barton, C. 1993. *The Sorrows of the Ancient Romans: The Gladiator and the Monster*. Princeton: Princeton University Press.

Benko, S. 1980. 'Pagan Criticism of Christianity During the First Two Centuries A.D.'. *Aufstieg und Niedergang der römischen Welt* II.23.2: 1055–1118.

———. 1985. *Pagan Rome and the Early Christians*. London: B.T. Batsford.

Berger, K. 1973. 'Die königlichen Messiastraditionen des Neuen Testaments'. *New Testament Studies* 20: 1–44.

———. 1974. 'Zum Problem des Messianität Jesu'. *Zeitschrift für Theologie und Kirche* 71: 1–30.

Blackburn, B. 1994. 'The Miracles of Jesus'. In *Studying the Historical Jesus: Evaluations of the State of Current Research,* eds. B. Chilton and C.A. Evans, pp. 353–94. Leiden: Brill.

Blomberg, C.L. 1992. 'Healing'. In *Dictionary of Jesus and the Gospels,* eds. J.B. Green, S. McKnight and I.H. Marshall, pp. 299–307. Leicester: InterVarsity Press.

Bultmann, R. 1968. *The History of the Synoptic Tradition,* 2nd ed. Oxford: Basil Blackwell.

Burke, P. 1990. 'Historians, Anthropologists and Symbols'. In *Culture Through Time: Anthropological Approaches,* ed. E. Ohnuki-Tierney, pp. 268–83. Stanford: Stanford University Press.

Carleton Paget, J. 2001. 'Some Observations on Josephus and Christianity'. *Journal of Theological Studies* 52: 539–624.

Charlesworth, J.H. 1995. 'The Son of David: Solomon and Jesus (Mark 10:47)'. In *The New Testament and Hellenistic Judaism,* eds. P. Borgen and S. Giversen, pp. 72–87. Aarhus: Aarhus University Press.

Choi, M. 1997. 'Christianity, Magic and Difference: Name-Calling and Resistance Between the Lines in *Contra Celsum*'. *Semeia* 77: 75–92.

Cohen, A.P. 1993. *Self-Consciousness. An Alternative Anthropology of Identity*. London: Routledge.

Cotter, W. 1997. 'Cosmology and the Jesus Miracles'. In *Whose Historical Jesus?* eds. W. Arnal and M. Desjardins, pp. 118–31. Waterloo: Wilfrid Laurier University Press.

Crossan, J.D. 1991. *The Historical Jesus: The Life of a Mediterranean Jewish Peasant*. Edinburgh: T&T Clark.

D'Angelo, M.R. 1999. 'Gender and Power in the Gospel of Mark: The Daughter of Jairus and the Woman with the Flow of Blood'. In *Miracles in Jewish and Christian Antiquity,* ed. J.C. Cavadini, pp. 83–109. Notre Dame: University of Notre Dame Press.

Davies, W.D. and D. Allison. 1991. *A Critical and Exegetical Commentary on the Gospel According to Saint Matthew,* vol. 2. Edinburgh: T&T Clark.

Demand, N. 1994. *Birth, Death and Motherhood in Classical Greece.* Baltimore: Johns Hopkins University Press.

Dickie, M.W. 2001. *Magic and Magicians in the Graeco-Roman World.* London: Routledge.

Doyal, L. 1995. *What Makes Women Sick? Gender and the Political Economy of Health.* Basingstoke: Macmillan.

Duling, D.C. 1975. 'Solomon, Exorcism and the Son of David'. *Harvard Theological Review* 68: 235–52.

———. 1985. 'The Eleazar Miracle and Solomon's Magical Wisdom in Flavius Josephus's *Antiquitates Judaicae* 8:42–49'. *Harvard Theological Review* 78: 1–25.

Dunn, J.D.G. 2003. *Christianity in the Making. Volume 1: Jesus Remembered.* Grand Rapids: Eerdmans.

Eitrem, S. 1966. *Some Notes on the Demonology in the New Testament. Symbolae Osloenses Supplement 20*. Uppsala: Almqvist & Wiksell.

Evans, C.A. 1997. '"Who Touched Me?" Jesus and the Ritually Impure'. In *Jesus in Context: Temple, Purity and Restoration*, eds. B. Chilton and C.A. Evans, pp. 353–76. Leiden: Brill.

Eve, E. 2002. *The Jewish Context of Jesus' Miracles*. London: Continuum.

Faraone, C.A. 1999. *Ancient Greek Love Magic*. Cambridge, MA, and London: Harvard University Press.

Faraone, C.A. and D. Obbink, eds. 1991. *Magika Hiera. Ancient Greek Magic and Religion*. New York and Oxford: Oxford University Press.

Fiorenza, E.S. 1995a. *Jesus: Miriam's Child, Sophia's Prophet*. London: SCM.

———. 1995b. *In Memory of Her: A Feminist Theological Reconstruction of Christian Origins*, 2nd ed. London: SCM.

Flusser, D. 1998. *Jesus*. Jerusalem: Magnes Press.

Fonrobert, C. 1997. 'The Woman With a Blood-Flow (Mark 5.24–34) Revisited: Menstrual Laws and Jewish Culture in Christian Feminist Hermeneutics'. In *Early Christian Interpretation of the Scriptures of Israel*, eds. C.A. Evans and J. Sanders, pp. 121–40. Leiden: Brill.

Fredriksen, P. 2000. *Jesus of Nazareth, King of the Jews: A Jewish Life and the Emergence of Christianity*. London: Macmillan.

Funk, R. and the Jesus Seminar. 1998. *The Acts of Jesus: The Search for the Authentic Deeds of Jesus*. San Francisco: HarperSanFrancisco.

Garland, R. 1995. *The Eye of the Beholder. Deformity and Disability in the Graeco-Roman World*. London: Duckworth.

Garrett, S.R. 1989. *The Demise of the Devil: Magic and the Demonic in Luke's Writings*. Philadelphia: Fortress Press.

Gledhill, C. 1988. 'Pleasurable Negotiations'. In *Female Spectators*, ed. E.D. Pribham, pp. 64–89. London: Verso.

Goode, W.J. 1949. 'Magic and Religion: A Continuum'. *Ethnos* 14: 172–82.

Gordon, R. 1995. 'The Healing Event in Graeco-Roman Folk-Medicine'. In *Ancient Medicine in its Socio-Cultural Context*, ed. P.J. von der Eijk, pp. 363–76. Amsterdam: Rodopi.

Graf, F. 1997. *Magic in the Ancient World*. Cambridge, MA and London: Harvard University Press.

Grmek, M.D. 1988. *Diseases in the Ancient Greek World*. Baltimore: Johns Hopkins University Press.

Grossberg, L. 1992. 'Is there a Fan in the House?: the Affective Sensibility of Fandom'. In *The Adoring Audience: Fan Culture and Popular Media*, ed. L. Lewis, pp. 50–65. London: Routledge.

Helman, C. 2000. *Culture, Health and Illness*, 4th ed. Oxford: Butterworth Heinemann.

Hooker, M. 1991. *The Gospel According to Mark.* London: A&C Black.

Horne, Simon. 1999. *Injury and Blessing: A Challenge to Current Readings of Biblical Discourse Concerning Impairment*, unpublished Ph.D. thesis: University of Birmingham.

Hull, J.M. 1974. *Hellenistic Magic and the Synoptic Tradition.* London: SCM.

Hulse, E.V. 1975. 'The Nature of Biblical "Leprosy" and the Use of Alternative Medical Terms in Modern Translations of the Bible'. *Palestinian Exploration Quarterly* 107: 87–105.

Illich, I. 1976. *Limits to Medicine.* London: Boyars.

Jackson, R. 1988. *Doctors and Diseases in the Roman Empire.* London: British Museum Press.

Janowitz, N. 2001. *Magic in the Roman World: Pagans, Jews and Christians.* London: Routledge.

Johnson, L.T. 1997. *The Real Jesus: The Misguided Quest for the Historical Jesus and the Truth of the Traditional Gospels.* San Francisco: HarperSanFrancisco.

Jones, W.H.S. 1957. 'Ancient Roman Folk Medicine'. *Journal for the History of Medicine* 12: 459–72.

Kee, H.C. 1986. *Medicine, Miracle, and Magic in New Testament Times.* Cambridge: Cambridge University Press.

Klauck, H.-J. 2000. *Magic and Paganism in Early Christianity: The World of the Acts of the Apostles.* Edinburgh: T&T Clark.

Klein, R. 1989. *The Politics of the National Health Service*, 2nd ed. Harlow: Longmans.

Kleinman, A. 1980. *Patients and Healers in the Context of Culture: An Exploration of the Borderland Between Anthropology, Medicine and Psychiatry.* Berkeley: University of California Press.

Kottek, S. 1994. *Medicine and Hygiene in the Works of Flavius Josephus.* Leiden: Brill.

Latham, R. and W. Matthews, eds. 1970–1983. *The Diary of Samuel Pepys*, 11 vols. London: G. Bell.

Levine, A.-J. 1996a. 'Second Temple Judaism, Jesus, and Women'. In *A Feminist Companion to the Hebrew Bible in the New Testament*, ed. A. Brenner, pp. 302–31. Sheffield: Sheffield Academic Press.

———. 1996b. 'Discharging Responsibility: Matthean Jesus, Biblical Law and Hemorrhaging Women'. In *Treasures New and Old: New Essays in Matthean Studies*, eds. M.A. Powell and D. Bauer, pp. 379–97. Atlanta: Scholars Press.

Lloyd, G.E.R. 1979. *Magic, Reason and Experience. Studies in the Development of Greek Science.* Cambridge: Cambridge University Press.

Malina, B.J. and J.H. Neyrey. 1996. *Portraits of Paul: An Archaeology of Ancient Personality.* Louisville: Westminster John Knox.

Meier, J.P. 1991. *A Marginal Jew: Rethinking the Historical Jesus. Volume One: The Roots of the Problem and the Person.* New York: Doubleday.

———. 1994. *A Marginal Jew: Rethinking the Historical Jesus. Volume Two: Mentor, Message and Miracles*. New York: Doubleday.
———. 2001. *A Marginal Jew: Rethinking the Historical Jesus. Volume Three: Companions and Competitors*. New York: Doubleday.
Meskell, L. 1999. *Archaeologies of Social Life*. Oxford: Basil Blackwell.
Meyers, E.M. 1997. 'Jesus and His Galilean Context'. In *Archaeology and the Galilee: Texts and Contexts in the Graeco-Roman and Byzantine Periods*, eds. D.R. Edwards and C.T. McCollough, pp. 57–66. Atlanta: Scholars Press.
Muela, S.H., J.M. Ribera and M. Tanner. 1998. 'Fake Malaria and Hidden Parasites – the Ambiguity of Malaria'. *Anthropology & Medicine* 5: 43–61.
Nutton, V. 1991. 'From Medical Certainty to Medical Amulets: Three Aspects of Ancient Therapeutics'. *Clio Medica* 22: 13–22.
———. 1992. 'Healers in the Market Place: Towards a Social History of Graeco-Roman Medicine'. In *Medicine in Society*, ed. A. Wear, pp. 15–58. Cambridge: Cambridge University Press.
Oakley, A. 1984. *The Captured Womb: A History of the Medical Care of Pregnant Women*. Oxford: Basil Blackwell.
Oliver, M. 1996. *Understanding Disability: From Theory to Practice*. Basingstoke: Macmillan.
Park, K. 1992. 'Medicine and Society in Medieval Europe, 500–1500'. In *Medicine in Society*, ed. A. Wear, pp. 59–90. Cambridge: Cambridge University Press.
Parsons, T. 1951. *The Social System*. Glencoe: Free Press.
Pilch, J.J. 2000. *Healing in the New Testament: Insights from Medical and Mediterranean Anthropology*. Minneapolis: Fortress Press.
Porter, R. 1985. 'The Patient's View: Doing Medical History From Below'. *Theory and Society* 14: 175–98.
Powell, M.A. 2000. 'The Magi as Wise Men: Re-examining a Basic Supposition'. *New Testament Studies* 46: 1–20.
Preuss, J. 1978. *Biblical and Talmudic Medicine*. New York: Sanhedrin Press.
Remus, H. 1997. *Jesus as Healer*. Cambridge: Cambridge University Press.
Roberts, C. and K. Manchester. 1997. *The Archaeology of Disease*, 2nd ed. London: Sutton.
Rosner, F. 1995. *Medicine in the Bible and the Talmud*. Hoboken: Yeshiva University Press.
Sande, S. 1999. 'Famous Persons as Bringers of Good Luck'. In *The World of Ancient Magic. Papers from the First International Samson Eitrem Seminar at the Norwegian Institute at Athens, 4–8 May 1997*, eds. D.R. Jordan, H. Montgomery and E. Thomasson, pp. 227–38. Bergen: Norwegian Institute at Athens.
Sanders, E.P. 1985. *Jesus and Judaism*. London: SCM.
———. 1993. *The Historical Figure of Jesus*. London: Allen Lane.
Seybold, K., and U.B. Mueller. 1981. *Sickness and Healing*. Nashville: Abingdon.

Selvidge, M.J. 1990. *Woman, Cult and Miracle Recital. A Redaction-Critical Investigation of Mark 5:24–34*. Lewisburg: Bucknell University Press.

Smith, J.Z. 1995. 'Trading Places'. In *Ancient Magic and Ritual Power*, eds. M. Meyer and P. Mirecki, pp. 13–27. Leiden: Brill.

Smith, M. 1978. *Jesus the Magician*. London: Gollanz.

———. 1980. 'Pauline Worship as Seen by Pagans'. *Harvard Theological Review* 73: 245–49.

Solomon, J. 1993. 'The Wandering Womb of Delos'. In *Woman's Power, Man's Game. Essays on Classical Antiquity in Honour of Joy King*, ed. M. DeForest, pp. 91–108. Wauconda: Bolchazy-Carducci.

Sontag, S. 1978. *Illness as Metaphor*. New York: Farrar, Straus & Giroux.

Sorensen, E. 2002. *Possession and Exorcism in the New Testament and Early Christianity*. Tübingen: J.C.B. Mohr.

Stanton, G. 2002. *The Gospels and Jesus*, 2nd ed. Oxford: Oxford University Press.

Strange, J.F. 1997. 'First Century Galilee from Archaeology and from the Texts'. In *Archaeology and the Galilee: Texts and Contexts in the Graeco-Roman and Byzantine Periods*, eds. D.R. Edwards and C.T. McCullough, pp. 39–56. Atlanta: Scholars Press.

Tenner, E. 1997. *Why Things Bite Back*. London: Fourth Estate.

Temkin, O. 1956. *Soranus' Gynecology*. Baltimore: Johns Hopkins University Press.

Theissen, G. 1983. *The Miracle Stories of the Early Christian Tradition*. Edinburgh: T&T Clark.

———. 1992. *The Gospels in Context: Social and Political History in the Synoptic Tradition*. Philadelphia: Fortress Press.

Theissen, G., and A. Merz. 1998. *The Historical Jesus: A Comprehensive Guide*. London: SCM.

Thomas, J.C. 1998. *The Devil, Disease and Deliverance*. Sheffield: Sheffield Academic Press.

Trunk, D. 1994. *Der messianische Heiler*. Freiburg: Herder.

Twelftree, G.H. 1993. *Jesus the Exorcist: A Contribution to the Study of the Historical Jesus*. Tübingen: J.C.B. Mohr.

———. 1999. *Jesus the Miracle Worker. A Historical and Theological Study*. Leicester: InterVarsity Press.

Vermes, G. 1973. *Jesus the Jew*. London: Collins.

White, R.J. 1975. *The Interpretation of Dreams: Oneirocritca by Artemidorus*. Park Ridge: Noyes Press.

Wright, N.T. 1996. *Jesus and the Victory of God*. London: SPCK.

PART II

MAGIC, CULTURE, SCIENCE

Chapter 5

All the Devils: Port-Royal and Pedagogy in Seventeenth-Century France

Nicholas Hammond

In this discussion of pedagogy, I have taken one of the roots of the word 'magic', namely that in French of the 'mage', which has the sense of learned person or scholar as well as magician. In seventeenth-century France, the first monolingual dictionaries appeared, crowned by the publication in 1694 of the first Académie Française Dictionary. This Académie dictionary explicitly defines 'mage' as relating to 'hommes sçavans' (learned men) who dabbled not only in astrology but also philosophy. The scholar and especially the teacher (the *magister*) would be deemed to have particular powers which were not available to others. At the beginning of *Hamlet*, for example, the character Horatio, upon the appearance of the Ghost, is called upon by Marcellus to speak to the ghost precisely because he is a scholar: 'Thou art a scholar; speak to it, Horatio' (I, 1).

I will return to this idea of the teacher/scholar later in this chapter, but first I would like to consider an extraordinary document, unpublished, which relates to a particularly fraught episode in an already fraught period of the life of Port-Royal, a religious community based both in and near Paris during the seventeenth century. Otherwise known as Jansenists (after their leading influence, the Flemish theologian

Cornelius Jansenius, who is perhaps best known for his massive tome, *Augustinus*), they regularly found themselves at odds with religious and political authorities of the day. A record was kept of the nuns' and confessors' daily lives, mostly consisting of visits to the abbey and other notable events. Yet, the *Journal de l'Abbaye de Port-Royal*, various manuscript copies of which exist in different libraries, is not a cosy collection of fond memories. On the contrary, with the airing of various fragmentary voices, the entries bear witness to a community in imminent danger of disintegrating. Detailed reports are given, often by the nuns involved, of their interrogation by various authorities who attempted to make the nuns sign a document known as the *formulaire*. This formulary, which included the words, 'I condemn through both my heart and mouth Jansenius's doctrine of the five propositions contained in his book *Augustinus*' effectively declared Jansenius, his friend Saint-Cyran (who had been a founding father at Port-Royal) and all who adhered to their beliefs to be heretical. In the journal from 1661, for example, all the nuns at Port-Royal and Port-Royal des Champs, including Agnès de Sainte Thècle Racine, Jean Racine's aunt, who would later become abbess, and Jacqueline Pascal, Blaise's sister, at that time mistress of the novices, record their interviews.

The Dying Nun

I have chosen to focus on an extract from the journal of 1664, for not only does it encapsulate the perilous situation in which the nuns found themselves but also it vividly rehearses some of the major problematics associated with writing their History. The extract consists of the closing moments of an interview, held on 12 February of that year, between an interrogator, M. de Longval, and a dying nun, whom he has been trying to persuade to sign the *formulaire*:

> M. de Longval: Why do you not follow the majority? You have the example of so many virtuous people from all communities who have signed. That ought to be obvious to you and make you unthinkingly obey what is demanded of you. You behold a great King who wants it, all the Church enacting it, the Bishops who have ordered it to be signed in all places. You owe that to everyone.
>
> The Sick Woman: I owe nobody anything other than what I owe to God.

> **M de Longval: In that case, since you are absolutely determined** to do nothing and since you wish to remain in this state of disobedience, I declare to you, on behalf of God, taking his place before you, that you are not in a state of salvation. Through my mediation, He is giving you a way to return from this disobedience, and you refuse Him. You will see after your death, even though there will be no more time to remedy the situation, that today he will have offered you his greatest means of grace, which are the reconciliation and reception of the Holy Sacraments, and that you will have scorned them, preferring to remain in your hardened state, and that is why there is no more salvation for you. I say to you once more, on behalf of God. *You will be damned along with all the devils.* I call you before God's judgement, where I will be your judge, and I will condemn you.[1]

Longval's assertion (underlined in the handwritten manuscript) that the dying nun will be indistinguishable from 'all the devils' is not unlike the terminology used in seventeenth-century witch hunts. One only has to think of the condemnation of Grandier in the affair of the possession of nuns at Loudun, where those condemning him were all too happy to ignore his prayers to God before his death, because, labelled as a 'magician', 'when he spoke of God, he was really speaking of the devil, and when he detested the devil, he was really detesting God; and what we were saying to him was true' (De Certeau 1970: 256). If we look more closely at Longval's interview with the dying nun, we find that the text is dominated by competing rhetorics: on the one hand, M. de Longval progressively uses more threatening (and masculine) means to terrify the dying nun into submission, investing his argument first with royal power ('a great King'), then with the might of the Church ('all the Church' and 'the Bishops'), followed by a sequence of clauses which stress his priestly role as God's spokesman ('taking his place before you', 'through my mediation', 'on behalf of God'), before assuming quasi-divine authority himself in the final sentence (with 'I' repeated three times); on the other hand, the rhetoric of Port-Royal itself plays a part, for the direct quotation of Longval's words (however truthful that transcription may be) allows him in effect to condemn himself through his own mouth (a technique which was used so effectively only a few years earlier by Pascal in his *Provincial Letters*). Moreover, the role which hagiography plays in many of the memoirs from the same time must allow for a plotting of narrative, in the same way that the term 'Relation' is often used to describe accounts of people or events. Yet overall, the very fact that Longval is able to call upon such an array of powerful examples to support his argument only serves to accentuate the vulnerability, isolation and ultimate courage of the dying nun.

In many ways, this tale is emblematic of the situation of Port-Royal as a whole, a community aware of its possibly imminent death and denied absolution by the Church authorities and finally the King himself. Moreover, the written account mirrors the difficulties which they faced in writing their History, for we have not only a documented account of a conversation which took place between two participants in this History but also a harrowingly vivid memoir which goes beyond the realm of objective reporting.

This one small incident in the continued persecution of Port-Royal has been chosen to convey a picture of what even the most humble nuns faced at the time. The inevitable question to ask is why the Church and of course the State felt so threatened by this relatively small group of nuns and attached *solitaires*.

The *Petites Ecoles* (the Teacher as Alchemist?)

There are many reasons for this, and this is not the place to go into all of them. However, one of the major causes of the sustained persecution lies in the threat posed by the schools (*petites écoles*) which Port-Royal had set up from 1637 and which were definitively closed not long before Longval's interview with the nun. Bearing in mind the overwhelming Jesuit dominance of education in France in the seventeenth century, it is clear that many of Port-Royal's education policies were defined in opposition to those of the Jesuit Collèges. The small number of pupils attached to a single teacher, for example, together with the teaching of subjects in the vernacular and the emphasis on translation, set the Port-Royal schools apart from the large Jesuit classes (often including as many as two hundred pupils in each class) where the students were made to memorise whole Latin texts. Moreover, for the first time Port-Royal educators preferred to view children not as incompletely formed adults (Taveneaux 1973) but rather as distinct beings. Those attached to Port-Royal were in little doubt why the Jesuits were instrumental in their persecution. The most famous of all the pupils to have attended the Port-Royal schools, Jean Racine (whom we shall meet again later in this chapter), for example, writes explicitly in his Memoir on Port-Royal that 'this instruction of the young was one of the principal reasons why the Jesuits were motivated to destroy Port-Royal' (Racine 1994: 90). Similarly, Robert Arnauld d'Andilly, the great translator of Augustine's *Confessions*, claims that the success of the Port-Royal schools was 'unbearable' (*insupportable*) to the Jesuits (Arnauld d'Andilly 1734: 138). We certainly find much mutual demonising in both camps. Whereas the Jesuits accuse the Port-Royal schools of teaching pupils 'the maxims of Jansenism' (Arnauld d'Andilly 1734: 139), various Port-Royal sympathisers repeatedly stress the great 'corruption' of the Jesuit colleges. Indeed, Saint-Cyran, one of the founding fathers of Jansenism, goes so far as to state that those in charge of education in his age deserve 'a terrifying succession of curses' from God (Lancelot 1738: 2: 333–34). If we consider the writings on education by such Port-Royal theorists as Pierre Coustel and Pierre Nicole, both of whom taught at Port-Royal, the explicitly Christian basis of the children's education, although shared by all educational establishments in France, was underlined precisely because of the perceived overemphasis on non-Christian authorities in Jesuit schools. The albeit jocular comment by Fontenelle, who was educated at a Jesuit school in Rouen, that 'our education familiarized us so much with the gods of Homer, Virgil and Ovid that in this regard we were born almost pagan' (Dainville 1978: 198),[2] cannot be too far from the perception held by those at Port-Royal of the Jesuit schools.

For those opposed to Port-Royal, on the other hand, the community and its education policies offered something new which was viewed with hostility. Even Louis XIV (Montesquieu's 'great magician') in his Memoirs, referring to the final destruction of Port-Royal in the early eighteenth century, writes that 'I was determined to destroy Jansenism and to disperse those communities where this spirit of novelty (esprit de nouveauté) was fomenting' (Louis XIV 1978: 56). This suspicion of what was seen as new is very similar to the pattern of how so-called sorcerers were identified at the time. Michel de Certeau has argued that those deemed to be 'sorcerers' were often learned people who in some way contravened the traditional image of the priest, doctor or scholar. As de Certeau writes, 'With these new "sorcerers", it was still a secret kind of learning (*savoir*) which was held to be threatening and which was treated as magic, but also it was a modern kind of learning, which distanced them even further from the crowd' (De Certeau 1970: 11). For the Port-Royal educators, many of their pedagogical methods were indeed modern and led first to the schools being disbanded and then to the whole community and its buildings being dismantled and in effect burnt at the stake, like so many witches of the time.

Whatever the horrors perpetrated on Port-Royal, the Jesuits recognised the transformative power which a teacher could exercise over his pupils. We should not forget the Latin root of the term 'education', literally 'e-ducere', to lead out, or even to transform, just as an alchemist might transform base metals into gold. On another level, the Port-Royal emphasis and concentration on translation is itself a kind of alchemy at work. The potential potency of the Port-Royal teachers would seem to have been noted by the Jesuits, especially when one considers the many outstanding thinkers who either taught at or were actively involved with the *petites écoles*. In addition to Saint-Cyran, Coustel and Nicole, already mentioned, Claude Lancelot, who wrote the Port-Royal Grammar, Antoine Singlin, a prominent spiritual director, and Nicolas Fontaine, whose Memoirs contain the famous Pascal text, *Entretien avec M. de Sacy*, all taught at the schools. Other prominent names like Antoine Arnauld, Le Maître de Sacy, and of course Pascal, who devised a reading method for the children as well as other pedagogical texts, were closely involved. Pascal's sister Jacqueline was herself Mistress of the novice nuns and particularly interested in questions of education.

The fact that each teacher at the boys' schools was assigned only five or six pupils makes it easy to discern the control which might be exerted over the children. The teacher is an alchemist who can transform his pupil definitively in the right or wrong direction. Indeed, the pedagogical theorists at Port-Royal are very aware of the potential dangers of such an influence, and careful consideration is given to appropriate reading material, the most effective ways of learning, and the need not to overburden the memory with useless facts. Coustel, for example, compares the pupil's soul to an empty sheet 'on which one can trace all kinds of figures' or even to soft wax, 'which is susceptible to all impressions which one may want to make on it'. For this reason, Coustel tells us, 'it is important to fill their minds first with the purest rays of truth and the most solid maxims of morality' (Coustel 1687: 1: 33–34). Moreover, as Lancelot stresses, the interaction between teachers and pupils is of supreme importance: 'We are their living dictionary, their rule, their commentary; everything is done through spoken communication' (Fontaine 1736: 2: 481).

Racine the Pupil

Racine's connection with the Port-Royal schools lasted for most of his childhood and adolescence. Both his aunt and grandmother were closely linked to the convent, and he moved between various Port-Royal schools between 1649 (when he was ten) and 1658. We have a better idea of his schooling than that of most pupils of the time, because many of his school notebooks and annotated texts have been preserved. Racine's career as a playwright led to alienation from Port-Royal, and it was only after writing *Phèdre* that he effected a reconciliation with Port-Royal.

Especially towards the end of his life, Racine wrote of his schooling. The high quality of the Port-Royal schools receives warm praise, and he mentions in particular the important influence of his teachers, whom he describes as 'extraordinary men' (Racine 1994: 89). Despite his separation from Port-Royal, it is perhaps not surprising therefore to find a number of examples of strong teacher figures in his 'secular' theatre. At this juncture, I must stress that I am not trying to make Racine into a Jansenist apologist in his Greek and Roman plays. However, the figure of the teacher is an important one in some of the plays.

Of those words used by Racine to describe his secondary characters, *gouverneur* is the term most directly related to pedagogy. As the Académie Dictionary of 1694 defines it, 'Gouverneur' is 'someone who has been assigned the role of educating and teaching a young Lord or Prince'.[3] In his annotations on Sophocles' *Electra*, Racine shows particular interest in Orestes' teacher, whom he calls 'gouverneur', and discusses the greater sagacity of the old man as opposed to the younger characters (Racine 1966: 2: 848–49). In Racine's theatre, we find three plays where characters are explicitly designated as *gouverneurs*: Phoenix in *Andromaque*, Burrhus and Narcisse in *Britannicus*, and Théramène in *Phèdre*.

As the *gouverneur* of Pyrrhus, Phoenix's role in *Andromaque* is negligible. The reason for this must stem mainly from the fact that Pyrrhus is already king and is less in need of advice from his teacher than a young prince might be. To a large extent, Phoenix represents the king's past, a past in which the teacher remains entrenched. Not only is he designated by Racine as 'gouverneur d'Achille, et ensuite de Pyrrhus' ('teacher of Achilles and later of Pyrrhus') but also his major response on hearing in II, 5 that Pyrrhus has overcome his passion for Andromaque is to compare his two star pupils, father and son (ll. 634–36). However, the very ineffectual nature of Phoenix (accentuated by his fragmentary utterances) plays an important structural role in *Andromaque*, for at the beginning and end of the play, his words are interrupted by Pyrrhus in a way which shows the pupil's autonomy. In Act I, scene 3, Phoenix's objections are swept aside by Pyrrhus at the arrival of Andromaque:

> Phoenix: Sir ...
> Pyrrhus: I will open my soul to you another time.
> Andromaque is here.[4]

Similarly, and fatally, Pyrrhus's final words involve the interruption of his teacher, at the end of Act IV:

> Phoenix: Orestes loves her still. And perhaps at this price ...
> Pyrrhus: Andromaque awaits me. Look after her son, Phoenix.[5]

Théramène's role in *Phèdre* is more central, precisely because Hippolyte is still a young prince and dependent on his tutor's advice. The close kinship between the two men is stressed by Hippolyte in the very first scene in his acknowledgement to the older man, 'You who have known my heart since I first took breath' (l. 66). Moreover, when Théramène recites tales of Thésée's brave deeds, Hippolyte responds not only to the stories themselves but also to the teacher recounting them (ll. 75–76).

Yet, Théramène knows the limits of his function as Hippolyte's *gouverneur*, for, unlike Oenone who attempts to change the course of events, he does not intervene at crucial moments, such as in II, 6, when Hippolyte responds to Phèdre's *aveu*, and III, 6, where he witnesses Hippolyte's meeting with his father. In the end, he is unable to prevent his charge's death. It is significant that, just before Théramène's long récit, Thésée draws direct attention to Théramène's role as Hippolyte's mentor. Not only has Théramène been given the duty of educating the young price, but also, as Thésée implies, his role has been to act *in loco parentis*: 'What have you done with him, Theramenes?/I put him as a boy into your hands.[6]

The fact that *Britannicus* features two *gouverneurs* rather than the one in *Andromaque* and *Phèdre* both highlights their presence and brings the role of education to the fore. Of all Racine's plays, *Britannicus* features the most lines spoken by *confident* figures (Worth-Stylianou 1999: 224). Much of the play revolves around the instruction of Néron by Burrhus and Narcisse and the dangers involved in teaching a young man who wields considerable power. The demons which are unleashed in the gradual indoctrination of Néron by Narcisse are paradoxically evoked in Britannicus's own reference to an 'envious demon' when he speaks to Junie. We as spectators are present at a form of reverse alchemy as Néron the potential golden pupil is transformed into something base and corrupt. In many ways, the focus of the play is as much upon the teachers as the pupil. The two central teacher-figures constitute what Barthes calls 'the double postulation of Nero' (Barthes 1963: 87). Yet other teacher/*conseiller* characters form part of the backdrop of the main action. Sénèque, for example, who, we are told, is 'occupied far away from Rome' ('occupé loin de Rome', l. 808) is referred to as another tutor figure for Néron. From the very beginning of the play, in a speech to Burrhus, before Narcisse is identified as a rival tutor, Agrippine, who almost obsessively refers to the different *gouverneur* figures in charge of her son, accuses both Sénèque and Burrhus of trying to erase her from Néron's memory: 'Are you and Seneca in competition/To see who first can erase me from his memory?/When I put you in charge of him, was it for this?'[7]

Agrippine wavers between wishing to give to others the authority to instruct Néron and attempting to maintain pedagogical authority herself. As she states in the same scene, 'I can at least teach him to keep his distance/When he indulges in confidences with his subjects'.[8] Burrhus's reply effectively summarises the various pressures involved in the teaching of Néron, such as the relinquishing of authority by the mother, the need for the *gouverneur* to remember the importance of his task, the conflict between family and state, and the question of how much one should teach the 'Maître du monde':

> Yes, you put the young Caesar in my hands,
> I agree, and certainly I should never forget it.
> But did I swear to betray him?
> Make him an emperor who could only obey?
> No. It is not to you I must answer now.
> He is no longer your son but master of the world.

I am responsible to the Roman empire
Which sees success or failure in my hands.
Ah, if it were ignorance he had to be taught,
Was there no one better than Seneca and I?
Why did you keep the flatterers away?
Why look among exiles for men to corrupt him?[9]

Pallas represents another tutor figure who features prominently in Agrippine's thoughts, especially as he has been banished by her son:

So, Burrhus, I was wrong in my suspicions?
And you were famous for your lofty precepts!
Pallas is exiled, his crime was, perhaps,
Raising your master to be emperor.
You know it well enough: he taught Claudius
And so it was that my son was adopted.[10]

The importance of the *gouverneur* figures is highlighted by the fact that both Narcisse and Burrhus are granted monologues in quick succession, II, 8 and III, 2. Burrhus's monologue is dominated by his worries about his decreasing authority as counsellor to Néron.

The struggle between Narcisse and Burrhus is in many ways akin to a struggle over Néron's memory. At several points, both advisers, and Agrippine, refer to words associated with memory and forgetting. Just as Burrhus appeals to Néron to remember his wife, so too does he try to make him forget his animosity towards Britannicus: 'Call your brother. Forget in his arms ...' ('Appelez votre frère. Oubliez dans ses bras ...', l. 1385).

In the opposing camp, in the very next scene, Narcisse manages to sway Néron by claiming that his mother has been praising herself for making him forget his previous decisions (ll. 1418–22). In almost the same breath, he asks Néron, 'Are you going to forget the memory of your own desires?' (l. 1435). As we know, it is this selfish memory which persists at the end of the play. Burrhus's final wish concerning Néron, 'May the Gods make this the last of his crimes' ('Plût aux Dieux que ce fût le dernier de ses crimes!' l. 1788), is not fulfilled.

Racine's final two religious dramas, *Esther* and *Athalie*, are of particular interest, not only because they coincide with Racine's reconciliation with Port-Royal, but also because their fundamental purpose was educational.

After having renounced the theatre in the years following *Phèdre*, Racine was named, along with Boileau, as the historiographer of Louis XIV. It was while he was in this post that he was called upon by Mme de Maintenon to review and correct the constitutions of the newly formed school for girls at Saint-Cyr. Although it would be wrong to discern too many similarities between Saint-Cyr and Racine's own education at Port-Royal, as the two institutions were in most ways very different from each other, some comparisons can usefully be made. Firstly, given the fact that Racine found himself involved once more in an educational establishment, it is significant that around this time he was to start writing extensively of his schooling.

Moreover, given Mme de Maintenon's wish to maintain simplicity within the school, Saint-Cyr, like the Port-Royal schools, was being formed in contradistinction to the practice of many of the Jesuit colleges (Piéjus 2000: 43–44). Again, the dominance of Jesuit educational establishments made it inevitable that new institutions would either model themselves on or shape themselves in opposition to the Jesuit schools.

It is perhaps inevitable that the religious subject matter of *Esther* and *Athalie* and Racine's reconciliation with Port-Royal a few years earlier would lead to both plays being interpreted in a Jansenist light. But of greater importance is the fact that the plays were interpreted by some readers and spectators at the time in this light. I shall limit myself as much as possible to evidence which is substantiated either by Racine's own words or by his sources.

One connection made by Racine between Port-Royal des Champs and the insecure situation of the Jewish people, which so dominates the action of *Esther* and *Athalie*, is worthy of comment. In his *Abrégé de l'histoire de Port-Royal*, composed in the years following *Athalie*'s first performance, he writes with reference to the schoolgirls at Port-Royal,

> Everyone knows with what feelings of admiration and recognition they have always spoken of the education which they received there, and there are those still who in the middle of worldly society and the court maintain the same love for the remains of this afflicted house as the ancient Jews maintained for the ruins of Jerusalem (Racine 1994: 97).[11]

Albeit retrospectively, Racine would seem to be inviting comparison between the plight of the Jewish people, played by schoolgirls at Saint-Cyr, and the children at Port-Royal.

Although in *Esther* there are no explicit teacher figures, the two counsellors of king Assuérus, Mardochée and Aman, recall in many ways the Burrhus/Narcisse axis of *Britannicus*, and their function is quasi-pedagogical. Whereas Mardochée's role is to teach the king the need to save the Jewish race, Aman (who is the king's favourite) attempts to steer the king away from the influence of the Jews. The play is dominated by the potential 'demons' (and the word is used) which the destruction of the Jews might unleash.

Joas, whose education underpins the whole of *Athalie*, is chosen by Racine to be between nine and ten years old, precisely, as he states in the Préface, 'in order to enable him to reply even at that age to the questions put to him' ('pour le mettre déjà en état de répondre aux questions qu'on lui fait'). This is very much consistent with theories of teaching at Port-Royal. According to theorists like Coustel, children under the age of seven should have only their memory cultivated, and only after that should other faculties like judgement be developed. The young Joas is posited by Racine as no different from other children in his ability to nurture these qualities. What makes him 'tout extraordinaire', according to Racine, is the special education which he receives from a very early age in his capacity as 'the unique hope of his nation' ('l'unique espérance de sa nation'). The obligation of Jewish children to write out the Book of Law and for Jewish kings, in particular to write it out twice and to have it 'continually before them' ('continuellement devant les yeux'), thereby keeping it continually within their memory, is seen by Racine as crucial to Joas's exceptional intelligence. Again, as we saw earlier, Port-Royal's education policies focused very much on similar methods, relying on the memorisation of books or extracts which were considered educationally and morally beneficial.

The combination of memory and the Law is integral to the education of Joas in *Athalie*. Racine is insistent on choosing Pentecost as the time to portray Joas's unveiling as the new King of the Jews, because, as he explains in the preface, 'the memory of the publication of the Law on Mount Sinai was celebrated then' ('on y célébrait la mémoire de la publication de la Loi sur le mont de Sinaï'). Joas himself explicitly links learning to read and write to the Law (ll. 662–64).

Throughout the play, all major characters seem to concern themselves with the effectiveness of the young boy Joas's education. Even Athalie, grandmother of Joas and follower of Baal, remarks to Josabet (the high priest Joad's wife), 'I like to see the way you instruct him' ('J'aime à voir comme vous l'instruisez', l. 690). Members of the chorus offer an ongoing commentary on the divine foundation of his education. In Act II, scene ix, for example, we find one girl's comment:

> O let him now rejoice,
> The child loved by the Lord,
> Who early hears His voice
> And whom God has instructed in His word![12]

This hymn of praise is then taken up by the whole Chorus, the members of which act as continuous agents of prayer and memory in the play: 'Blesséd, blesséd the child,/ Whom God instructs and keeps still undefiled!' ('Heureuse, heureuse l'enfance/Que le Seigneur instruit et prend sous sa défense!', ll. 776–77).

Joad is the character to assume principal responsibility for Joas's education, reminding him particularly of his important historical status. In IV, ii, for example, he stresses that 'You must, before the others, be instructed/ Of God's designs for you and for His race' ('Il faut que vous soyez instruit, même avant tous,/ Des grands desseins de Dieu sur son peuple et sur vous', ll. 1267–68).

Connected to this, from the outset, the play's action hovers between forgetfulness, which characterises those who have abandoned the Jewish God, and memory, which is exemplified by that same God's continual remembrance of his people. As Abner tells us in the first scene, apart from a few 'adorateurs zélés', 'everybody else shows a fatal forgetfulness of God' ('le reste pour son Dieu montre un oubli fatal', l. 17). By contrast, in Joad's words from the same scene, God's people 'are always present in his memory' ('est toujours présent à sa mémoire', l. 128). For this reason, Joad sees it as his pedagogical task to make the anointed king remember his historical status and to maintain that memory through the ages. We might usefully be reminded here of the innovative methods of teaching history, particularly ecclesiastical history, at the Port-Royal schools, where the teachers made use of cards to memorise important figures and dates; these cards acted as a *point de départ* for the pupils to discuss amongst themselves the significance of these events, in a way not unlike the constant retelling of Jewish history by Joad and Joas. Joad sees it very clearly as his and Josabet's duty in the education of Joas to recall the significance of that history.

Act II, scene vii, revolves most tellingly around the teaching of Jewish history. Athalie's invitation to Joas to enter her temple and to see her worldly *gloire* is perceived by the young boy as an attempt to induce forgetfulness of God, which is akin to stifling prayer (ll. 680–82). Joas's reluctance to follow Athalie results in a squabble between Athalie and Josabet about the pedagogical methods used to educate Joas. Athalie somewhat sourly notes the imprint of Joad and Josabet's teaching on the boy's mind, as she remarks to Josabet: 'I recognize the mark of both you and Joad, infecting his simple youth' ('De vous et de Joad je reconnais l'esprit./Voilà comme infectant cette simple jeunesse', ll. 702–703). Josabet's reply at first seemingly points to the incorruptibility of their shared history but is immediately undermined by her argument that Athalie has made full use of that same history for her own persuasive ends (ll. 707–708).

In this context, the question must be asked: how effective is Joad as teacher of Joas? As we have seen, the adult protagonists of *Athalie* are all equally anxious about the pedagogical effect that each of them may have on Joas. Whereas Josabet accuses Athalie of using their common history to achieve personal glory, the same accusation can justifiably be levelled at Joad. To a large extent, as John Campbell has shown (Campbell 1989), Joad and Athalie use their surprisingly similar image of their respective gods as weapons to assert political and personal power over each other. Joad may be temporarily victorious at the end of the play's action, but his obsession with vengeance and his bloodthirsty delight at Athalie's demise ('Grand Dieu, voici ton heure, on t'amène ta proie', l. 1668) suggest that his concerns as a teacher of the future king might not be entirely selfless or directed solely toward the divine. To use another analogy, each acts as a magician figure casting spells on each other in the name of their gods.

And, of course, as we saw in the earlier plays, such conflicting influences as a pedagogue are borne out by the events of post-dramatic time, namely the murder of Zacharie by Joas. The star pupil turns out to be somewhat less stellar than expected. Most significantly, the boy chooses to forget the spiritual duties which have so painstakingly been instilled in him. His final prayer to his God, which turns out to be less effectual than Athalie's curse, is sealed by a plea to remember God throughout his life. It is a prayer which remains fragmentary because of its lack of fulfilment. Yet, for the boy with the superlative memory, it is crushingly ironic that his last word should denote forgetfulness:

> God, who behold my sorely troubled heart,
> Avert her malediction far from me.

> Grant it may never come to pass, O Lord!
> If ever I forget You, let me die.[13]

The final lines of the play, spoken by Joad, cannot be divorced from their pedagogical context, for Joad the teacher is attempting to point out the educational value of Athalie's 'fin terrible' to his pupil:

> From this grim end, the sanction of her crimes,
> Learn and do not forget, King of the Jews,
> Kings have a judge in heaven, virtue a shield,
> And there's a father to the fatherless.[14]

The injunction to learn might be directed at us as an audience as well as the failed pupil.

Both *Britannicus* and *Athalie* end with what one might call an almost magical prescience of post-dramatic time. If, by way of conclusion, we return to the situation at Port-Royal in the final years of the seventeenth century, those at Port-Royal seemed all too prescient of their imminent destruction: the almost obsessive need to memorialise their deeds exemplifies this. At the beginning of this chapter, I wrote of the mutual demonization of Jesuits and Jansenists. The prayer which we find uttered by the Chorus in *Esther*, 'May the Demons and those who adore them be for evermore destroyed and confounded' ('Que les Démons, et ceux qui les adorent/Soient à jamais détruits et confondus', ll. 769–70), could perhaps be seen to have been partially fulfilled when, at the very time that the various memoirs related to Port-Royal rose, phoenix-like, from the ashes of their buildings, the Jesuits were expelled from France in 1764. This exile, however, was short-lived, and the only real traces of Jansenism remain in the many extraordinary books which emanated both directly and indirectly from their schools.

Notes

1. M.de Longval: Pourquoi ne suivez-vous pas le plus grand nombre. Vous avez l'exemple de tant de personnes vertueuses et de toutes les communautez qui ont signé. Cela vous devroit crever les yeux et vous porter à obeir sans discernement à ce qu'on vous demande. Vous voyez un grand Roy qui le veut. Toute l'Eglise qui le fait. Les Evesques qui l'ont ordonné partout. Vous devez cela à tout le monde.

La Malade: Je ne dois rien à personne au prejudice de ce que je dois à Dieu.

M.de Longval: Hé bien puisque vous étes absolument determinée à ne rien faire et que vous voulez demeurer dans votre desobeissance, je vous declare de la part de Dieu, et comme vous tenant sa place que vous n'étes pas en état de salut. Il vous donne aujourdhuy par mon entremise un moyen d'y rentrer et vous le refusez. Vous verrez après votre mort, mais il ne sera plus tems d'y remedier, qu'il vous aura offert aujourdhuy ses plus grandes graces, qui sont la reconciliation et la reception des SS et que vous les aurez meprisées, en aimant mieux demeurer dans votre endurcissement, c'est pourquoi il n'y aura plus de salut pour vous. Je vous le dis encore un coup de la part de Dieu. *Vous serez damnée comme tous les diables.* Je vous cite au jugement de Dieu où je seray votre juge, et je vous y condamneray.

2. Notre éducation nous a tellement familiarisés avec les dieux d'Homère, de Virgile et d'Ovide, qu'à cet égard nous sommes nés presque païens.
3. Celuy qui est commis pour avoir soin de l'education et de l'institution d'un jeune Seigneur, d'un jeune Prince.
4. Phoenix: Seigneur .../Pyrrhus: Une autre fois je t'ouvrirai mon Ame,/ Andromaque paraît (ll. 257–58).
5. Phoenix: Oreste l'aime encore. Et peut-être à ce prix .../Pyrrhus: Andromaque m'attend. Phoenix, garde son Fils (ll. 1399–1400).
6. Théramène est-ce toi? Qu'as-tu fait de mon Fils?/Je te l'ai confié dès l'âge le plus tendre (ll. 1488–89).
7. Entre Sénèque et vous disputez-vous la gloire/A qui m'effacera plus tôt de sa mémoire?/Vous l'ai-je confié pour en faire un ingrat? (ll. 147–49).
8. Je puis l'instruire au moins, combien sa confidence/Entre un sujet et lui doit laisser de distance (ll. 167–68).
9. Vous m'avez de César confié la jeunesse,
Je l'avoue, et je dois m'en souvenir sans cesse.
Mais vous avais-je fait serment de le trahir,
D'en faire un Empereur, qui ne sût qu'obéir?
Non. Ce n'est plus à vous qu'il faut que j'en réponde.
Ce n'est plus votre fils. C'est le Maître du monde.
J'en dois compte, Madame, à l'Empire Romain
Qui croit voir son salut, ou sa perte en ma main.
Ah! si dans l'ignorance il le fallait instruire,
N'avait-on que Sénèque, et moi pour le séduire?
Pourquoi de sa conduite éloigner les Flatteurs?
Fallait-il dans l'exil chercher des Corrupteurs? (ll. 175–86).
10. Hé bien, je me trompais, Burrhus, dans mes soupçons?
Et vous vous signalez par d'illustres leçons.
On exile Pallas, dont le crime peut-être
Est d'avoir à l'Empire élevé votre Maître.
Vous le savez trop bien. Jamais sans ses avis
Claude qu'il gouvernait n'eût adopté mon Fils (ll. 809–14).

11. On sait avec quels sentiments d'admiration et de reconnaissance elles ont toujours parlé de l'éducation qu'elles y avaient reçue; et il y en a encore qui conservent au milieu du monde et de la cour, pour les restes de cette maison affligée, le même amour que les anciens Juifs conservaient, dans leur captivité, pour les ruines de Jérusalem.
12. O bienheureux mille fois
    L'enfant que le Seigneur aime,
    Qui de bonne heure entend sa voix,
    Et que ce Dieu daigne instruire lui-même! (ll. 768–71).
13. Dieu, qui voyez mon trouble et mon affliction,
    Détournez loin de moi sa malédiction,
    Et ne souffrez jamais qu'elle soit accomplie.
    Faites que Joas meure, avant qu'il vous oublie (ll. 1797–1800).
14. Par cette fin terrible, et due à ses forfaits,
    Apprenez, roi des Juifs, et n'oubliez jamais,
    Que les rois dans le ciel ont un juge sévère,
    L'innocence un vengeur, et l'orphelin un père (ll. 1813–16).

References

Primary Texts

Arnauld d'Andilly, R. 1734. *Mémoires par Messire Robert Arnauld d'Andilly écrits par lui-même.* Hamburg: van den Hoeck.

Coustel, P. 1687. *Les Regles de l'Education des Enfans,* 2 vols. Paris: Estienne Michallet.

Dictionnaire de l'Académie Française. 1694. Paris: J.B. Coignard.

Fontaine, N. 1736. *Memoires pour servir à l'Histoire de Port-Royal,* 2 vols. Utrecht: aux dépens de la Compagnie.

Le Journal de l'Abbaye de Port-Royal, unpublished manuscript P.R. 64, Bibliothèque de la Société de Port-Royal.

Nicole, P. 1670. *De l'Education d'un Prince.* Paris: veuve Charles Savreux.

Pascal, J. 1665. *Reglement pour les enfans.* In *Les Constitutions du monastere de Port-Royal du S.Sacrement.* Mons: aux dépens de la Compagnie.

Racine, J. 1966. *Oeuvres complètes,* 2 vols. Paris: Gallimard.

———. 1967. *Andromaque, Britannicus, Berenice,* trans. J. Cairncross. Harmondsworth: Penguin, 1967.

———. 1970. *Iphigenia, Phaedra, Athaliah,* trans. J. Cairncross. Harmondsworth: Penguin.

———. 1987. *Britannicus, Phaedra, Athaliah,* trans. C.H. Sisson. Oxford and New York: Oxford University Press.

———. 1994. *Abrégé de l'Histoire de Port-Royal,* ed. A. Couprie. Paris: La Table Ronde.

Secondary Texts

Barthes, R. 1963. *Sur Racine*. Paris: Seuil.
Campbell, J. 1989. 'The God of *Athalie*'. *French Studies* 43: 385–404.
———. 1999. 'Racine and the Augustinian Inheritance: the Case of *Andromaque*'. *French Studies* 53: 279–91.
Carré, I. 1971. *Les Pédagogues de Port-Royal* (1887). Geneva: Slatkine Reprints.
Dainville, F. de, and M.-M. Compère. 1978. *L'Éducation des jésuites: XVI–XVIII siècles*. Paris: Minuit.
De Certeau, M. 1970. *La Possession de Loudun*. Paris: Julliard.
Hammond, N. 2000. 'Educating Joas: the Power of Memory in *Athalie*'. *Seventeenth-Century French Studies* 22: 107–114.
Jaouen, F. 1999. '*Esther/Athalie*: histoire sacrée, histoire exemplaire'. *Seventeenth-Century French Studies* 21: 123–31.
Lancelot, C. 1738. *Mémoires touchant la vie de Monsieur de S. Cyran*, 2 vols. Cologne: aux depens de la Compagnie.
Louis XIV. 1978. *Mémoires*. Ed. J. Longnon. Paris: Tallandier.
McBride, R. 1999. 'Mme de Maintenon – pédagogue chrétienne et raisonnable'. In *Autour de Françoise d'Aubigné Marquise de Maintenon*, ed. A. Niderst, vol. 2, pp. 411–24. Niort: Cahiers d'Aubigné.
McKenna, A. 1975. 'Les petites écoles de Port-Royal'. *Chroniques de Port-Royal* 24: 13–40.
Picard, R. 1976. *Nouveau Corpus Racinianum*. Paris: Centre National de la Recherche Scientifique.
Piéjus, A. 2000. *Le Théâtre des Demoiselles: tragédie et musique à Saint-Cyr à la fin du grand siècle*. Paris: Société Française de Musicologie.
Snyders, G. 1965. *La Pédagogie en France aux XVIIe et XVIIIe siècles*. Paris: P.U.F.
Stewart, W.McC. 1953. 'L'Éducation de Racine'. *Cahiers de l'Association internationale des études françaises* 3: 55–71.
Stone, H. 1998. 'Marking Time: Memorializing History in *Athalie*'. *L'Esprit Créateur* 38/2: 95–104.
Strosetzki, C. 1999. 'Madame de Maintenon et la tradition humaniste dans l'éducation des demoiselles de Saint-Cyr'. In *Autour de Françoise d'Aubigné Marquise de Maintenon*, ed. A, Niderst, vol. 2, pp. 425–46. Niort: Cahiers d'Aubigné.
Taveneaux, R. 1973. *La Vie quotidienne des Jansénistes*. Paris: Hachette.
Worth-Stylianou, V. 1999. *Confidential Strategies: The Evolving Role of the Confident in French Tragic Drama (1635–1677)*. Geneva: Droz.

Chapter 6

The Magic of French Culture: Transforming 'Savages' into French Catholics in Seventeenth-Century France

Sara E. Melzer

When we think of magic, our minds typically conjure up abracadabra-type magic tricks, like a man transforming a top hat into white doves. This transformation is so complete that it is hard to imagine the doves were ever once a hat. Defying all logic, such magic tricks are dismissed as irrelevant to the 'real' world. However, tricks such as these are not unlike what the seventeenth-century State and Church were doing: transforming 'savages' into civilised French Catholics.

This chapter will focus on the seventeenth-century Church and State's official colonial endeavour to transform 'outsiders' into 'insiders'. I will examine how magic played a major role in that transformational process, and how it was at the hidden heart of France's emerging sense of itself. French 'culture', in the seventeenth century, was charged with two related tasks: to transform 'outsiders', and to protect the 'insiders' from being contaminated by the newly assimilated Other. Given this heavy charge, no ordinary culture could do the trick, so to speak. Rather, it had to be endowed with special magical powers.

What do I mean by magic? (I will define 'culture' shortly). It is a tricky phenomenon, difficult to pin down. The seventeenth-century dictionaries do not offer a pertinent definition for my analysis. But this is not surprising. Nor is the fact that magic appears on the fringe of seventeenth-century thought. Magic can only cast its spell and exert its real force to the extent that it cannot be defined or seen. But its invisibility does not mean it does not exist or that it is marginal. Quite the contrary: its invisibility is what enables it to exercise its power.

To give a rough sketch of how I understand magic, I turn to Montesquieu's retrospective look back on the seventeenth century in his *Lettres persanes* (1721), where he described King Louis XIV and the Pope as magicians.

> [T]he King is a great magician, for he exercises dominion even over the minds of his subjects and makes them think as he wishes. If he has only a million écus in his treasury, and has need of two million, he has only to persuade them that one écu is worth two, and they believe it. If he has a hard war to sustain, and no money at all, he has only to put in their heads the notion that a piece of paper is money, and they are instantly convinced (Montesquieu 1964: XXIV, 42–43).

After criticising the king, the speaker then moved on to the Pope.

> [T]here is an even greater magician than he, who is master of the king's mind, even as the king is sovereign over his subjects. This magician is called the pope. Sometimes he makes the prince believe that three is only one, or that the bread he eats is not bread, or that the wine drunk is not wine, and a thousand similar things.

For Montesquieu, magicians transform objects by convincing others that they have meanings that do not adhere in them. His description drips with irony and works to demystify royal and religious power. The real power behind the throne is magic tricks that the mind plays on itself by fabricating symbols.

Montesquieu's irony helps answer a subsidiary question to my primary one. Given that my inquiry is mainly about the transformation of 'outsiders', the next logical question is how one constructs the instruments of that transformation. Montesquieu addressed that issue by showing how ordinary objects such as bread, wine and paper are themselves transformed so that they can in turn possess the ability to transform one's ways of perceiving and thinking.

At the most basic level, bread, wine and paper are ordinary objects that do not have much meaning other than their practical use value. However, they can take on added meanings which signify mental concepts so powerful they can profoundly alter one's consciousness, a process that Roland Barthes has described in *Mythologies* (Barthes 1957). When outsiders to a given system of meaning look at bread, wine or paper, they see them starkly, in their nakedness, devoid of any larger, symbolic meaning. The outsider's naive perceptions highlight the magic central to most signifying systems, for there is a mysterious process that frames ordinary objects so they signify something more than themselves. And this 'something more' appears lodged in the objects themselves, as if it were natural. Any object, no matter how banal, can be transformed in this way. What changes are not the objects themselves, but our perceptions of them. This transformational process is a 'magic' that can only cast its signifying spell if it does not have a flashing neon sign pointing to itself. Magic must disguise itself and masquerade as natural. This is precisely why magic is not and cannot be named directly in the contexts I will be considering.

Returning now to the State and Church's efforts to transform 'outsiders' into 'insiders', my goal is to understand magic's role in that process. It is well known that the nineteenth- and twentieth-century French State sought to transform 'peasants into Frenchmen', as part of an internal colonisation, an assimilation process that Eugen Weber has described (Weber 1976). What is not well known, however, is that the seventeenth-century external colonisation of the New World 'savage' provided an important foundation for this assimilationist strategy. I propose to examine the foundation of France's assimilation policy in the seventeenth century. My argument is that French culture came to assume important magical properties and it did so partly in relation to some key problems posed by the assimilation of the 'savage' Other.[1]

I will focus on two different kinds of 'outsiders'. The first is an internal Other, French peasants, the inhabitants of the French-Spanish border in the Labourd region. The Church and State accused the Labourdins in 1609 of witchcraft in the largest and most important witchcraft trial of the seventeenth century (De Lancre 1982). France's internal colonisation of its peasants was linked to its external colonisation of the New World 'savages' in that the State and Church viewed the Labourdins as 'savages' akin to the New World 'savage'. They saw them as creatures in cahoots with each other, threatening France's political, social and religious order. In the trial, the

State sought to map the Labourdin witch onto the New World, as we will see.

The New World 'savage' is the second form of 'outsider' I will discuss. This choice calls for greater explanation since the most important and threatening form of Otherness is always the one closest to home. It thus might seem more appropriate to turn to various groups inside France, such as the Protestants, lapsed Catholics, Jews, peasants, or libertines. Nevertheless, I focus on the New World 'savage' for several reasons. First, in seventeenth-century France, the Other was defined negatively, by what it lacked; not positively by what it possessed. What each form of Otherness lacked was the same: Frenchness and Catholicity. In their Otherness, they were essentially similar. Disparate groups such as Protestants, lapsed Catholics, Jews, peasants, and libertines, along with Amerindians, were all lumped together in an indistinguishable mass, all viewed as 'savage' in a generic way. The specificity of their differences did not really matter.[2] They were all particular instances of what I call the 'Universal Other'.

The New World 'savage' best embodied this Universal Other. The 'savage' was a composite figure; it was both a mythical creature as well as a real world, flesh and blood being. As a myth, the prototypical image of the 'savage' was invented long before the New World had made its way on to the map of the Western consciousness. It dates back to Ancient Greece and Rome (White 1972). But the 'discovery' of the real world Amerindian breathed new life into the pre-existing myth. It served as the primary real world referent for this archetype (Ellingson 2001: 4). The New World 'savage' came to function as the stripped-down model of Otherness. Reduced to its most primitive form, stripped of its particularities, the New World 'savage' lurked behind all forms of Otherness. I will examine how the image of the New World 'savage' shadowed the French peasant. However, the same dynamic would apply to the perceptions of multiple forms of Otherness: the lapsed Catholic, Protestant, Jew, or libertine, as well as other groups. For each group, the shadowy image of the New World 'savage' was conjured up even when it was not directly mentioned.[3]

The New World 'savage' was also important as a real world flesh and blood creature. It posed the problematic of assimilation in its most stark and extreme form. As a real world being, the New World 'savages' were at the furthest remove from French civilisation. They roamed the woods half-naked, half-dressed in animal skins tied with intestinal gut. When not dining on human flesh, they would make do with moose lips, bear fat, or soups cooked with shoes in them. Many travellers described them as living without law, engaging in wild sexual orgies.

And yet, despite these differences, the State and Church still eagerly sought to educate and assimilate them. This meant that the boundaries separating an 'us' from the 'them' had to be stretched to the furthest extreme to accommodate them.[4] The New World 'savage' thus constitutes an important 'limit case'. It highlights issues about assimilation that might otherwise pass unnoticed in cases closer to home. Because the New World 'savage' posed these problems in their most clear form, I begin with this case before moving on to the 'inside-outsiders', the inhabitants of the French-Spanish border.

Assimilation and Culture

Assimilation was a colonising strategy that cultivated the power of culture to the greatest extent. Culture had to possess sufficient force to function as an alternative to military might. There are basically three different colonising choices. The first would kill off the indigenous peoples to take possession of the land. The reliance on physical force meant that the colonised did not need to depend as much on its cultural resources. A second colonising strategy would dominate the population in one of several forms, such as enslaving the inhabitants, beating them into submission or separating them on reservations, as did the English in creating an Indian reservation system. Such a strategy would still necessitate considerable physical force, and rely on a cultural force to some significant degree. Assimilation, as the third alternative, would use the least amount of physical force. To develop a strong military presence would undermine the trust and cooperation upon which assimilation was based. This meant that a cultural power had to be cultivated to the highest degree. It would dominate through its magnetic, seductive force.

To be sure, each nation employed a mixture of different approaches, always using military might and cultural influence to some extent. But there was always one that predominated. France was the only early modern European nation in which assimilation was the official, dominant mode of colonisation, thus explaining, in part, why France developed its culture more self-consciously than did England, Holland, Spain or Portugal.

I use the term 'culture' in several interrelated senses. In the seventeenth century, the term 'culture' had a very different meaning than it does today. It was used more in its etymological sense, for it derived from agri*culture* and referred to the cultivation of the earth and of plants.[5] It was applied metaphorically to humans as plants; they were capable of cultivation. If humans were left in their original state of nature, they would, like plants remain wild and 'savage'. (Hence the term 'savage' to designate the uncultivated, wild Amerindians.) But they could be cultivated to be brought within the order of 'civilisation'.[6] The French concept of *civilisation* was based on the Roman *civitas,* etymologically linked to the *civil* quality of a citizen and the moral order of the city. The first meaning in which I use the term 'culture' is akin to the Roman *civitas.* The *civitas,* like the Greek *polis,* was not one place amongst many. It was the only place, at least for Roman theorists such as Cicero, in which the cultivation of the human was truly possible (Pagden 1995: 11–28). Those who dwelled outside its walls were less than human. A second meaning for the term 'culture' refers to the material objects that are part of its civil society, such as food and clothing. While material objects exist at a 'primitive' level, they can be refined and 'cultivated' to take on the value of an art. Such objects reflect a set of beliefs and values about the perfection of the civil order. The Romans believed that the *civitas* possessed the power to transform those who came in contact with it. It had an almost magical quality that could 'cultivate' and 'civilise' those deemed 'savage'. It is here that we come to the third meaning for my use of the term 'culture', for it needs to be understood not as a thing but as a process. Aspiring to be the 'New Rome', France thought that its civilisation would produce the same magical, transformative effect (Pagden 1995: 21). In short, then, I use the term 'culture' to designate a type of community marked by its civility, objects within it, and a process whereby they can together transform outsiders into members of that perfected, civilised community (Greenblatt 1995: 225–32).

To understand the most important elements of French 'culture' for this context and how they had to function, it is important to realise the problematic nature of assimilation in the seventeenth century. As a strategy, it was open to gradations, ranging from minimal to maximal levels of contact with the colonised. Unlike its nineteenth- and twentieth-century counterpart, where the French State sought to minimise the level of contact between coloniser and colonised, the seventeenth-century Church and State interpreted assimilation in its most maximal form, adopting an 'integrationist' approach (Jaenen 1976: 153–89). The French State and Church were more open to the Other than they were at any other point in their history. Their level of openness is best conveyed by the fact that both the Church and State aggressively promoted intermarriage between the French and the 'savages' at varying moments in this period. For example, in 1613 Capucin Father Claude d'Abbeville brought several Brazilian men to France to be publicly baptised and then married to young French women before the King and Queen.[7] Father d'Abbeville had staged these ceremonies as elaborate, public relations spectacles to dramatise the Capucins' great success in converting the 'savages'. The King, to signify his approval, became the godfather to these Toupinambou men, who were all re-named Louis.

In the 1630s when the Jesuits wrested the colonial endeavour away from the Capucins, they also favoured a maximal form of assimilation at first, including intermarriage.[8] For example, in his *Relation* of 1636, Jesuit Father Le Jeune urged that 'these little savage girls [be] brought up as Christians and then married to Frenchmen'.[9] The success of their endeavour 'will lie in our succouring them, in giving them a dowry, in helping them to get married'.[10] The Jesuits offered dowries to promote more stable intercultural unions.

The colonising ideal was what we would today call 'passing'. Jesuit Father Paul Le Jeune described it in praising a young Amerindian girl who had been sufficiently educated so that now 'this child has nothing savage about her except her appearance and colour; her sweetness, her docility, her modesty, her obedience, would cause her to pass for a young well-born French girl' (Thwaites 1896: IX: 104).[11] Passing is the transformation of an individual from one form into another so that all traces of one's former existence vanish into thin air.

I am calling this colonising ideal 'assimilationist' although the term had not yet been coined. The concept, however, did exist and was conveyed by the phrase 'one people', an entity created out of the Amerindians' ability to pass for French. The phrase was first used by the Capucins in reference to the Toupinambou Indians of Brazil (Mercure François 1617). Since the Church had spearheaded much of the colonising work in the New World, at least until 1650, much of their terminology continued to endure. After the 1650s the State began to take the lead, but continued to support the creation of 'one people'. Colbert, King Louis XIV's minister, was one of the strongest supporters of an integrationist approach to assimilation, and added the phrase 'one blood' to 'one people'. He wrote: 'If it is possible to mix them, over time, having the same law and the same master, they will constitute *one people and one blood*' (my emphasis) (*Rapport de l'Archiviste de la Province de Québec* 1930–1 XL: 72; Provost 1964 I: 36).[12] To achieve this goal, he insisted, 'it is necessary to employ all of our temporal authority to attract the savages amongst our French, which can be done through marriage' (Clément 1865: III: 404).[13] It was necessary to 'instruct the children of the savages and to render them capable of being admitted into the common life of the French, so that they only compose *one people*' (my emphasis) (Clément 1865: III: 452). Colbert continually repeated that the Amerindians should be 'instructed in the maxims of our religion and in our manners', so that 'they can compose along with the inhabitants of Canada *one people* and by this means fortify the colony (my emphasis) (*RAPQ* 1930–1: 147).[14] The repetition of 'one people' underlines the strong and intimate connection between the French and a people whom they consistently called 'savages' and 'barbarians'.

The most hotly debated question was how much contact the French should maintain with the 'savages'. That this should have been the case is not surprising. Assimilation, especially in its most maximal form, was a problem, for it had two conflicting needs. It was, on the one hand, expansionist, with an extraordinary level of openness to the Other. Creatures as far out on the scale of civilisation as flesh-eating cannibals could be transformed and brought within the civilised order to form 'a single people and a single blood' with the French. This transformational process implied a willed transgression of the boundaries separating the 'civilised' from the 'savage'. It temporarily dissolved the radical 'us/them' dichotomy to expand the 'us' portion of the divide.

On the other hand, this openness needed a corresponding closedness to ensure the identity of that 'us'. Like a rubber band, the expanded boundaries needed to be snapped back in place to reaffirm the same basic principles of the division to make sure that whatever it was that constituted the 'us' remained intact and was not influenced by the 'them'. Assimilation thus posed a double-edged dilemma: the question was how to allow for expansion, yet preserve the identity and the 'purity' of the 'us'.

French culture was charged with negotiating these contradictory needs. In this context, France's material culture became particularly important since its more refined 'art' would have been inappropriate and less appealing for such a primitive Other as the New World 'savage'. However, the same principles would apply to the more elite forms of culture and Otherness. My goal now is to turn more specifically to the links between how France's material culture emerged as part of a self-conscious strategy to respond to the contradictory need of assimilation. Culture was constructed to perform the offensive and defensive functions that the military would have otherwise assumed. I explore three of its major functions: seduction, transformation and protection, each of which seemed to take on the properties of magic. I separate them out for the sake of clarity but they were all intertwined.

Seduction

As an alternative to brute force, France's material culture took the offensive by operating through seduction. The French State self-consciously sought to create a culture so alluring and charming that people the world over would want to imitate the French. As if by magic, French culture would conquer through charm, enchanting people. The French would not have to impose force because their culture would do the trick. It would stimulate in others the desire to become like the French, seducing them into voluntarily imposing a form of colonisation on themselves. If French culture continues to this day to be associated with the art of seduction, this was no accident. It resulted from a self-conscious strategy of cultural imperialism.

To colonise was to seduce; culture was its prime agent. The material aspects of French culture worked on the 'savage' Other by a series of hidden attractions and desires as well as repulsions. Many missionaries and colonists presented this process of seduction as a naturally occurring phenomenon, a logical and voluntary choice to improve their lives and 'civilise' themselves.[15] The French were there simply to help.

France's material culture lured them through its 'sweetness of life'.[16] Once the 'savages' had tasted it, they would be magnetically drawn towards the French world. Throughout the *Relations Jésuites*, the missionaries described how they were providing the 'savages' with French food, clothes and lodging, for 'having tasted the sweetness of life that does not always cry out in hunger, as do these Barbarians' (Thwaites 1896: VI: 106),[17] the 'savages' would prefer to remain with the French and leave their past life behind. The 'savages'

> ... will become so accustomed to our food and our clothes, that they will have a horror of the Savages and their filth. We have seen this exemplified in all the children brought up among our French. They get so well acquainted with each other in their childish plays, that they do not look at the Savages except to flee from them or mock them (Thwaites 1896: IX: 106).[18]

The seductiveness of French culture also had a strong protective force built in. The power of the seduction was so strong that the 'savages', in crossing the cultural divide, would not hesitate to burn their bridges behind them, severing all ties to their ancestral culture. Father Le Jeune told the story of a young Amerindian boy, 'notre petit Fortuné', who was one of several young children who were sent to France each year, on the equivalent of a Study Abroad programme. When the chosen Amerindian would return home transformed, he would serve as a model and a lure, making his companions desirous of becoming just like him: French and Catholic. The Amerindian child, 'having been [in France] two years, would return with a knowledge of the language, and having already become accustomed to our ways, he will not leave us and will retain his little countrymen' (Thwaites 1986: VI: 85).[19] Ideally, this strategy was to produce a domino effect.

The strategy was to make French culture act upon their desires, making the 'savages' wish to 'demeurer volontiers' ('remain voluntarily') amongst the French settlers (Thwaites 1896: VI: 86). The French colonists envisaged the proverbial carrot approach as opposed to the stick so that they could manage 'by gentle treatment to constrain them to do better and by good example to incite them to correct living'.[20]

The missionaries and colonists did not use the term 'magic', but spoke rather in terms of a series of hidden attractions and revulsions operating beneath the surface of their culture. There was something almost magical about French food, clothing and lodging, as if it had cast a spell over the 'savages' to bring them into the fold. The first function of France's material culture, then, was that it had to have a magnetic quality, with the power to charm or entice.

Transformation

The seductive function of culture was allied with a second one: transformation, since the 'savages' had to be transformed into members of the French, Catholic world. If culture were to serve as an instrument of that transformation, towards what ideal would outsiders be transformed? And how would it be achieved? Thus far, I have been speaking about the Church and State as if they functioned in almost perfect harmony with each other. To a large extent, they did work in tandem, for their interests often overlapped or were interdependent. However, they did not always coincide (Jaenen 1976; Goddard 1990; Phillips 1997). Given their competition, it is important to separate out their respective goals and I will focus mostly on the political goal. As Samuel Champlain had put it, the 'savages' would acquire 'a French heart and spirit' (Champlain 1929: 264–65).

Father Paul Le Jeune in his *Relations Jésuites* described how France's material culture would magically help give the Amerindians 'a French heart and spirit'. He told of a young 'savage' baby who was baptised, given a French name, Francois Olivier, and then handed over to a French godmother and godfather. His birth parents noticed that he was, presto-chango, magically transformed by his contact with things French.

> They had swaddled this little Christian in the French fashion; its mother, holding it, said to her husband: 'I do not know what ails our little Francois Olivier; when he is dressed in the French way he laughs all the time, when he is dressed in our way he cries and grieves; when I hold him he is quite sad and mournful, and when a French woman holds him he acts as if he wants to jump all the time.' She wished by these words to show her satisfaction at seeing her son become French, as it were (Thwaites 1896: IX: 14–16).[21]

This passage is told from the supposed perspective of the birth mother who observed a marked change in her baby when he was 'dressed in the French way'. His new attire were not ordinary garments, for they miraculously stimulated an immediate and magical change. The baby suddenly began to smile and was happy, as opposed to his former sadness 'when he [was] dressed in the [savage] way'. It was as if the French godmother was a fairy godmother and had sprinkled fairy dust over him, for he became a new person. Similarly, as soon as his French godmother held him, the baby instinctively felt the difference and began to jump with joy. What the French godmother did to produce this effect was not evident. But clearly she had a certain 'je ne sais quoi'[22] – an indefinable, ineffable something to make him smile and jump. And whatever that quality was, the birthmother did not have it.

In another vignette, Le Jeune described the magical effects of French dress. '[When t]hese little girls are dressed in the French fashion, they care no more for the Savages than if they did not belong to their Nation' (Thwaites 1896: IX: 102–3).[23] The wearing of French clothes stimulated a change of identity, with the twin effects of causing the Amerindian girls to identify themselves more with the French, and disassociate themselves from the 'savages'.

Thus far I have discussed only one kind of transformation, focusing on the 'savages' themselves. But given that French culture was to be the instrument of their transformation, select elements of French culture themselves had to be transformed to be endowed with properties capable of performing the desired change. As I mentioned earlier, specified elements of French material culture, such as clothes, food, lodging could not be seen simply as ordinary objects but had to be transformed so they could conjure up other worlds of meaning. Like Montesquieu's example of money, bread and wine, clothes can be transformed so they can enter into a symbolic system that moulds the mind in such a way as to create a new French heart.

'Frenchification' was modelled on religious conversion. French clothes came to function like the dipping of a baby in baptismal water. They were to be endowed with the power to transform the soul and spirit so that one can be born anew, with a new French heart and spirit. This magical transformation of clothes is part of a sacralisation of French material culture, making it capable of performing functions similar to that of conversion. Magic would give French culture a sacred aura so that the state could compete with the Church for the souls of the savages.

If conversion aspired to a new Christian heart, Frenchification sought to create a new French heart. Both transformations were like heart transplants where the old is ripped out, replaced by a new improved version. They both began with imitating outer signs. In a religious conversion, the non-believer had to imitate the outer signs and practices of the believer. Pascal, in his wager argument, put forth a behaviouralist notion of conversion that featured imitation as a key role in the transformational process. He advised the non-believer to imitate the outward gestures, the rituals and practices of the believer, even if at first they were simply empty signs. The non-believer must first act *as if* he or she believes. Over time, one's inner world would come to align itself with one's outer practices and the non-believer would come to have faith. The same would be true of 'Frenchification', a cultural, social and political transformation. It would begin by imitating the outer signs of Frenchness. One would act *as if* one were French, and over time one would develop a 'French heart and spirit' in alignment with its outer signs. Soon one would be born anew, 'comme devenu Français'. Akin to baptism, 'Frenchification' produced a mystical change of heart, stripping the 'savages' of their old identity and giving them a new one. Soon all traces of their former life would vanish as if they never existed.

But what were the outer signs of Frenchness? That was an issue that was in the process of being worked out. Unlike Catholicism, Frenchness had not yet been formulated and codified into a series of rituals, a set of beliefs, behaviours, and practices. But that was clearly the goal: to construct an alternative signifying system that could compete with Catholicism. The elements of French material culture needed to be transformed to produce its own magic.

Protection

The combined seductive/transformative function of culture slides into a third one, protection. To protect 'insiders' from the Other was particularly important because assimilation made it impossible to fix clearly defined physical boundaries separating the 'savage' from the 'civilised'. Moreover, to the extent that some boundaries did exist, they were stretched to their furthest extreme to include outsiders on the edge of civilisation. It was thus necessary to develop alternative boundaries, even if they were invisible. And that was of course the only kind they could come up with. The invisibility of the boundaries was precisely what allowed for the flexibility of French expansion, enabling a continued re-mapping of borders as the French were expanding their empire outward, pushing back the supposed frontiers of barbarism.

Although these boundaries were invisible and elastic, they were not any the less powerful. This is where magic enters the picture. The elements of French culture had to be made to work like a magic charm that could draw an imaginary, protective circle to shelter the insiders from the negative influence of outsiders. The line of demarcation, although invisible, was keenly felt through its effects, just like the newly baptised infant intuitively felt the difference when he was dressed 'in the French way' and was held by his French godmother. Clothes were part of a mysterious, underlying system that caused the Amerindians to be magnetically drawn towards French life and repelled by 'the savage way'.

Protection was built into magic's sudden, presto-chango kind of transformation. Like a top hat transmuted into doves, one's first existence as a 'savage' can vanish in a puff of smoke, without any residue left over to mix in with a new hybridised concoction. Just as the cross between a hat and a dove would seem absurd, so too would that of a 'savage' and a French Catholic. Assimilation did not mean a mixture between the two cultures. Each would remain separate. It was only when the 'savages' were as fully transformed as the top hat that they could gain entry into the inner circle. The seductive power of French culture would ensure that the French would not have to accommodate the 'savages' or compromise since the lesser beings would do all the changing, with the French remaining fixed in their Frenchness.

While this was the theory, the historical reality was of course quite different. In the *Relations,* many of the stories implicitly challenge that theory as well as support it. But there was a kind of magical thinking involved in the *Relations*' efforts to convey that the boundaries were nevertheless imposing themselves spontaneously. The *Relations* sought to give the impression that physical boundaries were not necessary since the objects of French culture constituted powerful, naturally occurring boundaries that produced the same effect.

The magical aura of the protective circle was so strong that both the Amerindians and the French felt its effects. For example, Father Le Jeune described a young 'savage' girl who was now living with the French and had been brought up 'in the French way' ['à la francoise'] (Thwaites 1896 XI: 92–93). When she 'goes back to the Cabins of the Savages, her father, very happy to see his daughter well clothed and in very good condition, does not allow her to remain there long, sending her back to the house *where she belongs*' (Thwaites 1896 XI: 93

my emphasis).[24] The girl's clothes and appearance constitute a boundary. Even her father felt their effects since he understood that his own daughter belonged on the opposite side of the imagined divide.

Not only did the apparent differences between the 'savage' and the French ways of life constitute boundaries, but the Amerindians themselves were instinctively policing these borders. So completely transformed were these 'savages' that they would flee their past life once they had crossed the imagined divide. Pierre the Montagnais was a young boy sent to France by the Recollet Fathers to learn French. When he returned home, 'he fled from the Savages; he was compelled to return among them, in order to learn the language which he had forgotten; he did not wish to go ...' (Thwaites 1896: VI: 86).[25] The boundaries remained intact since the 'savages' had internalised French values, identifying with the French and against themselves as 'savage' (White 1972; Melzer forthcoming). Or such was the idealised view that the French *relateurs* projected onto the Amerindians, a view which enabled assimilation to take place.

There was, of course, another 'insider' who needed protection: the French colonists and missionaries who risked being colonised by the 'savages'. Missionary Father Le Jeune articulated this danger when he wrote Richelieu: 'I do not know if I am becoming savage conversing with the savages everyday' (Thwaites 1896: VII: 238).[26] If one could anchor oneself in French culture, this would prevent the colonists and missionaries from slipping down the slippery slope into savagery. But French culture could not be maintained in its purity in the New World (Melzer 2001).

The greatest threat, however, was not the real world, flesh and blood Amerindians, but the 'savage within': the 'savage' within the French themselves. This danger was built into the way the French conceptualised the 'savage' itself. The French could not construct the 'savage' as something of a totally different order from the 'civilised', protected by impermeable boundaries. But rather the 'savage' and the 'civilised' had to be on the same continuum, with the savage on the bottom and the civilised at the top. If they were of totally different orders, it would be hard to imagine how the 'savages' could ever be transformed into French Catholics. A transformation was suggested by the definition of the term 'savage'. As all of the seventeenth-century definitions made clear, the 'savage' meant, amongst other meanings,[27] 'uncultivated' or 'wild'. Its wildness came not from an inherent quality, but from external circumstances that could be changed. The savage could be cultivated and brought within the order of the civilised; however, there always lurked a fear that the reverse would transpire, that the civilised French could slide back on that continuum and be sucked back down into primitivism and wildness.

The idea of being pulled back into a 'state of nature'[28] was not an abstract, remote possibility. It seemed like a real, potentially imminent danger because of the speculation about the origins of the New World 'savage'.[29] In response to the much debated question of who the Amerindians were, Marc Lescarbot, a seventeenth-century coloniser, proposed in his 1605 *History of New France* (Lescarbot 1968) that they could have been French sailors, merchants or even noblemen who were shipwrecked and forced into a state of nature. Finding themselves naked, these French sailors would have been compelled to live by hunting and fishing and to clothe themselves in the skins of the animals they had killed. Over time, they would have lost their knowledge of God and French ways. Lescarbot based this theory on the supposedly true story of a French nobleman, the Marquis de la Roche of Brittany, who in 1598 sought to colonise New France. His vessel was shipwrecked. He and his crew remained in the New World for five years, living on fish and the milk of some cows they had brought over. Finally they were rescued and when they returned, they presented themselves to the king dressed in walrus skins. The unpredictable forces of nature could make even the French nobility resemble 'savages' in the state of nature. The greatest fear then was ultimately not so much the real world, flesh and blood 'savage', as the 'savage within', since the savage Other was not quite so Other.

Black Magic

The notion that French culture could serve as a protective magic shield against the 'savage within' was dramatically conveyed in the biggest witchcraft trial of the century. It took place in the Basque region in the Labourd province, on the border of Spain in 1609. The State and the Church competed with each other to conduct the trial, for both saw the Labourd as rife with witches. The State won out since King Henri IV appointed Pierre de Lancre, a magistrate from Bordeaux, as the prosecutor. De Lancre framed the Labourdins' 'crime' as a function of their relationship to French culture. What they were really accused of was refusing to fully integrate into the French community.

After conducting the trial, Pierre de Lancre wrote a book about his findings, *Tableau de l'inconstance des mauvais anges et demons, ou il est amplement traicté des sorciers et de la sorcellerie* in 1609. One of the main questions that he asked was why the Labourd had more witches than in any other part of France. De Lancre had estimated that almost everyone single one of the Labourd's 30,000 inhabitants had engaged actively in satanic practices and associations at some time. His main goal was to figure out what made them so susceptible to the devil. His response came in the form of a narrative constructed out of the hundreds of depositions he took for the trial. This book was so popular and widely read that there were several editions of it in the years immediately following its first publication in 1610. The story he told was essentially about the dangers of non-assimilation.

Politically, the Labourdins were French. Ever since 1451, the Labourd was an official part of France when it was annexed, as one of three provinces of the Basque region. Politically, this province fit into the centralising political unity of France, subordinated to Royal authority and connected through a magistrate. By 1609, however, the Labourdins were still not yet acculturated and assimilated.

This witchcraft trial was a vehicle through which the French State sent the following message: if the inhabitants of France failed to live inside the boundary stones of 'civilisation', the State would be powerless to protect them. The boundary stones were not marked by physical boundaries so much as by a set of emerging codes of Frenchness. If the inhabitants did not become schooled in them and abide by them, they would become easy prey for the devil and his black magic. Their geographic location on the periphery of France was at the root of the problem. Living on the edge of France and Spain, in between the mountains and the sea, not fully committed to one space or another, they led 'halfway' lives 'à demi' or 'à moitié'. Such a location meant they inhabited a place of a cultural *métissage*, the French mixed in with the Spanish and the Basque. De Lancre described how the Labourd was situated 'on the edge of three Realms, France, Navarre, Spain' (De Lancre 1982: 72). The Labourdins mixed with the inhabitants of Navarre and Spain, with its culture bearing the mark of that mixture. Situated 'on the frontier of France and Spain, half in the mountains and half on the coast', they spoke a language that was 'a mixture of three languages, French, Basque and Spanish' (De Lancre 1982: 72). As for its inhabitants, De Lancre asked, do they belong 'among us who are French' or are they foreigners? (De Lancre 1982: 72).

De Lancre's portrait of the Labourdins was of a people so distant from France's civilising influence that they could barely qualify as French. Unlike 'these *gentilshommes* who frequent the Court, ... having been raised in the French way' (De Lancre 1982: 78), they were more like strangers: 'Their commercial dealings which take place more in Navarre and Spain than in France, keep them indifferent to French manners, customs, sentiments'.[30] Their physical distance from Paris, the centre of civilisation, made them indifferent to what were emerging as the defining characteristics of Frenchness: manners, clothes and the proper sentiments.

The diversity of their region diluted the impact of the Frenchness on them and made this region fertile ground for the devil. 'All these diversities provide Satan with the means to make this a fertile ground for his assemblies and Sabbaths' (De Lancre 1982: 72).[31] Heterogeneity was to be shunned in favour of a cultural and linguistic homogeneity. They needed to speak a separate language that was incomprehensible to the Spanish and distinctly French to keep out the devil.

De Lancre wrote as if the Amerindians were stacked behind the Spanish, as in Chinese boxes. This confusion was due to the fact that most male Labourdins were fishermen who had travelled to the New World in pursuit of whales, cod and *loups de mer*. When they returned home they had to enter via Spain, for their ports were in Spain, not France, such that there was a strange triangulated relationship between France, Spain and the New World, with Spain as an intermediary or half-way house between 'civilisation' and 'savagery'. The Labourdins, 'returning from the Indies, the New World, Canada and other places, must use Spanish ports, where [the Labourdins] are kept under wraps in a position of submission as in enemy territory' (De Lancre 1982: 74).[32] The devil's main outpost was in the New World but he also developed more proximate strategic bases in Spain from which to launch his attack. The New World 'savage' was the deeper, archetypal layer of Otherness behind the Spanish Other.

For De Lancre, the devil was, in effect, remapping the world, breaking down geographic boundaries to situate Spain on the edge of France without sufficient protective borders, and then placing the New World behind Spain. It was as if the devil were able to pick up the New World, unhook it from its mooring like moveable furniture and place it right near France, just beyond Spain. De Lancre used this remapped understanding of the world to explain all that appeared illogical or *invraisemblable* about the fact that seemingly normal housewives could engage in satanic orgies. The New World normalised all that seemed implausible otherwise.[33] While satanic orgies would not seem possible on French soil, American soil was a different story. There, such orgies seemed the norm. But the next question was how did they get there? After all, the New World was not exactly around the corner, or even remotely in the vicinity.

The devil made France and the New World seem in such close proximity that the women of the Labourd could travel there with a speed that would put Superman or even the Concord to shame. Jeannette d'Abadie of Siboro, aged sixteen, reported in her deposition that she would fly to the New World in a mere two to three hours. Lest she succumb to the proverbial fear of flying, she could be escorted by older women, on whose coattails she could hang. Once when Jeannette d'Abadie arrived in the New World, lo and behold, what did she find there but all the other Sorceresses from her home town. 'In the New World she saw witches there who had been transported from all the parishes in the Labourd'. The devil had devised a veritable mass transportation system. Marie d'Aspilcouette, aged nineteen, claimed in her deposition that 'she saw troupes of witches, still in spasms of joy, flying through the air, together en masse, back from the New World (De Lancre 1982: 145).[34] The New World would get closer by the minute, the two or three hour travel time getting whittled down to mere seconds. In a variation on her first deposition, Jeannette d'Abadie reported that 'she was often carried to the New World by hanging on to the coattails of Grataiane, and they got there in an instant, in the company of several other witches whom the Devil transported all at the same time. When she was there, she saw practically her entire village' (De Lancre 1982: 151).[35]

The men were also drawn to the New World. Unlike the women, however, they were not lured by satanic sex, but by fish! The devil used whales and cod as his bait to lure their husbands away from home for over half the year. He wanted easy access to their wives. Without their husbands, the women lived in a topsy turvy, carnivalesque world where misrule was the proverbial rule. They would yield to their 'inner savage', their baser impulses and consort with the devil. And so they engaged in fantastic, wild orgy-like Sabbaths, De Lancre argued. When their husbands returned, the women did not resume a normal, civilised life since the men felt estranged from them: 'They hardly love their wives, and don't really know them well because they are not even home half the year'.[36] Similarly, their children led a lawless life of freedom: 'As for their children, they live in complete liberty, and live together with women before marrying them in a kind of trial marriage'.[37] De Lancre's descriptions of their witch-like behaviour mirrored the descriptions of the New World 'savages' as promiscuous and lawless.[38]

The State's most pressing agenda was to unify the nation by developing an internal colonisation of its inhabitants. The trial was an important part of that internal colonisation, staging a cautionary drama about assimilation. As long as France's inhabitants were disconnected culturally, socially and politically from the State, they remained vulnerable to the devil's influence. The best defence against sorcery was to be fully assimilated into the French community. The trial dramatised a tug of war between the State and the devil, between the centre and the periphery, locked in battle for the souls of France's inhabitants.

The trial was also a battle about boundaries and their crossings. The construction of 'civilisation' was haunted by the need to establish boundary lines to separate it from 'savagery'. The witch was a kind of 'savage'. Witches were creatures who, by definition, knew no boundaries. By day, they seemed like normal housewives; by night they turned into libidinous creatures dancing in satanic orgies. By day, they lived inside of French borders; by night they flew off to the New World or to other such places to consort with 'savages'. Witches could fly in and out of worlds with an ease that any traveller would envy. No security checks. No nothing. Just a presto-chango changing of places and identities. All of these 'crossings' were made possible by the fact that they were in cahoots with the devil, the protean character *par excellence*.

The devil's 'black magic' was the shadowy counterpart to the 'white magic' of the State and the Church when they sought to transport transformed 'savages' across the divide and bring them into the French, Catholic community. In the expanding world of the seventeenth century, where trade and evangelism were bringing the French into increasing contact with the Other, it was necessary to establish some kind of invisible new boundaries to compensate for the stretching of the old ones to accommodate 'outsiders'. The new 'white magic', transforming 'outsiders' into 'insiders' was an invisible magic, but it worked to stimulate a belief in the transformative, protective function of French civilisation. It worked to stimulate the belief that French civilisation was magic itself.

Notes

1. I do not mean to suggest that the relationship between assimilation and culture was causal in any simple sense, since they developed in a reciprocal relationship to each other.
2. There has been significant work to show how the Church viewed its missionary work inside and outside of France as essentially the same. As long as one lived far from God, it did not really matter whether one lived in France or in the New World. See Venard 1980, Vincent 1990, Dompnier 1996, 1997, Deslandres 1997, 1999 and Codignola 1997.
3. See Pagden 1993 and 'The Barbarian' in Pagden 1986; White 1972; Dickason 1984; Gliozzi 2000.
4. While the general phenomenon I am describing referred to many groups, it did not apply to all. It depended on the needs of the French State and Church. I discuss the relationship between the New World 'savages' and groups inside of France in Melzer forthcoming.
5. For a more nuanced discussion of the difference between 'culture' and 'civilisation', see Elias 1973 and DeJean 1997. DeJean sees in 'culture' the seeds of a notion of relativity of values, whereas 'civilisation' implies a hierarchy, with France as the most civilised in the seventeenth century. I am using the term 'culture' more in line with her discussion of 'civilisation'. I prefer the term 'culture' because of its link to cultivation and the capacity for transformation. But ultimately there is no good term for the phenomenon I am discussing.
6. The term 'civilisation' had not yet been coined, although the related terms of 'civilité' and 'civilser' had, as Starobinski 1989 has pointed out.
7. This event was the subject of a veritable media blitz, with fifteen books and pamphlets reporting on it. See Boucher 1989. The most important documents published were Abbeville 1614, and Evreux 1615.
8. There are no good comprehensive studies of the assimilation policy. For the best studies on assimilation available see Jaenen

1966 and Jaenen 1976. See also Bailey 1937; White 1991; Jacquin 1996; Melzer 2001.

9. Ces petites filles, étant nourries à la façon des Chrétiens, puis mariées à quelques Français ou à des Sauvages baptisez, retireront tant d'enfants de leur Nation que nous voudrons.
10. Consistera à les secourir, à les doter et à les ayder dans leur mariage. Thwaites 1896: IX, 102.
11. Cet enfant n'a rien de sauvage que le teint et la couleur, sa douceur, sa docilité, sa modestie, son obeisance la ferait passer pour une petite Francaise bien née.
12. S'il se peut les y mesler, afin que par la succession du temps, n'ayant qu'une mesme loy et un mesme maitre, ils ne fassent plus ainsy qu'*un mesme peuple* et *un mesme sang.*
13. Il faut ... employer toute l'autorité temporelle pour attirer les sauvages parmy les Francois, ce qui se peut faire par les mariages ....
14. Instruits dans les maximes de notre religion and dans nos mœurs ... ils puissent composer avec les habitants de Canada *un mesme peuple* et fortifier, par ce moyen, cette colonie là.
15. This was an attitude that Aimé Césaire criticised (Césaire 1972).
16. This notion of a 'sweetness of life' went back to the Middle Ages and still exists to this day. See the discussion of the parity debate in recent years in 'Liberty, Equality, Sorority ...' 2000.
17. Ayant gouté *la douceur d'une vie* qui ne crie pas toujours à la faim, comme font ces Barbares ... .
18. ... s'accoutumeront tellement à nos vivres, et à nos habits, qu'ils auront horreur des Sauvages et de leurs saletez. Nous avons veu l'exemple de cecy en tous les enfans nourris parmy nos François; ils font telle connaissance les uns avec les autres dans leur jeux d'enfants, qu'ils ne regardent les Sauvages que pour les fuir, ou se mocquer d'eux.
19. Ayant été [en France] deux ans, il y reviendra sachant la langue, estant deja accoustumé à nos façons de faire, il ne nous quittera point et retiendra ses petits compatriotes.
20. *Avec douceur* les contraindre à faire mieux, et par bons examples les esmouvoir à correction de vie. (Champlain 1929: III: 145), my emphasis.
21. On avait emmaillotte ce petit Chrestien à la Françoise, sa mère le tenant disoit à son mary, je scay qu'a nostre petit Francois Olivier; quand il est accommodé à la Francoise, il rit toujours, quand je l'accommode à nostre façon il pleure et se chagrine, et quand je le tiens il est tout triste et tout morne, et quand une Française le tient, vous diriez qu'il veut toujours sauter. Elle vouloit par ce discours tesmoigner le contentement qu'elle avoit de voir son fils comme devenu François.
22. See Scholar 2005. In his study of the *Je ne sais quoi,* his analysis of the bourgeoisie as 'outsiders' reveals similar patterns as my examination of the 'savages' as 'outsiders'.

23. Ces petites filles sont vêtues à la Françoise; elles ne se soucient non plus des Sauvages, que si elles n'estoient pas de leur Nation.
24. ... s'en retourne par fois [aux] Cabanes des Sauvages, son père extremement aise de voir sa fille bien couverte, et en fort bon point, ne lui laisse pas demeurer longtemps la renvoyant en la maison, où elle demeure.
25. Il fuyoit les Sauvages: on le contraignit de retourner avec eux pour apprendre la langue, qu'il avoit oubliée; il n'y vouloit pas aller ...
26. Je ne scay pas si je deviens sauvage conversant tous les jours avec les sauvages...
27. The most significant alternative meaning was linked to cruelty or animal-like behaviour.
28. Hobbes' description of the 'state of nature' was stimulated in part by his readings of the *Relations* about the New World. See Ashcraft 1972.
29. For a discussion of these speculations, see Lestringant 1995, 1999; Doiron 1995 and Gliozzi 2000.
30. Le commerce qu'ils ont presque plus en Navarre et Espagne qu'en France, les tient en quelque indifference de moeurs, d'habits et d'affection.
31. Toutes ces diversités donnent à Satan de merveilleuses commodités de faire en ce lieu ses assemblées et Sabbats ...
32. [En] revenant des Indes, de Terre-neuve, de Canada, et autres lieux, que leurs vaisseaux prennent port en Espagne ... chez lesquels ils sont sous la verge, et en toute soumission comme en terre ennemie ... les Espagnols les tiennent sous boucle.
33. For an excellent discussion of De Lancre and of witchcraft in general, see Houdard 1992.
34. Elle a vu les sorcières partant du sabbat voler par l'air à troupes, et au retour se jacter avec grande joie, qu'elles venaient d'exciter la tempête sur la mer vers Terre-neuve.
35. Elle a été portée fort souvent en Terre-Neuve par Gratiane, comme si elle eut volé, se tenant à la robe de ladite Gratianne, où elles allaient et revenaient en un instant en compagnie de plusieurs autres sorcières que le Diable emportait toutes à la fois. Qu'étant là elle y voyait presque de toute sorte de gens de Labourd.
36. Ils n'aiment guère leurs femmes, et ne les connaissent pas bonnement, parce qu'ils ne les pratiquent que la moitié de l'année.
37. Pour leurs enfants, la liberté qu'ils prennent d'essayer leurs femmes quelques années avant de les épouser et les prendre comme à l'essai.
38. The lewdness of the Amerindians had been a *topos* ever since Amerigo Vespucci's letters (Vespucci 1992). See in particular the First Letter, 1504. Such descriptions were a standard part of the travel literature to the New World.

References

Abbeville, C. d'. 1614. *Histoire de la mission des pères capucins en l'isle de Maragnan et terres circonvoisines.* Paris: Huby.

Ashcraft, R. 1972. 'Leviathan Triumphant: Thomas Hobbes and the Politics of Wild Men'. In *The Wild Man Within: An Image in Western Thought from the Renaissance to Romanticism*, eds. E. Dudley and M. Novak, pp. 141–81. Pittsburgh: University of Pittsburgh Press.

Bailey, A.G. 1937. *The Conflict of European and Eastern Algonkian Cultures, 1504–1700.* Sackville, N.B.: The Tribune Press.

Barthes, R. 1957. *Mythologies.* Paris: Seuil.

Boucher, P.P. 1989. *Les Nouvelles Frances: France in America, 1500–1815. An Imperial Perspective.* Providence, R.I.: John Carter Brown Library.

Césaire, A. 1972. *Discourse on Colonialism*, trans. J. Pinkham. New York and London: Monthly Review Press.

Champlain, S. de. 1929. *The Works of Samuel de Champlain. 1615–18*, ed. H.P. Biggar, Vol. 3. Toronto: The Champlain Society.

Clément, P., ed. 1865. *Lettres, Mémoires et Instructions de Colbert, publiés d'après les ordres de l'empereur.* Paris: Imprimerie impériale.

Codignola, L. 1997. 'Les Frontières de la mission: Efficacité missionnaire, acculturation réciproque et centralisation romaine'. In *Les Frontières de la mission, (XV–XIX): Mélanges de l'Ecole Française de Rome. Italie et Méditerranée.* Vol. 109, pp. 785–92. Rome: Ecole française de Rome.

DeJean, J. 1997. *Ancients against Moderns: Culture Wars and the Making of a Fin de Siècle.* Chicago: University of Chicago Press.

De Lancre, P. 1982. *Tableau de l'inconstance des mauvais anges et démons où il est amplement traité des sorciers et de la sorcellerie*, ed. N. Jacques-Chaquins. Paris: Aubier.

Deslandres, D. 1997. 'Les Missions francaises intérieures et lointaines, 1600–1650. Esquisse géo-historique'. In *Les Frontières de la mission, (XV–XIX): Mélanges de l'Ecole Française de Rome. Italie et Méditerranée.* Vol. 109, pp. 505–38. Rome: Ecole française de Rome.

———. 1999. 'Mission et altérité: Les missionnaires français et la définition de *l'Autre* au XVIIe siècle'. In *French Colonial Historical Society Proceedings*, ed. J. Pritchard, pp. 1–13. Cleveland: University Press of America.

Dickason, O. 1984. *The Myth of the Savage and the Beginnings of French Colonialism.* Edmonton: University of Alberta Press.

Doiron, N. 1995. 'Discours sur l'origine des Amériquains'. In *Figures de l'Indien*, ed. G. Thérien, pp. 46–60. Montreal: Typo.

Dompnier, B. 1996. 'La Compagnie de Jésus et la mission de l'intérieur'. In *Les Jésuites à l'age baroque, 1540–1640*, ed. Luce Giard and L. de Vaucelles, pp. 155–79. Grenoble: J. Millon.

———. 1997. 'La France du premier XVIIe siècle et les frontières de la mission'. In *Les Frontières de la mission, (XV–XIX): Mélanges de l'Ecole Française de Rome. Italie et Méditerranée*. Vol. 109, pp. 621–52. Rome: Ecole française de Rome.

Elias, N. 1973. *La Civilisation des moeurs*. Paris: Calmann-Lévy.

Ellingson, T. 2001. *The Myth of the Noble Savage*. Berkeley: University of California Press.

Evreux, Y. d'. 1615. *Suite de l'histoire des choses plus mémorables*. Paris: Payot.

Gliozzi, G. 2000. *Adam et le nouveau monde: La naissance de l'anthropologie comme idéologie coloniale: des généalogies bibliques aux théories raciales, 1500–1700*. Lecques: Théétète.

Goddard, P.A. 1990. 'Christianisation and Civilisation in Seventeenth-Century Colonial Thought', unpublished D.Phil. thesis, Oxford.

Greenblatt, S. 1995. 'Culture'. In *Critical Terms for Literary Study*, eds. F. Lentricchia and T. McLaughlin, pp. 225–32. Chicago: University of Chicago Press.

Houdard, S. 1992. *Les Sciences du Diable: Quatre Discours sur la Sorcellerie*. Paris: Cerf.

Jacquin, P. 1996. *Les Indiens blancs*. Montreal: Libre expression.

Jaenen, C. 1966. 'Problems of Assimilation in New France 1603–1645'. *French Historical Studies* 4: 265–89.

———. 1976. *Friend and Foe: Aspects of French-Amerindian Cultural Contact in the Sixteenth and Seventeenth Centuries*. Toronto: McClelland and Stewart.

Lescarbot, Marc. 1968. *History of New France*. New York: Greenwood.

Lestringant, F. 1995. 'Mornay, Lescarbot, De Laet, Claude d'Abbeville'. In *Figures de l'Indien*, ed. G. Thérien, pp. 61–97. Montreal: Typo.

———. 1999. *Le Huguenot et le sauvage*. Paris: Klincksieck.

'Liberty, Equality, Sorority. French Women Demand Their Share'. *The New Yorker*, 29 May 2000: 112–23.

Melzer, S. 2001. 'The Underside of France's Civilizing Mission: Assimilationist Politics in "New France"'. *Biblio 17* 131: 151–64.

———. Forthcoming. *France's Hidden Colonial Histories: Assimilating the 'Savage' Other in French Literature and Culture of the Classical Age*.

Mercure Francois. 1617. *Devise en deux livres. Le premier contenent La Suite de L'histoire de L'Auguste Régence de la Reine Marie de Medecis et Le Second L'Histoire de Nostre Temps, Commençant à la Majorité du Tres-Chrestien Roy de France et de Navarre, Louis XIII*. Vol. 3. Paris: Estienne Richer.

Montesquieu, C., baron de. 1964. *The Persian Letters*, trans. G.R. Healy. Indianapolis: Bobbs-Merrill.

Pagden, A. 1986. *The Fall of Natural Man: The American Indian and the Origins of Comparative Ethnology*, 2nd edn. Cambridge: Cambridge University Press.

———. 1993. *European Encounters with the New World*. New Haven: Yale University Press.

———. 1995. *Lords of All the World: Ideologies of Empire in Spain, Britain and France, 1500–1800*. New Haven: Yale University Press.

Phillips, H. 1997. *Church and Culture in Seventeenth-Century France*. Cambridge: Cambridge University Press.

Provost. H. 1964. *Le Séminaire de Québec. Documents et biographies*. Quebec: Université de Laval.

Rapport de l'Archiviste de la Province de Québec. RAPQ 1930-1. Québec: Imprimerie de Sa Majesté le Roi.

Scholar, R. 2005. *The 'Je Ne Sais Quoi' in Early Modern Europe: Encounters with a Certain Something*. Oxford: Oxford University Press.

Starobinski, J. 1989. *Le Remède dans le mal: critique et légitimation de l'artifice à l'âge des Lumières*. Paris: Gallimard.

Thwaites, R.G. 1896. *The Jesuit Relations and Allied Documents; Travels and Explorations of the Jesuit Missionaries in New France, 1610–1791*. Cleveland: Burrows Brothers.

Venard, M. 1980. 'Missions lointaines ou/et missions intérieures dans le catholicisme français de la première moitié du XVIIe siècle'. In *Actes du colloque de Lyon: les réveils missionnaires en France du Moyen Age à nos jours, XII–XX siècles (29–31 mai 1980)*, pp. 83–89. Paris: Société d'histoire ecclésiastique de France et Société du protestantisme français.

Vespucci, A. 1992. *Letters from a New World: Amerigo Vespucci's Discovery of America*, ed. L. Formisano. New York: Marsilio.

Vincent, B. 1990. 'Les Jésuites et les "Indes"'. In *Structures et cultures des sociétés ibéro-américaines. Au-delà du modèle socio-économique*, pp. 273–78. Paris: C.N.R.S.

Weber, E.J. 1976. *Peasants into Frenchmen: The Modernization of Rural France, 1870–1914*. Stanford: Stanford University Press.

White, H. 1972. 'The Forms of Wildness: Archeology of an Idea'. In *The Wild Man Within: An Image in Western Thought from the Renaissance to Romanticism*, eds. E. Dudley and M. Novak, pp. 3–38. Pittsburgh: University of Pittsburgh Press.

White, R. 1991. *The Middle Ground: Indians, Empires, and Republics in the Great Lakes Region, 1650–1815*. Cambridge: Cambridge University Press.

CHAPTER 7

A MAGUS OF THE NORTH? PROFESSOR JOHN FERGUSON AND HIS LIBRARY[1]

David Weston

Before Carl Gustav Jung discovered alchemy he experienced a series of dreams with a recurrent theme in which he saw another wing or annex to his house where he had never been.

> Finally came a dream in which I reached the other wing. I discovered there a wonderful library, dating largely from the sixteenth and seventeenth centuries. Large, fat folio volumes, bound in pigskin stood around the walls. Among them were a number of books embellished with copper engravings of a strange character, and illustrations containing curious symbols such as I had never seen before. At the time I did not know to what they referred; only much later did I recognize them as alchemical symbols. In the dream I was conscious only of the fascination exerted by them and the entire library' (Jung 1963: 193–94).

In this quote Jung could quite easily have been describing the Ferguson Collection, one of the most important of the many collections preserved in Glasgow University Library and the subject, along with its creator, of this study.

Professor John Ferguson's personal library was extensive, containing in the region of 18,000 volumes. While it had been his intention to bequeath his collection intact to a public institution, very likely Glasgow University, his will could not be found after his death. Consequently the contents of his estate, books, jewellery, silver and wines were sold at auctions in

Glasgow and London in order to satisfy the claims of inheritors. Fortunately the principal part of his library dealing with alchemy, early chemistry, metallurgy, mineralogy, the Rosicrucians, Paracelsus, witchcraft and the Romany language, was preserved from dispersal when the University purchased it in 1921.

Ferguson's name is well-known among scholars and students of alchemy for his bio-bibliographic survey of alchemical writers and their books, the *Bibliotheca Chemica* (Ferguson 1906). This was, in its initial conception, a catalogue of the alchemical collection of James Young (1811–1883), 'Paraffin Young', a self-made Scottish entrepreneur who amassed a considerable fortune from his discovery of paraffin. Young collected alchemical books because he believed that a survey of alchemy was indispensable for an understanding of the history of chemistry, rather than through a deep interest in alchemy for its own sake. He was able to gather a collection of some 1,300 books and seven manuscripts, which was given in the late nineteenth century to the Andersonian Institute in Glasgow where, by attending classes in his early years, Young had been able to gain his knowledge of chemistry. The collection is now housed in the Department of Special Collections in the Andersonian Library of the University of Strathclyde.

However because of this catalogue, this collection is so linked with John Ferguson, that few are aware that Ferguson's own collection of alchemical books and manuscripts far outweighs the Young Collection in size and scope. The Ferguson collection as it stands today comprises some seven thousand printed books (including 104 incunabula, books printed before 1501) and 337 manuscripts, and is considered to be among the finest collections of alchemical materials available anywhere. The full extent of its holdings is yet to be fully appreciated by many scholars because only now is there full access to information regarding its holdings.

A two-volume comprehensive catalogue of the printed books *was* published during the Second World War (University of Glasgow Library 1943), but due to the rationing of paper only forty copies were printed for presentation to various major libraries throughout the world. With the support of the Bibliotheca Philosophica Hermetica in Amsterdam all the catalogue entries for the Ferguson collection were keyed into a database during the early 1990s and may now be consulted via the Library's on-line web-based catalogue. In addition a facsimile reprint of the 1943 publication was published in 2002 by Martino Books in the United States.

John Ferguson was born on 24 January 1838 at Alloa in Clackmannanshire, the second of three children. His father moved from Alloa at an early date, settling in Glasgow as a merchant. Ferguson was educated at the old High School of Glasgow, and subsequently matriculated at the University of Glasgow for the session 1855–1856. In total he spent nine years as a matriculated student, most of these in the Faculty of Arts, graduating B.A. in 1861 and M.A. with honours in 1862. As an undergraduate he distinguished himself, winning several prize essay competitions, with titles as diverse as the 'Historical Account of the Papacy as a Temporal Power in Europe', and 'On Cohesion'. However, rather than proceeding to Oxford or Cambridge, the typical course for brilliant Arts faculty students to follow, he remained in Glasgow to develop his increasing interest in science, which had begun in the late 1850s. At that time Professor William Thomson (later Lord Kelvin) was engaged on his research into electric telegraph cables and Ferguson was employed by him, both in the laboratory and on field trips, to carry out numerous electrometric experiments. In addition to experimental work, Ferguson was also required to prepare an abstract of some of Thomson's lectures for the use of students. This resulted in the publication of *Elements of Dynamics. Part I* (Kelvin 1863), the first occurrence of his name in print. In 1863 he matriculated in the faculty of medicine in order to pursue studies in chemistry. After a time working as a student in the chemistry laboratory he became assistant to the professor, Thomas Anderson, and in 1868 was appointed University Assistant with responsibility for tutorial classes and the supervision of students in the laboratory. By 1869 ill health forced Anderson to hand over general responsibility for running the chemistry department to Ferguson, who became intimately involved in planning its transfer to the new University site at Gilmorehill. Following Anderson's death in 1874, Ferguson at the age of only thirty-six, was appointed to the Regius professorship. By all accounts Ferguson was an excellent teacher to which the number of his students subsequently occupying chairs of chemistry, both in Britain and throughout the Commonwealth, bears eloquent testimony. However, already in 1867 with the publication of a paper on Geber in *The Laboratory* (Ferguson 1867), discussing the identity of this writer with the Arabic author

Jabir ibn Hayyan, Ferguson had established the historical and bibliographical character of almost all his subsequent output. It was this bias towards the more developmental and philosophical aspects of his subject that was to cause some contemporaries to criticise the absence of experimentation from his work. But as John Millar Thomson, his assistant and subsequently professor of chemistry at King's College, London, remarked, 'from the record of the work done by those who came immediately under his influence, it is clear that he encouraged experimental research in others' (Thomson 1918: 8).

Ferguson lamented the lack of interest shown in the history of science in Britain and determined to use his position to redress this imbalance some small degree. After settling into his new position as professor, a steady stream of papers and articles flowed from his pen: 'On the Study of the History of Chemistry' (Ferguson 1875), an attempt to periodise the history of chemistry; 'Recent Enquiries into the Early History of Chemistry' (Ferguson 1876), dealing largely with Greek manuscript sources from the second to the fifth centuries AD; an article on Sir Humphrey Davy for *Good Words* (Ferguson 1879); and five entries for the ninth edition of the *Encyclopaedia Britannica* (1879–80) on Geber, Christopher Glaser, Joseph Louis Gay-Lussac, Paracelsus, and Karl Wilhelm Scheele. Between 1882 and 1915 he published a series of bibliographical notes on histories of inventions and books of secrets based on talks delivered to the Archaeological Society of Glasgow. In these he focused on the early writers of compendia, Albertus Magnus, Vincent de Beauvais, Polydore Vergil, Roger Bacon and Conrad Gesner, and books of technical recipes. (For a full bibliography, see Alexander 1920 and 1934). Also, from the mid-1870s until its eventual publication in 1906, Ferguson was working on what has become his most enduring monument, the *Bibliotheca Chemica*. According to the sub-title this purports to be 'A Catalogue of the Alchemical, Chemical and Pharmaceutical Books in the Collection of the Late James Young of Kelly and Durris', but in fact it was transformed by Ferguson into a detailed reference work on alchemical and early chemical writers which has yet to be superseded. By establishing and defining the corpus, the *Bibliotheca Chemica* has become the primary reference work for anyone commencing research in the area. Jung, for example, referred to it often in his books on psychology and alchemy. Although only describing 1,300 books (a fraction of what Ferguson was to possess himself), it runs to over a thousand pages in two quarto volumes due to the wealth of bibliographical and biographical information provided for each entry.

In addition to his scholarly pursuits, Ferguson enjoyed music. He was a competent instrumentalist and attended concerts frequently. Thomson in his memoir reports that whenever the violinist Joseph Joachim was playing in Glasgow he would come to visit Ferguson. He also liked to travel and was often abroad representing the University in an official capacity. As a person he was well liked and possessed a keen if somewhat caustic sense of humour, a fact which may account for his nickname 'Soda'. He was president of the Royal Philosophical Society of Glasgow, 1892–95, and of the Glasgow Archaeological Society, 1891–94, and a fellow of the Royal Society of Edinburgh, the Society of Antiquaries, the Chemical Society and the Institute of Chemistry in London. He was also an honorary member of the Imperial Military Academy of Petrograd.

Ferguson died a bachelor on 3 November 1916, the year following his retirement. In the absence of Ferguson's will David Murray, a close friend, and a Assessor to the University Court applied for, and received the powers of Judicial Factor over Ferguson's estate and was instrumental in securing the purchase of the major part of his library for the University. Murray may also have been responsible either intentionally or unintentionally for the total absence of any correspondence files amongst Ferguson's papers.

Alchemy is almost as protean and elusive to define as the processes which lie at its centre. While it may have originated in China, the form in which it reached the Western mediaeval world had its roots in Hellenistic Greek science, most probably in an Egyptian context; the very term, 'alchemy', an Arabic term, 'al-kimia', is, according to some etymologies, derived from the ancient name for Egypt, – *kmt*, Demotic *kmy*, or 'land of the black soil'. From there it was transmitted through Arabic works in Latin translations. Common to all alchemy is the belief in the unity of matter and the possibility of effecting change from one state to another, hence of transmuting base metals into gold, either literally or metaphorically. But it is the search for the principle by which this may be achieved which constitutes its principal goal. This latter is called variously the Philosopher's Stone, the Stone, the Tincture, the Elixir, the Quintessence, the Arcanum ... Lyndy Abraham in her exhaustive *Dictionary of Alchemical Imagery* lists some forty different names for it (Abraham 1998). The *opus alchimicum* or alchemical work can be summarised in an abstracted, simplified form as follows.

In the initial, black, *nigredo*, or putrefaction stage of the process, impure metal is dissolved into *prima materia* (sulphur and mercury) so that it can be reborn into a new state. This stage is also known as the raven's head. Next follows a lengthy, delicate distillation process during which the matter is sublimated and purified, changing colour through all the colours of the rainbow, or of the peacock's tail, *cauda pavonis*, until it is purified at the point of the *albedo* or the formation of the White Stone. The *rubedo*, or preparation of the red stone, is reached by the decoction of the albedo in a dry fire until it transforms into a deep red or purple. This red elixir, or red rose is the Philosopher's Stone, which apart from the ability to transmute all metals, can according to different authors, cure all disease, confer eternal life and even raise the dead. In some texts it is identified explicitly with Christ. The obscurity of the language used on the part of the alchemists was deliberate and they seem to have delighted in multiplying the terms used for the various stages and phenomena.

In an engraving from Johann Daniel Mylius' *Philosophia reformata* (1622: 316), seven stages are depicted within roundels around a tree under which the adept stands with his student. In this case the *nigredo* is depicted by a crow perched on a skull at the top of a tree, the *albedo*, and a unicorn with a rosebush represents the *rubedo*, the white turning to red. In the last roundel a female figure emerging from a tomb signifies the Philosopher's Stone.

To be sure there were enough alchemists who conformed to the standard caricature: charlatans driven by unabashed greed of the sort lampooned by Jonson and others, bringing ruination on themselves and those dependent on them. But of the authors we encounter in the collection, we can identify two broad camps. On the one hand there are practical workers in metallurgy, in smelting of ores and mineralogy. While they were inducted into the alchemical lore and conventionally employed its terminology in their writings, they doubtless soon realised for instance that mercury and sulphur combined results in nothing very spectacular but mercuric sulphide, or cinnabar, the material used by painters for red. That is probably why we often encounter in alchemical writings the terms philosophical mercury and philosophical sulphur and even philosophical gold, i.e., some other substance than simply mercury must have been intended by the authority being consulted. In this unsystematic way these practical alchemists amassed a considerable body of important, but isolated chemical facts, as well as developing incidentally some enduring processes, such as distillation, and equipment, such as the alembic.

In contrast there is another group of *philosophical* alchemists for whom the philosopher's stone holds the key to an understanding of the essentially unified nature of everything above and below, celestial and mundane, with man specially placed as mediator, who, possessed of arcane knowledge of the nature of things, or as Newton termed it 'the whole frame of Nature' (Dobbs 1975: 231), can effect transformations, and transmutations, which can to the uninitiated appear miraculous. This is the Magus or natural magician, which we already encounter in the writings of the Florentine humanists. They claimed, as do these later writers, legitimacy for their enterprise from antiquity, drawing on neo-Platonism and especially on the secret knowledge preserved in the Hermetic Corpus. It is interesting to note that Newton, whose intense involvement with practical alchemy was hardly known in Ferguson's time (White 1998: 1–5), and who anyway published nothing in that sphere, did believe that such a secret knowledge could be found.

Of these two outlooks, the one, exoteric and practical, eventually becomes increasingly experimental, invoking reason and careful, quantitative observation as the only arbiters of truth, whereas the other, the esoteric, the Rosicrucian and essentially fideist, requiring the belief of the adept, is banished eventually to the periphery of an emerging enlightened Europe.

What were Ferguson's motives in forming his collection? Apart from the normal requirements of his professional life, he was keenly interested in the history of his chosen subject in all its manifestations. This may be seen from the several papers he presented to learned societies, such as those to the Philosophical Society of Glasgow on such topics as 'The First Editions of the Chemical Writings of Democritus and Synesius' in 1884, and 'The First History of Chemistry' in 1886, a study of the *De veritate et antiquitate artis chemicae* ... by Robert Duval or Robertus Vallensis of Rouen, printed at Paris in 1561. In his researches he was greatly aided by the access he had to the Young Collection, but he also seems to have made a point of actually acquiring for himself every book that he had recourse to mention in his papers. As a consequence, his historical statements not only display a heavy reliance on bibliographical evidence, but increasingly become in fact bibliographical in inspiration. In a paper to the Archaeological Society in 1885 on Antoine Mizaud's *Memorabilium ... centuriae* (Ferguson 1888: 5) he states, 'I have a copy of the [Frankfurt] 1592 edition here' (undoubtedly the Young copy, see Ferguson 1906: 97). At that time, as today, the University Library and the Hunterian Museum each had copies of an earlier edition of 1572, which he employed in writing his article. It is clearly the case that Ferguson did not own any copy of the Mizaud in 1885. By the end of his life, however, he had acquired the first edition of 1566 in October 1905, his own copy of the 1572 edition on 11 July 1899, and two further editions of 1584 and 1613. The bibliographer's zeal is also eloquently evidenced by the frequent presence in the collection of two, three and sometimes more copies of a particular edition. Another reason behind his avid collecting was to provide the necessary foundations for his magnum opus, the *Bibliotheca Chemica*, a work which could not have been so easily produced had reliance been placed simply on the items actually held. There is also a suggestion made by his own bibliographer Elizabeth Alexander (1920: 3) that he had been planning to write a comprehensive history of chemistry.

Ferguson did not employ a book plate. Ownership if marked at all is done with the minimum intrusion: an upper case 'F' in pencil on the front endpaper sometimes accompanied by the date of acquisition. On occasion he does wax more expansive. For example, in a fifteenth-century manuscript, *Summma perfectionis*, of Geber, formerly in the Sir Thomas Phillipps Library, he wrote 'Glasgow Tuesday 22 June 1897, the Queen's Diamond Jubilee Day. This is my memorial of it ... It was acquired from the London book dealers Bernard Quaritch.' Or, in Michael Scot's Latin translation of Avicenna's *De animalibus* of ca. 1500: 'Everything comes to him who can wait (when he knows what he is waiting for). This gives me all M. Scot's books wh[ich] were published.' Ferguson, as others have noted, managed to compete favourably in terms of completeness with major libraries in areas which attracted his interest. Michael Scot for instance, the Scottish (or more probably Irish) alchemist who was considered a 'great master of black magic' by Boccaccio and was consigned by Dante to Inferno, was the subject of an unpublished paper to the Glasgow Archaeological Society in 1888. Ferguson owned thirty-six editions of his

pre-1600 published corpus, of which around fifteen may be assigned to the fifteenth century.

Of the seven thousand or so printed volumes in the collection by far the majority, some four thousand items counting duplicates, is devoted to alchemy in the broadest sense, i.e., including early mineralogical, Hermetic, Rosicrucian and Paracelsian works, and most have pre-1800 imprints. The remainder embraces an exceptionally valuable collection of 670 works dealing with witchcraft and demonology, 120 on Romany language and culture, and around 1,300 miscellaneous books mainly on medicine, science, bibliography, herbalism, cosmetics and conjuring.

The particular strength of the collection lies in its possessing many editions of key works, enabling the scholar to access not only every significant work in several editions, but also many rare and, occasionally, uniquely surviving titles. While it is always difficult to make sensible comparisons of the holdings of major libraries since each has its own strengths and weaknesses, it is true to say that the Ferguson Collection ranks amongst the strongest of those possessing early printed alchemical collections, such as the Bibliotheca Hermetica Philosophica in Amsterdam or the Duveen Collection at the University of Wisconsin.

The collection holds virtually every conceivable author considered relevant to the subject. The Jabirian corpus, from the name of the eighth-century Arab scientist Jabir ibn Hayyan, embraces works which may have been penned by him, but under the Westernised form, Geber, and includes many which were probably originally composed in Latin. Geber is especially important as the transmitter to the West of the key Hermetic text, the Tabula Smaragdina. More than twenty editions are held in the collection, including the first printed in Rome in 1483. There are numerous editions of the compendia of mediaeval writers Albertus Magnus, Arnold of Villanova and Raymond Lull; thirty editions of the obscure, but highly influential Basilius Valentinus in Latin, French, German and English; a staggering seventy-two editions of the German occult philosopher Heinrich Cornelius Agrippa von Nettesheim, about whom Ferguson published a paper; works on distillation and natural magic by the Italian Giambattista della Porta; and over two hundred works in English, translations of standard texts and original works, published during the seventeenth century when England was experiencing something of an alchemical revival. There are also twenty-eight editions of Sir Kenelm Digby's works. The seventeenth-century German alchemist, expert on furnaces, distilling and the discoverer of sodium sulphate, or Glauber's salt, Johann Rudolph Glauber, is represented by fifty-four editions. The collection is also strong in the works of the new era of chemistry inaugurated by Robert Boyle. Despite his being a practising alchemist, it is to him that we owe our modern understanding of an element. There are fifty-two editions of his works, including his seminal, *The sceptical chymist: or chymico-phisical doubts and paradoxes, touching the experiments whereby vulgar spagirists are wont to evince their salt, sulphur and mercury, to be the true principles of things ....* The phlogiston theorists Johann Joachim Becher and Georg Ernst Stahl are represented by twenty-two and sixteen editions respectively.

Robert Fludd was a leading English Rosicrucian and a proponent of Paracelsian ideas. He was the archetypal magus figure, seeking out knowledge of God through an exhaustive examination of the natural order, which was seen as paralleling the revelation of Holy Scripture. The *Utriusque cosmi maioris scilicet et minoris ... historia* , or history of the macrocosm and the microcosm of 1617, was commenced after his return from travelling on the Continent and is considered his major work. More of an encyclopaedia than a history, it attempts to treat in volume one the macrocosm, that is the external world as formed by God and man, and in the second volume, the microcosm, man himself, his God-given faculties and physical make-up. It was sumptuously produced with many fine engravings by the Palatine firm of Jan De Bry, prominent in the publishing of Rosicrucian and Hermetic texts requiring illustrations. The engraved title page reveals the intimate correlation between the universe and man with corresponding inner and outer circles of planetary bodies, the zodiacal signs and the four humours all being turned by winged Time on the upper right of the plate. Ferguson's copy is of particular interest, being one of the sixteen copies sent to Fludd from the publishers, which, according to the annotation on the front end-paper, he presented to his colleague and friend, the physician William Harvey. It is amusing for us today, but indicative of the contemporary outlook, that Fludd was able to postulate a theory of the circulation of the blood around the body 'through the branches of the aorta to the South, that is, the liver, and the north, or the spleen' (Debus 1965: 116) five years prior to Harvey, based on the circular motion of the planets around the earth (He was not a heliocentrist!).

Another work produced in Oppenheim by the firm of De Bry is possibly the most attractive alchemical publication, benefiting as it does from the fine engravings of Matthaeus Merian, *Atalanta fugiens, hoc est, emblemata nova de secretis naturae chemica*, 'new chemical emblems on the secrets of nature', by Michael Maier in 1618. Ferguson owned two copies of this work in addition to seventeen other works by Maier in twenty-four editions and in thirty-six copies. After medical studies at Rostock, and several years of practical medical experience, Maier was summoned to Rudolph II's court at Prague where he served as the emperor's personal physician. When Rudolph died in 1612 Maier left Prague spending several years on the Continent, and in England where he met, amongst others, Sir William Paddy, court physician to King James, and Robert Fludd. *Atalanta fugiens*, which is Maier's best-known work, comprises fifty emblematic engravings, which symbolically depict, but in no particular sequence, the alchemical process. It is distinctive also in having these paralleled by an equal number of musical canons for two voices over a third *cantus firmus*. In this way Maier hoped to unite the visible and verbal with the audible in the presentation of his message.

Another subject which was to engage Ferguson over several years was the elusive figure of Theophrastus Bombastus von Hohenheim, or Paracelsus. Like Copernicus who challenged Ptolemy in astronomy, Paracelsus rejected the stranglehold the classical authorities, Galen and Hippocrates, had on medicine. For him alchemy dealt primarily with the preparation of medicines, which were appropriate to the condition of the sufferer, hence the term, 'iatrochemistry', for his school. While his methods were unconventional, frequently involving metal and mineral compounds, he achieved notable successes. The collection holds two hundred volumes of his writings, some 180 of which are separately published editions before 1800. This remarkable collection appears to have been amassed carefully over a period of twenty or so years, commencing with Ferguson's first essay in Paracelsian research, a paper to the University Dialectic Society in 1873 entitled simply 'Paracelsus', and culminating in the purchase of the extensive Paracelsia belonging to Dr Eduard Schubert sometime in 1894 from the London scientific booksellers and publishers William Wesley & Son. Schubert with his friend Karl Sudhoff, published *Paracelsus-Forschungen* between 1887 and 1889 (Schubert 1887). They also collaborated on a comprehensive bibliography of Paracelsus editions.

To this outstanding collection of early printed works must be added of course the manuscripts, no fewer than 337, of which thirty-five possess coloured illustrations, making the Ferguson Manuscript Collection one of the largest currently in existence. Unlike some other collections of alchemical manuscripts, only a small percentage of the Ferguson collection is taken up with obscure volumes of recipes. Transcriptions and translations of key texts and some unique works dominate, with a tangible emphasis on manuscripts reflecting the spiritual or philosophical side of alchemy.

The earlier, pre-sixteenth century manuscripts in general consist of copies of works by mediaeval writers such as Raimon Lull, Geber, Constantinus Africanus, Albertus Magnus, Roger Bacon, and there is also a 'Turba Philosophorum' or 'Philosophers' Convention', dated 1470 and written by a north Italian scribe who gives his name as Johannes Visto.

There is a sixteenth-century copy, with six illuminations on vellum, of Thomas Norton's poem, 'The Ordinall of Alchemy', once the property of Sir Roger Arundell of Trerice. This work was first published in a Latin translation in a collection of three tracts by Michael Maier at Franckfurt am Main in 1618, the original English version having to wait until 1652 to be printed in Elias Ashmole's *Theatrum Chemicum Britannicum*. Ms Ferguson 6 has been given the general title in German, *Spruch der Philosophien* ('sayings of the philosophers') which is stamped on its late sixteenth-century binding. It was owned and perhaps written by a certain Petrus Wintzig, whose name appears on the recto of the first leaf. This manuscript is significant as it contains a number of the classic alchemical pictorial series, executed in watercolour: the twelve figures of 'Pretiotissimum Donum Dei', the eighteen drawings from the 'Margarita preciosa novella' of Petrus Bonus, the twenty images from the 'Rosarium philosophorum', and the thirty-eight pictures from the 'Aurora Consurgens'. In addition there are a number of figures unique to this manuscript. The 'Rosarium philosophorum' or 'Rosary of the philosophers' is recognised as one of the most important texts of European alchemy, being extensively quoted in later writings. (It is the source, for example, of several mottoes in Maier's *Atalanta fugiens*.) There are six manuscripts of it in the collection including English, French and German translations.

The seventeenth-century manuscripts have many treasures amongst them. Ms Ferguson 149, a seventeenth-century German manuscript unusually, and possibly uniquely, depicts

the sequence of the 'Rosarium' figures taking place within flasks. Ms Ferguson 4 is a seventeenth-century copy of the 'Buch der heiligen Dreifaltigkeit', 'the book of the holy Trinity', called in our manuscript the 'Buch von Wunder werken'.

Ms Ferguson 21 is a previously unknown (1691) English translation of the 'Monas hieroglyphica'. In it John Dee provides an explanation of the planet sign for mercury in which he discerns a mystic expression of all truth, because the signs of the sun and moon, and the cross are conjoined in it. Dee also adds the four elements. The 'Coronatio Naturae' or 'Crowning of Nature', also called in some manuscripts the 'Angelorum opus', is one of the most important symbolic representations of the alchemical process. The series of sixty-seven or sixty-eight illustrations is represented in the collection by no fewer than eight manuscripts, dating from the seventeenth and eighteenth centuries, and mostly in Latin, but two manuscripts have English translations. The cycles of transformation, involving the four elements, in the production of the white and red stones are depicted as taking place within flasks. Ms Ferguson 230 is a handsomely produced presentation copy for Sir Henry Berkley of a collection of alchemical treatises in English translation which also includes the illustrations of the 'Coronatio naturae'. An unillustrated, composite manuscript, Ferguson 322, contains a very interesting alchemical diary, in English, of experiments conducted over the period 4 December 1687 to 7 December 1689, much of which consists of notes by a certain 'Sir Joseph *** of Loughton'. This is an unusual, personal notebook in which the writer's alchemical experiences are written up in a clear and straightforward way.

There are 149 eighteenth-century items, including several eighteenth-century French manuscripts. Some of these are copies or translations of key alchemical works, but a number are especially important in their own right. There are two illustrated copies of Nicolas Flamel's 'Figures hiéroglyphiques', one of which, Ms Ferguson 17, has thirteen full-page, vividly coloured paintings. Ms Ferguson 271 has a series of twenty coloured figures of a symbolic alchemical process, which appears to be unique. There are three copies of a work ascribed to 'Solidonius philosophus', a series of eighteen illustrations with text in French. Ms Ferguson 45, a text by a certain Ortelius, again in French, presents the alchemical process in a highly naturalistic manner using images of mining and agriculture. Ms Ferguson 210 contains an eighteenth-century English translation of the text of the 'Rosarium philosophorum' with twenty miniatures pasted in.

In 1853, while Ferguson was still a lad of fifteen, Alphonse-Louis Constant published a book in Paris entitled *Dogme de la magie,* to be followed shortly by *Rituel de la magie*. This Catholic ex-priest, from that time on to be known by the Hebraised version of his name, Eliphas Lévi, recapitulated in his writings the ideas of eighteenth-century French occultists, such as Martines de Pasqually and Louis Claude de Saint-Martin, becoming the cornerstone of a French, and ultimately European, occult revival (McIntosh 1972). Amongst his extensive writings on Cabala and magic he also touched on the esoteric aspects of alchemy. The many disciples drawn into his ambit included Papus (alias Dr Gérard Encausse) who published several treatises on the occult during the 1890s; François Jollivet-Castelot, the author of *Comment on devient alchimiste* (Paris, 1897) with a preface by Papus, and many other works treating the relation of alchemy to modern chemical theory; Albert Poisson, who published French translations of key mediaeval alchemical texts in addition to modern practical treatises such as his *L'initiation alchimique* of 1900; and Stanislas de Guaita, poet and mystic whose extensive library of works of esoteric subjects and alchemy furnished Ferguson with two of his manuscripts. The Theosophical Society, founded in 1875 by Madame Blavatsky and Henry Olcott, and the Order of the Golden Dawn, formed in 1888, both had associations with this esoteric revival.

We find in Ferguson's collection works by all the aforementioned writers and founders of this revival. What was his relationship to this phenomenon? What was the nature and level of his engagement if any? Once again in the absence of a body of correspondence, diaries or notebooks, there appears little that can be said with any certainty. One might conjecture that, given the completeness of his collecting of earlier editions, which posed considerable difficulties to acquire, he would have found it easy to form complete sets of the works of the authors and movements mentioned. Instead we find he has purchased particular works. The books present in the library of an individual are of course no sure guide to the owner's thinking, but it is interesting to note that Ferguson is acquiring (and reading) these works towards the latter part of his life, i.e., in his sixties as they are being published. At the age of sixty-eight in 1906 he publishes, at last, the work by which his name has been preserved, the *Bibliotheca Chemica*. Suddenly his vast erudition and knowledge of the subject of alchemy is revealed to a wider public than had attended meetings of the Philosophical Society of Glasgow or the Glasgow archaeological and bibliographical societies. In 1912 the Alchemical Society was established by a group of enthusiasts interested in both the academic history of the subject and its esoteric aspects. One of its vice-presidents was Arthur Edward Waite, an original member of the Order of the Golden Dawn and the instigator in 1902 of the more mystical, breakaway organisation the Independent and Rectified Order (Gilbert 1987: 116–23). Ferguson already owned several of his works including his *Studies in Mysticism* and *Certain Aspects of the Secret Tradition*, which appeared in the same year as the *Biblitheca Chemica*. In 1914, the year before his retirement, Ferguson was elected Honorary President of the Alchemical Society, delivering as his inaugural address an essay, subsequently published, entitled 'The Marrow of Alchemy' (Ferguson: 1915).

Ferguson was appointed to his chair in a period dominated by scientific materialism. His mentor and inspiration as a collector, James Young, had made his fame and fortune from chemical discoveries, and this could have been Ferguson's path. Sir James Dewar, a fellow Scot, born in Kincardine, became professor of experimental chemistry in Cambridge, and in Glasgow, Lord Kelvin, with whom Ferguson had served, forged scientific advances in so many areas. Ferguson turned his back on what many would have seen as his incumbent duty, to devote his energies and attention to an abstruse, and at the time, what must have been viewed as a decidedly inappropriate subject for a man of science.

Ferguson probably felt ill at ease and isolated in his post. There were probably few if any in Glasgow with whom he could discuss his interest in alchemy except under the guise of antiquarianism. At the same time it is highly unlikely that Ferguson ever did or would even have contemplated attending the meetings of the Theosophical Society or of visiting Amen-Ra Temple No. 6 of the Golden Dawn established in Edinburgh in 1893 (Colquhoun 1975: 138). I do think, however, that as his fascination with the alchemical texts he was acquiring *grew*, he began to view it not merely as an earlier manifestation of his professed subject, but also as something he could engage with on a more psycho-spiritual level.

However, enough of speculation. What *is* certain is that Ferguson left a major legacy to the world in his monumental

Bibliotheca Chemica. Ironically, this has for too long eclipsed the magnificent legacy to his University, the unrivalled collection which gave his magnum opus its authority and depth.

Note

1. Part of this paper appears in the *Oxford Dictionary of National Biography*.

References

Abraham, L. 1998. *A Dictionary of Alchemical Imagery*. Cambridge: Cambridge University Press.

Alexander, E.H. 1920. *A Bibliography of John Ferguson, M.A., LL.D., F.S.A., Regius Professor of Chemistry in the University of Glasgow, 1874–1915*. Glasgow.

———. 1934. *A Further Bibliography of the Late John Ferguson, M.A., LL.D., F.S.A., Regius Professor of Chemistry in the University of Glasgow, 1874–1915*. Glasgow.

Colquhoun, I. 1975. *Sword of Wisdom: MacGregor Mathers and 'The Golden Dawn'*. London: Spearman.

Debus, A.G. 1965. *The English Paracelsians*, London: Oldbourne

Dobbs, B.J.T. 1975. *The Foundations of Newton's Alchemy, or, The Hunting of the Greene Lyon*. Cambridge: Cambridge University Press.

Encyclopaedia Britannica: A Dictionary of Arts, Sciences, and General Literature. 1879–80. Edinburgh: A. and C. Black.

Ferguson, J. 1867. *Geber*. Extracted. [London].

———. 1875. 'On the Study of the History of Chemistry'. *Proceedings of the Philosophical Society of Glasgow* 10: 27–39.

———. 1876. 'Recent Enquiries into the Early History of Chemistry'. *Proceedings of the Philosophical Society of Glasgow* 10: 368–89.

———. 1879. 'Sir Humphry Davy'. *Good Words* 20: 112–16, 185–88, 304–8.

———. 1888. *Bibliographical Notes on Histories of Inventions and Books of Secrets. Part IV*. Glasgow: Strathern & Freeman.

———. 1906. *Bibliotheca chemica: A Catalogue of the Alchemical, Chemical and Pharmaceutical Books in the Collection of the Late James Young of Kelly and Durris*. Glasgow: Maclehose.

———. 1915. *'The Marrow of Alchemy': Being an Address Delivered to The Alchemical Society on Friday, 9 October, 1914*. London: The Alchemical Society.

Gilbert, R.A. 1987. *A.E.Waite: Magician of Many Parts*. Wellingborough: Crucible.

Jung, C.G. 1963. *Memories, Dreams, Reflections*, ed. A. Jaffe, trans. R. and C. Winston. London: Collins, Routledge & K. Paul.
Kelvin, W.T. 1863. *Elements of Dynamics*, ed. J. Ferguson. Glasgow: [University of Glasgow].
McIntosh, C. 1972. *Eliphas Lévi and the French Occult Revival*. London: Rider.
Mylius, J.D. 1622. *Philosophia reformata continens libros binos. I. Liber in septem partes divisus est... II. Liber continet authoritates philosophorum*. Francofurti: Jennis.
Schubert, E. 1887. *Paracelsus-Forschungen. Mit drei Tafeln in Lichtdruck*. Frankfurt a. M.: 1887–89.
Thomson, J.M. 1918. *Professor John Ferguson*. [Glasgow].
University of Glasgow Library. 1943. *Catalogue of the Ferguson Collection of Books Mainly Relating to Alchemy, Chemistry, Witchcraft and Gipsies in the Library of the University of Glasgow*. Glasgow: Maclehose.
———. 2002. *Catalogue of the Ferguson Collection of Books Mainly Relating to Alchemy, Chemistry, Witchcraft and Gipsies in the Library of the University of Glasgow*. Mansfield Centre, CT: Martino.
White, M. 1998. *Isaac Newton: The Last Sorcerer*. London: Fourth Estate.

CHAPTER 8

THE GOLDEN FLEECE AND HARRY POTTER

Amy Wygant

At the end of *Harry Potter and the Philosopher's Stone*, the stone itself, 'a blood-red stone', has seemingly been destroyed (Rowling 1997: 212). Albus Dumbledore, 'considered by many the greatest wizard of modern times' and 'particularly famous for [...] his work on alchemy with his partner Nicolas Flamel' (Rowling 1997: 77), informs the injured Harry that following Harry's struggle over the stone with the great dark wizard Voldemort, Dumbledore has had a chat with Nicolas and that they have decided that the stone's capacity to confer unlimited wealth and freedom from death is something that the world can do without. This means that Flamel, an historical alchemist who was born around 1330 and supposedly died in 1418, although, Elvis-like, he was sighted by believers and disciples in odd places for the next three hundred years, will die, really die, at last.

But the terms of Harry's struggle with Voldemort and Dumbledore's explanation of his success suggest that a new alchemist has appeared to carry on the stone's work of transfiguration. That is, a structure is set in place in the book's closing pages which has characterised the study of alchemy since its heyday in the early modern period. Harry, rather than the great dark wizard, managed to find the philosopher's stone by looking into a magical mirror that will show its subject doing whatever it is that he wants most in the world to do. And the stone came to Harry because he saw himself simply finding it, not actually using it to gain wealth and eternal life (Rowling 1997: 217). A distinction is thus put in place between the true alchemist engaged in a properly philosophical project of finding, and the false 'souffleur', the 'puffer', who wants only to gain worldly wealth by turning base metals into gold and living forever. 'You must always distinguish carefully between true philosophers and false ones, in order to weed out the latter and pay homage to the former', a 1684 apology for alchemy recommends, 'for the abuses practiced in chemistry by all of these puffers, ramblers, and charlatans are detestable. But this divine art itself merits our continual love and support.'(D'Atremont 1684: 231).[1] This distinction lasted, and can still be read, for example, in connection with the most prominent attempt to formulate a properly effective alchemy for the twentieth century, that of Carl Jung. The French translation of his autobiography still responds to Jung's discussion of the christological nature of the alchemical quest with a note explaining that Jung's discussion goes only to *les alchimistes les plus sérieux*, 'the most serious alchemists', who understood that their work was not about literal gold but rather about spiritual transformation (Jung 1973: 245, n. 4).

So, despite the stone's ostensible destruction, it seems that a new alchemist has been born at the end of the first of the Harry Potter books. Indeed, the fourth book in the series, *Harry Potter and the Order of the Phoenix* (Rowling 2003), claims in its title the ultimate alchemical bird, 'a symbol of renewal and resurrection signifying the philosopher's stone, especially the red stone attained at the rebedo, capable of transmuting base metal into pure gold' (Abraham 1998: s.v. 'phoenix'), and this is only one of many plot references that encourage a reading of the series based upon alchemical imagery.

But it is far less interesting to play a critical game of spot-the-alchemy, a game which has been played for many hundreds of years and surely cannot offer any insight beyond itself, than it is to ask what the cultural status is of the playing of such a game. My project here will not be to tie down detailed references and lock up a sealed alchemical reading of texts. Instead, I would like to ask what kind of difference an alchemical patina on a text makes. Does the history of its reception then become in any sense itself alchemical? A quick look at some aspects of the reception of the wizarding Harry Potter will enable us to pose this question in turn for another powerful and magical figure, from ancient and early modern history this time, the great witch and barbarian, the infanticidal, regicidal, and, I will argue, alchemical, Medea.

When *Harry Potter and the Philosopher's Stone* first appeared on the *New York Times* bestseller list in December 1998, its description read, 'A Scottish boy, neglected by his relatives, finds his fortune attending a school of witchcraft.' About six weeks later, 'Scottish' was changed to 'British', but, remarkably, the plot summary stood (Nel 2002: 262). Anyone who has read the book will know that Harry precisely does not 'find his fortune'. The plot is not about fortune-finding but rather about a boy's finding within himself a kind of naïve, Parsifal-like capacity for finding as such. It is, as I have claimed above, about the search of the good alchemist for spiritual, not material, gold. What seems to have happened to the *New York Times* summary is that the all-too-material force of the reference to the stone has carried away the plot and skewed it in a way that completely misses the point. A bad alchemist, in other words, wrote that summary.

But this first volume of the series was of course not published in the United States under the title *Harry Potter and the Philosopher's Stone* but rather under the title *Harry Potter and the Sorcerer's Stone*, the leading example among many of a controversial translation of the British text into American English which led to general critical accusations of the 'dumbing down' of American society and of the 'global arrogance of the American' (Nel 2002: 261) against the text's American editor, Arthur Levine of Scholastic, who had worked with Rowling on the translation. But what exactly was the problem with 'philosopher's'? Was the thinking that Americans would not know what a philosopher was? Does anyone, we might wonder, understand what the possessive here refers to?

A warning signal sounds when we remember that the French expression is not *pierre philosophique* or *pierre des philosophes* on the model of the German *Stein der Weisen*, but rather *pierre philosophale*. 'Philosophale' is attested from the fifteenth century (Bloch and Wartburg 1986: s.v. 'philosophe'), and its only use in French is in the expression 'la pierre philosophale'. The 'al' suffix, from the Latin 'alis', means 'of, like, or suitable for' (*Webster's* 1982: s.v. '-al'), but when the book was actually translated into Latin, it became *Harrius Potter et Philosophi Lapis*, and any sense that the adjective might be problematic, or refer to something complicated, was lost. The first meaning of 'philosophe' in Antoine Furetière's 1690 *Dictionnaire* (*Dictionnaires* 1998), however, is not 'philosopher' but rather 'chemist'. 'The term "philosophe" is used particularly by chemists, who prefer to call themselves philosophers'.[2] The entry goes on to name historical figures with well-known alchemical leanings: 'Raymond Lull, Paracelsus, Basil Valentine, and Sedenvogius were great philosophers'. And it ends by naming the primary alchemical ingredients: 'salt, sulphur, and mercury are the principles of the philosophers' (*Dictionnaires* 1998, s.v. 'philosophe').

There really is, then, a translation problem with this adjective. At the historical moment when alchemy was vital, the first meaning of 'philosopher' was 'alchemist'. Much more recently, Françoise Bonardel, who treated this problem at length, formulated it as the occupation by 'philosophale' of the position of the other with respect to 'philosophique', her weighty claim then being that alchemy is in the position of poetry relative to philosophy, its 'Orient' (Bonardel 1993: 3–26).

So, the philosopher's stone does not really belong to the philosophy of which we might first think. It is not Kant's or Hegel's, and it is certainly not Descartes'. It is the hermetic philosopher's stone, the alchemist's stone, the chemist's stone, the poet's stone, and – why not? – the sorcerer's stone. The American translation, I would argue, confuses suitably a matter about which it is a very good thing indeed not to be too confident in our knowledge. It is a first, familiar instance of an alchemical patina on a text skewing its reading in a way which disregards utterly those elements which to us make a text what it is: its plot, for one; its title, for another. These two brief episodes in the Harry Potter reception history seem to show that the possibilities for an alchemical reading which the text contains are both extremely forceful and surprisingly diffuse. It seems that, to find the philosopher's stone must necessarily mean to find one's fortune, whatever the text may actually say, but, at the same time, the object of the exercise, the stone, can lose its alchemical specificity and assume another name without damaging the plot's internal coherence or its immense appeal to readers. Whatever this stone might be called, J.K. Rowling is now, among those whose wealth is earned, the wealthiest woman in Britain, and the stone has clearly brought her both unlimited gold and eternal life (Chittenden 2003).

The encounter with the alchemist, be it Harry's series-long apprenticeship with Dumbledore or the reader's engagement with the character complex that is Harry Potter, seems to produce a narrative of youth and education. It is always in some sense a *Bildungsroman*, and always in some sense allegorical, and this was just as true in the early modern period as it is today.

There circulated in manuscript form from the beginning of the sixteenth century, a collection of alchemical treatises entitled *Aureum vellus*, the author of which was reportedly Salomon Trismosin, who was the teacher, or so claims a later title page, of Paracelsus (Trismosin 1612). The treatises were gathered together at the end of the sixteenth century as a compendium, *Aureum vellus oder guldin Schatz und Kunstkammer* (Trismosin 1598), one of the first alchemical treatises not to be issued in Latin, and it begins with a five-page 'Tractat unnd Wanderschafft dess hochberhümpten Herren Salomonis Trismosini'. This short allegory-autobiography puts in place a number of standard plot elements and, while readers will immediately see that Trismosin is no Potter-prototype, curious convergences with the twentieth-century plot nevertheless appear, alongside even more curious divergences.

It begins with a youth meeting an alchemist. 'When I was a young fellow, I came to a miner named Flocker, who was also an alchemist.' That the alchemist is a miner brings in to the narrative all of the notions of depth and toil, labour and luck, which coincided for early modern people in a relation between mining and alchemy. Minerals were thought to mature slowly in the earth until they reached a state of perfection in gold, just as they achieved their perfection more quickly with the alchemist's help in his laboratory (Eliade 1977).

'But he kept his knowledge secret, and I could get nothing out of him. I was grieved at heart that I could not have this art, but he refused to tell his secret process. Shortly thereafter he tumbled down a mine and no one could tell what the artifice was that he had used.' The young man wants the alchemist to teach, but the very nature of this art is to be secret, its essence hidden and known only through allusion. But he does not understand this yet; and the fall of the teacher, his loss, launches the young man into the world to find another, a good alchemist, encountering numerous bad alchemists on the way. At last he comes to understand the work and make gold, and becomes secretive in his turn: 'I was then put on oath not to reveal my Art to anyone. To make a long story short, everything had to be kept secret, as it should be. If someone boasts of his art, even if he has got the truth, God's justice will not let such a one go on. Therefore be silent, even if you have the highest tincture, but give charity.' When at last Trismosin has found the treasure of the Egyptians, his one reaction is precisely silence, struck dumb as he is in awe: 'Darab Ich mich entsetz.'

From the compendium of alchemical treatises of the *Aureum vellus*, of which Trismosin's short autobiography is the opening text, one treatise only, the *Splendor solis*, was translated into French, paraphrased, and published in 1612 as *La Toison d'or ou la fleur des thresors* (Trismosin 1612). The title page of the French, that is, translates the title for the complete collection, but the text is a translation of only about sixty pages of some four hundred in the original. So, a book of practical alchemy comes into the French language called 'the golden fleece', with 'Toison d'or' appearing as a running title at the top of its pages. The translator's fifteen-page prologue and commentary on the two-page German Vorrede, moreover, is an extended metaphor of the conquering of the fleece by Jason and the Argonauts. 'The deep folds of the Golden Fleece' are like 'this inexhaustible labyrinth' which is the alchemical work (Trismosin 1612: 3),[3] and which requires valour and virtuous application: 'The brave Argonauts, after performing many deeds and led over the waves by the powerful hand of destiny, finally conquered the rich Fleece thanks to their own valour, armed and aided by hard work, experience, and patience, which are the real foundation of the calm expressly required for this divine effect (Trismosin 1612: 9–10)'.[4]

The reference to the golden fleece indeed frames the treatise in its French version, which concludes by positioning the conquest of this fleece firstly as a matter for initiates only and secondly as a matter of grace even for the Knights of the Fleece:

> For the Fleece allows itself to be conquered only in its own good time by the faithful perseverance of these clever Knights of the Fleece. And it gives itself only to them, not indiscriminately to everyone, and even then not always, but only when its season comes, when the golden grain ripens, when the fruits of the earth have lain uncorrupted for years, and when the settled minds of its inheritors have shown themselves adequate to receive this wedding dowry (Trismosin 1612: 217–18).[5]

This is a beautiful series of metaphors of the alchemical project. The grain turns precisely to gold in its own good time and season, and the mention of the wedding dowry in the text's concluding lines is immensely dense. It references firstly the history of the creation by Philippe le Bon of Burgundy in 1429 of the knightly order of the Golden Fleece, and his marriage to Isabelle of Portugal in the same year (Faivre

1990: 20, 23). Secondly, the image refers to the symbology of the alchemical process, which utilises the figure of marriage to describe the various combinings of elements and colours which the work requires. 'The first marriage is performed in the crucible; the second, in the glass' (Hamilton-Jones 1960: 149). Finally, the most ancient reference for this wedding dowry is the famous princess of Colchis, the great magician, barbarian and traveller, Medea, who protected Jason with her magic as he undertook heroic tasks to win the fleece, actually procured it for him in some versions of the tale, and then returned to Greece with him and it. This is a highly equivocal and dangerous reference, and one with which Pierre Corneille will struggle when he comes to depict it in his vast machine play composed for the marriage of Louis XIV in 1660, *La Conquête de la toison d'or* (Wygant 1994, 1995).

But, apart from this careful framing of the 1612 treatise by the reference to the fleece, the text produces only scattered references and does not follow the story of Jason or develop its symbolic implications in any systematic way. It is enough, it seems, to gesture to the golden fleece, which is self-evidently the image of the goal of the alchemical work. And it will remain so, from the eighteenth-century *Dictionnaire mytho-hermétique* of Pernety, 'This fleece is the symbol of the matter of the great work' (Pernety 1758: s.v. 'Toison d'or'),[6] to the most recent alchemical dictionary, in which the golden fleece is 'the goal of the opus alchymicum' (Abraham 1998: s.v. 'golden fleece').

It is into this loose network of references, then, that a second early modern tale of the meeting between a youth and an alchemist fits. In 1643 there appeared Tristan L'Hermite's *Le Page disgracié*, a first-person novel of a young page at the court of Henri IV, his flight from it, travels and misadventures. While it now seems to read as an adventure story, and indeed a *Bildungsroman*, its title then read, 'Le Page disgracié où l'on void de vifs caractères d'hommes de tous temperamens & de toutes professions', 'The page fallen from grace, in which we find lively portraits of people of all complexions and beliefs' (L'Hermite 1643). This was, in other words, a gallery, and one of its pictures was perhaps of an alchemist.

The page has fled the court and put up at an inn. During the night, he sees someone, at first called only 'celui' 'that one' (L'Hermite 1994: 63) and 'cet honnête artisan' 'this respectable artisan' (L'Hermite 1994: 64) making gold coins. 'I was overjoyed at this encounter, and imagined that Heaven had sent me a cure for all of my bad luck' (L'Hermite 1994: 64).[7] So this character minting money may at first have struck the reader as perhaps a counterfeiter, a suspicion which was widespread in the early modern period. Alchemy's nineteenth-century historian gives a wonderful description which connects this kind of bad alchemist with the counterfeiter:

> People with no theoretical method, working wherever, whenever, they were looking for the philosopher's stone to be sure, but only empirically. Meanwhile, they did industrial chemistry, selling soap, fake jewels, acids, alloys, and dyes. They were the ancestors of the chemists, and they profited from selling the secret of how to make gold. Charlatans, crooks, and counterfeiters, more than one puffer was hung on a gilded scaffold, the torment allotted to this kind of impostor (Poisson 1891: 3).[8]

But the Tristan-character's imagination is engaged, 'je [...] m'imaginai que c'était un remède', 'I imagined that this was a cure', and what next enters his construction of the stranger is a series of alchemy books which he has read: 'Jacques Coeur, Raymond Lulle, Arnold de Villeneuve, Nicolas Flamel et autres, jusqu'à Bragardin' (L'Hermite 1994: 64). It is through the logic and the lenses of these books that the dodgy stranger becomes in the narrator's eyes an alchemist: 'I believed therefore that this one was a minor version of them, and that this man was capable of setting me up so that I would be better off than any prince or king (L'Hermite 1994: 64).[9]

Once the encounter is declared alchemical, however, its schema has many of the standard plot elements: the alchemist, secretive, is reluctant to take the student on, but, once cornered, warns him of the extreme difficulty of the task, for which the term is 'la toison d'or': 'He let me know who his teachers had been, and how difficult it had been to acquire this golden fleece that I so desired' (L'Hermite 1994: 67).[10] Called now 'this great philosopher' (L'Hermite 1994: 70), 'this learned alchemist' (L'Hermite 1994: 71), and 'this great chemist' (L'Hermite 1994: 73), he engages the page in a christological exercise of confession and prayer. The need for secrecy is impressed upon him. And then the alchemist disappears. We do not learn where he has gone; he does not fall down a mine as did Trismosin's teacher. The page accompanies him to the edge of town, and 'after much embracing and a great outflowing of tears on both sides' (L'Hermite 1994: 74), he goes, propelling the page, *le page*, out of the country, across the Channel to London, and propelling the page, *la page*, on a narrative which is split and unsettled by the imagination as is the structure of the good alchemist and the bad. The storm-tossed crossing which the page endures for the next twenty-four hours is a good metaphor for this.

In these three examples, then, *Harry Potter and the Philosopher's Stone*, Trismosin's 'Tractat unnd Wanderschafft', and Tristan L'Hermite's *Le Page disgracié*, we find a story of a boy and his education. The great teacher, the magus, is met and lost, and this loss propels the boy through a series of adventures in his search to find the alchemist's secret. Even the great Dumbledore spends much of the 766 pages of *Harry Potter and the Order of the Phoenix* completely ignoring Harry and his problems, and on page 549 he disappears completely from Hogwarts School of Witchcraft and Wizardry. His final words are, 'You will understand' (Rowling 2003: 549). The alchemical narrative, then, is what we would call a narrative of childhood, although this must be understood for the early modern texts through an anachronistic idealisation of the child which developed only much later. But the alchemical imperative to tell the story of a child makes it at once much more interesting and much more problematic to understand the reading of the golden fleece and the involvement in it of the infamous child-killer, Medea.

The alchemical literature from the Renaissance to the present has already been combed through for references to the golden fleece, and these may be found in Antoine Faivre's 1990 study *Toison d'or et alchimie* (Faivre 1990). Faivre notes that the allegorisation of Greek myths was a characteristic trait of Renaissance thinking, and that the story of Jason and the fleece is not unusual in this (Faivre 1990: 29). This perhaps glosses over the specificity of the story of the Argonautic journey, that is, that it was often considered to be not myth but rather history, a pre-Homeric foray to the east (Morse 1994: 102). But it is nevertheless undoubtedly generally true, as is Faivre's observation that even in the first third of the seventeenth century, when the hermeneutic of the fleece was relatively prominent, references to it rarely go beyond the generally allusive (Faivre 1990: 48). However, it is precisely the status of alchemical allusion which seems interesting to try to understand, and, in this connection, there is a history which Faivre did not take on, the history of the alchemical Medea. For she was not just a child-killer. She also rejuvenated an aged king, and it is this episode of her chequered career which involved her figure in the mechanics of the alchemical process.

Taken from Ovid's *Metamorphoses*, the 'Rejuvenation of Aeson' was a powerful theme in sixteenth- and seventeenth-century visual art, and was believed to transcribe the struggle of medicine against age, the etymologies of which were believed to be related to the names of Medea and her father-in-law Aeson (Bardon and Bardon 1969: 84, n. 2). Something of the power of this theme may be seen in Macchietti's 'Medea and Aeson' (1570–73), for the so-called Studiolo of Francesco I de'Medici in the Palazzo Vecchio, Florence (Figure 8.1).

Figure 8.1 G. Macchietti, 'Medea and Aeson'. Palazzo Vecchio, Florence. © 2005 photo Scala, Florence.

Figure 8.2 'Medea and Pelias' [sic], painted enamel, Victoria and Albert Museum, London.

This is indeed the medicinal Medea, stirring the liquid with which she will replace the blood she will drain from Aeson's body with, according to Ovid, a withered stick of an olive branch, itself become green and new. In the foreground, as in Ovid, flowers and soft grass spring up where her cauldron has boiled over. The altar upon which the old man's throat will be slit is dominated by the statues of triple-formed Hecate and Youth. And, if Aeson's body looks little in need of rejuvenation in the Macchietti painting, the sign of the problem which Medea's operation will address is clearer in a panel from the Salting collection of Limoges painted enamels in the Victoria and Albert (Figure 8.2) (Mitchell 1911–12: 84, where the panel is misidentified as 'Medea and Pelias'). Here, Aeson's limpness is openly displayed and forms a clear contrast with the soft body of Youth, holding an erect palm frond. In the image accompanying this passage in the 1558 edition of the most famous Italian version of the *Metamorphoses*, Ludovico Dolce's *Le Trasformationi*, a naked Medea actually straddles the body as she bends to slit Aeson's throat (Figure 8.3) (Dolce 1979). The operation will be successful. 'Quickly his beard and his hair

Figure 8.3 'Medea rejuvenates Aeson'. L. Dolce, *Le Transformationi*, 1558. Beinecke Rare Book and Manuscript Library, Yale.

lost their whiteness, and turned dark once more. [...] New flesh filled out his sagging wrinkles, and his limbs grew young and strong. The old king marvelled at the change in himself, recalling that this was the Aeson of forty years ago' (Ovid 1955: 162–63).

This fantasy of new life is, in general terms, part of the great Ovidian stockpile of metamorphoses which map, point for point, onto what Panofsky formulated as 'the Renaissance man's sense of "metamorphosis"' (Panofsky 1960: 37). In France, *La Metamorphose d'Ovide figuree* of Bernard Salomon (Salomon 1557), includes six images from Medea's story. 'Medee rajeunit Eson' (Figure 8.4) has turned the two flaming

Medee rajeunit Eſon.

Medee ayant inuoqué la puiſſance
Du noir Pluton, & de ſa Proſerpine,
Fait apporter le corps plein d'impuiſſance,
D'Eſon vieillard, faiſant piteuſe mine,
A demi mort, ſommeillant, qui s'encline:
Puis eſtanchant tout ſon ſang de vieilleſſe
(Cas merueilleus) quand ſa vie il termine,
Elle lui rend nouueau ſang & ieuneſſe.

Figure 8.4 'Medee rajeunit Eson'. B. Salomon, *La Metamorphose d'Ovide figuree*, 1557. Courtesy of the Department of Special Collections, Glasgow University Library.

altars to Hecate and to Youth specified by Ovid into one sacrificial table, surrounded by seven enormously erect torches. On the table are inscribed geometric figures, concentric circles and transecting lines meeting within them, which suggest alchemical symbols. The body of Aeson stretched out in front of this imposing altar is, according to the accompanying verse, 'plein d'impuissance'. And in the course of Medea's operation, that body becomes, additionally, quite dead: the 'cas merveilleus' is, in addition to being a transfusion of youth, a resurrection, and the text is explicit on this point: 'Quand sa vie il termine, /Elle lui rend nouueau sang & jeunesse'.

But there is in fact no mention in Ovid that Aeson actually dies before Medea rejuvenates him. She slits his throat, drains his blood, and refills his veins with her potion. 'Aeson absorbed it, both by mouth and through the wound she had made'. Yet at this moment in the 1557 text accompanying the Salomon image, Aeson must die in the course of his Medean operation. The text is quite independent here of Ovid, and antiquity's dream of rejuvenation has become one of a christological and accordingly profoundly culturally resonant renaissance. This is the macrological pressure which has been brought to bear on the textual event. The interesting divergence is not about birth or rebirth but rather about death.

In the early pages of *Science and Civic Life in the Italian Renaissance*, Eugenio Garin described the Renaissance as a burial: 'It did amount to a solemn burial of a dead, if noble, interpretation of reality. [...] People, instead of being conscious of a beginning, were dimly aware that something was ending' (1978: 2–3). This is an historical dynamic which scholars have since emphasised. It was formulated by Thomas Greene as the light in Troy: 'The ubiquitous imagery of disinterment, resurrection, and renascence needed a death and burial to justify itself; without the myth of medieval entombment, its imagery, which is to say its self-understanding, had no force' (1982: 3).

If Garin and others are right in arguing for this structure, then Aeson as the generalised body of antiquity must indeed die before being brought back to life by a Medea who represents the 'new convergence between rational understanding and occult forces' (Garin 1978: 163) which enabled the project of rebirth. This would be the macrological reason why the notion of Aeson's dying was important to the sixteenth-century text. 'Notre thème était trop compliqué pour survivre à l'humanisme de la Renaissance', concluded Françoise and Henry Bardon in their survey article of the theme of Medea and Aeson (1969: 93). And yet, I would think that the theme's apparent complication or simplicity, like that of the framing story of Medea's chequered career, is less crucial to its interest than is its macrological ability to figure an urgent historical and cultural project. That project completed, set aside, or given up as a bad job, 'Medea Rejuvenating Aeson' becomes a micrological figure for an alchemical knowledge.

This micrological pressure works to depict Medea as the operator of the grand alchemical work. She is at once the alchemist, effecting the king's death and his rebirth, and the figure of the alchemical process. Eighteenth-century commentators are explicit about this. Pernety's *Dictionnaire mytho-hermétique* observes that 'once the golden fleece is conquered, it is the alchemical powder and the panacea which Medea used to rejuvenate Aeson, the father of her lover Jason'(1758: s.v. 'Toison d'or').[11] Indeed, the eighteenth-century twilight of the gods includes at least one startling alchemical reading of Medea's Senecan and Euripidean tragedy in Corinth.

The name of its author, Ehrd de Naxagorus, is probably a pseudonym. In the *Aureum vellus, oder, Güldenes Vliess* Medea's rejuvenation of Aeson is cited as a clear example of her alchemy, and, at the same time, she is identified with the moon, an element internal to the alchemical work. 'In sum, there is also in the alchemical work a Medea, which the alchemists call their moon' (Naxagorus 1733: 32).[12] Medea's figuration as a chemical had by this time a certain history. René Alleau described an inscription on a marble plaque, dated 1680, in the square Victor-Emmanuel in Rome, left over from the destruction of the villa of the marquis Palombara. It reads, 'Villae Ianuam Trahendo Recludens Iason Obtinet Locuples Vellus Medeae', or, 'Pushing open the door of the villa, Jason discovers and conquers the precious fleece of Medea', the first letters of which in the Latin spell 'vitriolum', vitriol, the secret shining crystalline body which symbolises the philosopher's crude matter (Alleau 1953: 11–12; Abraham 1998: s.v. 'vitriol'). The inscription is described as well in a manual of practical alchemy by Eugène Canseliet, one of the best-known of the twentieth-century French alchemists (Canseliet 1972: 202).

This accordingly hints that there was in place a conceptual structure within which the elements of Medea's story could be given technical alchemical meanings within a broadly alchemical narrative, and the text of Naxagorus pursues this. Firstly, any mention of fire, the central alchemical mystery, was apt to attract a technical reading. The fire-breathing bulls which Jason had had to harness in order to plough the *champ de Mars* in Colchis, for example, had been read in the 1695 *Dictionnaire hermétique* of Ledoux as a teaching device, 'which teaches us that fire needs to be handled with skill, for the initiates understand their nostrils to be the dampers of the furnace' (Ledoux [1695] 1979: s.v. 'Toison d'or).[13] So, why stop at the details of the Argonautic voyage? Why not include in the alchemical reading the details of Medea's tragedy in Corinth? For Naxagorus (1733), then, the burning dress by means of which Medea assassinates her husband Jason's new princess bride does not represent a gristly killing but rather a part of the alchemical work (Naxagorus 1733: 46). Then, when Medea flies off to Athens in a car pulled by two dragons [*sic*], this is a representation of the spiritus mercurii, which must rise through the air in the alembic (Naxagorus 1733: 46–47). And further, if Jason decides to marry Hypsipyle [*sic*] in Corinth, this demonstrates that the material must change in the course of the work, and take on other names, because the original material must marry many times (Naxagorus 1733: 47–48).

Those familiar with the drama of Medea, her regicides, her infanticides, her barbarity and alienation and all of her desperate misdeeds, will have noticed that the plot summary given by Naxagorus in the course of this alchemical reading is just about as accurate as that of the first Harry Potter book, 'Scottish boy finds his fortune'. Medea does not fly off to Athens in a car drawn by two dragons in any known version of the tragedy, and Jason does not marry Hypsipyle in Corinth. This brings us back to the question I had originally posed concerning the possible difference that an alchemical patina on a text could make.

It is clear, firstly, that the force of the alchemical quest as the *Bildungsroman*, the story of a child's education, is incompatible with a story of child killing. Indeed, the deaths of Medea's innocent children in Corinth, killed by her own hand in revenge for Jason's infidelity, are completely excised from the alchemical reading of the tragedy. Not only are the children she has borne to Jason simply not mentioned, but her killing of her brother Absyrtus in order to discourage pursuit as she and Jason fled Colchis is read as the alchemical material purifying itself (Naxagorus 1733: 45). Medea herself is mentioned in relation to children only as a successful mother, the birth of Medus in Athens signifying the mid-point of the alchemical process (Naxagorus 1733: 47).

Secondly, alchemy warps plots, or perhaps, somewhat astonishingly, just considers them to be irrelevant. Harry Potter does not find his fortune, and Medea does not fly off to Athens in a car drawn by two dragons. She either flies off to Athens in the chariot of her father, the sun, in Euripides, or she flies off to some unspecified place, called 'beyond good and evil' by Martha Nussbaum, in a chariot drawn by two dragons, in Seneca (Nussbaum 1997: 240). Further, Jason does not marry Hypsipyle. He seduces and abandons her, and he most certainly does not marry her in Corinth, where his new alliance is effected through a young woman called either Creusa in Seneca, or nothing at all in Euripides and Glauke in a later commentary. Although the details of the plot and the disposition of the characters are warpable and variable according to the usual processes of what we call reception history – Pierre Corneille had had Absyrtus marry Hypsipyle in the 1660 machine play, *La Conquête de la Toison d'or*; and Jason does indeed marry Hypsipyle in the 1649 Venetian opera, Cavalli's *Giasone* – the alchemical take on the tragedy seems to be of a different order altogether. That is, an originary problem posed by an event sequence that is plot, call it Medea's divided self (Foley 1989), or a spectacle of violence so extreme that no discussion or reception of it can do it justice (Segal 1996), or a qualifier, 'philosophale', slippery enough to represent anything from a general counterweight to philosophy to a practical chemistry, is torched in favour of something else. Tragedy and its sacrifices are incinerated without a second thought in a kind of meta-sacrifice that is the alchemical furnace. The alchemical patina on a text, it turns out, is something much closer to an aura.

Notes

1. Qu'on fasse un sage discernement des faux & des vrays Philosophes, pour extirper les uns, & honnorer les autres; que l'on deteste les abus qu'ont apporté dans la Chimie tous ces malheureux souffleurs, circulateurs, & impostures: mais qu'on ne laisse pas d'aymer & d'approuver cet Art tout divin.
2. Philosophe se dit particulierement des Chymistes, qui s'appliquent ce nom par preference à tous les autres. [...] Raymond Lulle, Paracelse, Basile Valentin, Sedenvogius, ont été de grands Philosophes. [...] Le sel, le soulphre & le mercure sont les principes des Philosophes.

3. Les vagues replis de la Toison doree [...] ce Dedale inespuisable.
4. Apres mille travaux les sages Argonautes, conduits entre les ondes par la puissante main des longues Destinees, conquirent seuls en fin cette riche Toison, à la pointe de la valeur, armee & secourue: de l'industrie, de l'experience & la patience, vrays conducteurs de la bonace expressement requise à ce divin effect.
5. Car elle [la toison] prend son temps pour se laisser vaincre à la fidelle perseverance de ces sages Cavalliers de la Toyson, auxquels seuls elle se communique, non indifferamment à tous, & non tousiours encor, ains en certaine saison, puis qu'elle attend son temps; que les espics blonds tournent à maturité, que le fruict de la terre se soit ia conservé plusieurs annees, & que les cerveaux posez de ses coheritiers soient capables de ce dot nuptial.
6. Cette toison est le symbole de la matiere du grand oeuvre.
7. Je n'eus pas une petite joie de voir que j'avais fait cette rencontre, et m'imaginai que c'était un remède du Ciel pour adoucir ma mauvaise fortune.
8. Gens dépourvus de théorie, travaillant l'aventure, ils cherchaient il est vrai la pierre philosophale, mais empiriquement; entre temps, ils faisaient de la chimie industrielle, trafiquant des savons, de fausses pierres précieuses, des acides, des alliages, des couleurs; ce sont eux qui donnèrent naissance aux chimistes; ce sont eux qui vendaient pour de l'argent la secret de faire de l'or. Charlatans et filous, ils faisaient de la fausse monnaie; plus d'un souffleur fut pendu au gibet doré, supplice réservé à cette sorte d'imposteurs.
9. Je crus donc que celui-ci en était quelque petite copie, et que cet homme-là seul était capable de me mettre mieux à mon aise que tous les princes et les rois.
10. Il m'apprit sous quels maîtres il avait étudié, et quelles peines il avait eues pour acquérir cette toison d'or dont j'avais envie.
11. La Toison d'or conquise est la poudre de projection, & la médecine universelle, de laquelle Médée fit usage pour rajeunir Eson, pere de Jason son amant.
12. Kurz, man hat in Opere Philosophico auch so eine Medeam, welche von den Weisen ihre Luna genennt wird.
13. Ce qui nous enseigne que le feu doit être ménagé adroitement, & que les Sages prennent les narines pour les registres du fourneau.

References

Abraham, L. 1998. *A Dictionary of Alchemical Imagery*. Cambridge: Cambridge University Press.

Alleau, R. 1953. *Aspects de l'alchimie traditionnelle. Textes et symboles alchimiques*. Paris: Minuit.

Bardon, F. and H. Bardon. 1969. 'Médée rajeunissant Eson'. In *Hommages à Marcel Renard*, ed. J. Bebauw, pp. 83–93. Brussels: Latomus.

Bloch, O. and W. von Wartburg. 1986. *Dictionnaire étymologique de la langue française*, 7th edn. Paris: PUF.
Bonardel, F. 1993. *Philosophie de l'alchimie. Grand OEuvre et modernité.* Paris: PUF.
Canseliet, E. 1972. *L'Alchimie expliquée sur ses textes classiques.* Paris: J.J.Pauvert.
Chittenden, M. 2003. 'Harry Potter Author is Richer than Queen'. *The Sunday Times Scotland*, 27 April.
D'Atremont. 1684. *Chymie des savants, ou la pierre des philosophes.* Lyon: Esprit Vitalis.
Dictionnaires des XVIe-XVIIe siècles. 1998. Paris: Champion.
Dolce, L. 1979. *Le Trasformationi, Venice 1568, including, as an appendix, the eighty-five illustrations from the edition of Venice, 1558.* New York and London: Garland.
Eliade, M. 1977. *Forgerons et alchimistes.* Paris: Flammarion.
Faivre, A. 1990. *Toison d'or et alchimie.* Milan: Archè.
Foley, H. 1989. 'Medea's Divided Self'. *Classical Antiquity* 8: 61–85.
Garin, E. 1978. *Science and Civic Life in the Italian Renaissance*, trans. P. Munz. Gloucester, MA: Peter Smith.
Greene, T. 1982. *The Light in Troy. Imitation and Discovery in Renaissance Poetry.* New Haven and London: Yale University Press.
Hamilton-Jones, J.W., ed. 1960. *Bacstrom's Alchemical Anthology.* London: John N. Watkins.
Jung, C. 1973. *Ma Vie. Souvenirs, rêves et pensées.* Paris: Gallimard.
Ledoux (dit de Claves). 1695. *Dictionnaire hermétique*, Paris: D'Houry. Reprint, Paris: Gutenberg Reprints, 1979.
L'Hermite, T. 1643. *Le Page disgracié où l'on void de vifs caractères d'hommes de tous temperamens & de toutes professions*, 2 vols. Paris: Toussainct Quinet.
———. 1994. *Le Page disgracié*, ed. J. Prévot. Paris: Gallimard.
Mitchell, H.P. 1911–12. 'The Limoges Enamels in the Salting Collection'. *The Burlington Magazine* 20: 77–89.
Morse, R. 1994. *The Medieval Medea.* Woodbridge: Boydell and Brewer.
Naxagorus, E. de. 1733. *Aureum vellus, oder, Güldenes Vliess.* Frankfurt am Main: Stock, Erben, and Schilling.
Nel, P. 2002. 'You say "Jelly", I say "Jell-O"? Harry Potter and the Transfiguration of Language.' In *The Ivory Tower and Harry Potter. Perspectives on a Literary Phenomenon*, ed. L. Whited, pp. 261–84. Columbia and London: University of Missouri Press.
Nussbaum, M. 1997. 'Serpents in the Soul: A Reading of Seneca's Medea'. In *Medea. Essays on Medea in Myth, Literature, Philosophy, and Art*, ed. J. Clauss and S. Johnston, pp. 219–49. Princeton: Princeton University Press.
Ovid. 1955. *The Metamorphoses*, trans. M. Innes. Harmondsworth: Penguin.
Panofsky, E. 1960. *Renaissance and Renascences in Western Art.* Stockholm: Almquist & Wicksell.

Pernety, A. 1758. *Dictionnaire mytho-hermétique*. Paris: Bauche.

Poisson, A. 1891. *Théories & symboles des alchimistes. Le grand-oeuvre. Suivi d'un essai sur la bibliographie alchimique du XIXe siècle*. Paris: Bibliothèque Chacornac.

Rowling, J.K. 1997. *Harry Potter and the Philosopher's Stone*. London: Bloomsbury.

———. 2003. *Harry Potter and the Order of the Phoenix*. London: Bloomsbury.

Salomon, B. 1557. *La Metamorphose d'Ovide figuree*. Lyon: Ian de Tournes.

Segal, C. 1996. 'Euripides' *Medea*: Vengeance, Reversal and Closure'. In *Medée et la violence. Colloque international organisé à Toulouse-Le Mirail*, pp. 15–44. Toulouse: Presses universitaires du Mirail.

Trismosin, S. 1598. *Aureum vellus oder guldin Schatz und Kunstkammer*, 2 vols. Rorschach am Bodensee: n.p.

———. 1612. *La Toyson d'or ou la fleur des thresors. Traduict d'Alemand en François, & commenté en forme de Paraphrase sur chasque Chapitre par L.I.* Paris: Sevestre.

Webster's New World Dictionary. 1982. Ed. D. Guralnik. New York: Simon and Schuster.

Wygant, A. 1994. 'Pierre Corneille's Medea-Machine'. *Romanic Review* 85: 535–50.

———. 1995. 'Corneille, Rubens, and the Heroic Emblem'. *Emblematica* 9: 111–32.

CHAPTER 9

COWBOYS AND MAGICIANS: BUFFALO BILL, HOUDINI AND REAL MAGIC

Ronald G. Walters

This begins as the story of two giant figures in early twentieth-century North American popular culture, Buffalo Bill Cody and Harry Houdini. Each was an innovator, enormously popular in his day, and has a reputation that lingers today, not just in the United States. Buffalo Bill's ghost haunts a recent novel, *The Congress of Rough Riders* (2001), by the young Irish writer, John Boyne, as Houdini's does a 2002 Norwegian short film, entitled *Houdinis Hund*. Such continuing homage is appropriate. For several decades, each man was an international star, with extensive European tours, including such cities as Glasgow, where Houdini shot scenes for one of his dreadful movies and Buffalo Bill added a hundred Zulus to his cast (Walsh 1928: 294). Buffalo Bill persists in historical memory for his Wild West shows, Houdini as a leading practitioner of 'modern magic', a term I will discuss later. But each man also met a medium he could not master: film.

Taken together, their cinematic failures reveal the instability of two diametrically opposed claims Americans made about early motion pictures: that they portrayed reality in a new and compelling manner and that they were a realm of magic. Exploring that instability takes us to what is at the heart of my project, the question of what performance practices changed, and what did not change, with the invention of cinema, especially narrative cinema.[1]

In making my case, I will be taking issue, albeit respectfully, with two recent, and quite fine, biographers of each man, Joy Kasson and Kenneth Silverman. Both of them want to push their heroes forward in time, into modernity, a term I find problematic. What Kasson calls 'paradoxes' in Buffalo Bill's shows are, for her, 'a crucial sign of the Wild West's modernity'. For Silverman, Houdini's 'career was an icon of modernity', a judgment Houdini himself might have endorsed (Silverman 1996: 414; Kasson 2000: 221). Each biographer has a point, although there is the hard fact that neither could conquer the most modern of media in the early twentieth century, cinema.

Buffalo Bill and Harry Houdini failed as movie stars, in part, because their acts rested upon older performance practices, some of which flowed effortlessly onto film and some of which did not. Examining the latter will eventually take us further back in time, to the mid-nineteenth century, and to another towering figure of U.S. popular culture, a mystery guest whom I will introduce at the proper moment. His success before the film era serves to mark what changed in performance practices between his day and the advent of motion pictures.

To anticipate the conclusion: by the end of the nineteenth century larger cultural shifts, combined with the rise of film, worked against a long-standing 'aesthetic' in American popular entertainment. It was an aesthetic that imagined a certain kind of relationship between performance and audience and compelled the latter to determine the line between the 'real' and the 'supernatural' or between 'authentic' and 'inauthentic'. Cinema challenged the assumptions and practices of this aesthetic. And that was a big problem for two otherwise successful performers, Buffalo Bill and Harry Houdini.

Now for the stories. I will start with the claim to represent reality or 'authenticity' – a claim some scholars, such as Miles Orvell, see as central to the more general 'modernist' project and an important part of the cultural shift to which I just alluded (Lears 1981: 345–78; Levine 1988; Orvell 1989). From there we will move to the contrary, and ultimately no more stable, claim that movies were a realm of magic.

Buffalo Bill was born William F. Cody in 1846 in the American Midwest, on the edge of the great open plains on which he would make his reputation. He served in the Civil War and worked at a variety of frontier jobs – hunter and guide, farmer, cattle rancher. His hunting skills and knowledge of the land made him valuable to the United States

Army, which employed him as a scout to lead military detachments through unfamiliar territory. In 1872 he even won the United States military's highest award, the Medal of Honor. His fame spread and his list of clients expanded to include gentlemen hunters, European royalty and other foreign dignitaries. He quickly passed into popular fiction, some of it written by himself, as a frontier hero. By the 1870s he occasionally played himself on stage.

What made his career, however, was the conjunction of two things that occurred when he was thirty years old. The first was a traumatic event for white Americans: the death of General George Armstrong Custer and 215 of his soldiers at the hands of Sioux Indians in June 1876. The second came about three weeks later, when Cody was part of a military unit seeking revenge, which it exacted on a different group of Indians, among them a warrior called Yellow Hair. The details are vague, but Cody ended up with Yellow Hair's scalp, which he proclaimed to be 'the first scalp for Custer'. This episode enhanced his credentials as a real frontier hero and figured in the failure of his grandest movie venture in 1913.

By 1883 he had created the Wild West Show that led to his greatest fame. It was a mix of cowboys and Indians, real Indians, including, at times, ones involved in the attack on Custer. It featured stirring recreations of frontier battles and of a famous stagecoach robbery, along with demonstrations of marksmanship and horseback riding skills. At its core was an assertion, made time and time again (although not necessarily correct), that Cody's Wild West was real, the genuine thing, a piece of history enacted before the spectator's eyes. 'Unlike the majority of actors presenting border [frontier] plays', a reporter noted, 'Mr. Cody has had actual experience in the scenes which he so vividly portrays on the stage and under the canvas' (Anonymous 1897b: 615; Langman 1992; Reddin 1999; Kasson 2000: 55–63).

By the 1890s those claims became muddled as the show itself grew more spectacular. Rechristened a 'Congress of Rough Riders of the World', it now included non-American horsemen. When touring the British Isles in 1902, for example, it featured a riding exhibition with a 'Cowboy, Cossack, Mexican, an Arab, a Gaucho, and an Indian', along with British Cavalrymen from the Boer War (Buffalo Bill's Wild West Show 1902). Initially, the Wild West was primarily a story white Americans told about themselves, about their conquest of the West and of the Indians. With the Congress of Rough

Riders the message was less clear. Was it now a story about empire? About stages of civilisation? About the universal cowboy? When Buffalo Bill later tried once again to tell a coherent narrative about the American West, this time on film, he could not do it.

In 1913 any questions about the Congress of Rough Riders became moot. Buffalo Bill lost his show to bankruptcy. He had, however, a plan to recoup his fortune. It was to make a movie. He had been in pictures before, from the very beginning. There exists a kinetescope, a precursor to movies, dating from 1894, a year before the birth of cinema. It is of Buffalo Bill shooting a rifle. He and his troupe were in a number of short early films, at least one of them available for viewing on the Internet. In 1900 the Edison laboratory announced that it was making arrangements 'for the taking of the biggest moving picture ever attempted ... a series of scenes illustrating the entire performance of Buffalo Bill's Wild West' (Anonymous 1900: 1).

Cody himself was the subject of a film biography in 1912, but the 1913 project was something much grander. Bearing various titles – I will use *The Indian Wars* – it was to become an eight reel, two and a half hour epic, shot on location in some very difficult terrain, with, whenever possible, both Indian and white participants in the events it recounted. As publicity for the film proclaimed, 'correctness, historical correctness, that is the slogan of the men who are working' on it (Moses 1996: 232). Nothing magical here. Quite the opposite.

The movie was plagued by two problems that stemmed directly from Buffalo Bill's insistence on 'reality' and on 'authenticity'. The first was that there were multiple versions of reality. One of the key figures participating in the project was General Nelson Miles, a distinguished soldier in the Indian Wars and a man whom Cody greatly admired. He, too, was a stickler for 'realism' to the point where he insisted that the movie show all eleven thousand soldiers present at the surrender of the Sioux. Since eleven thousand soldiers were not available, the director had to keep marching the same men past the camera (Walsh 1928: 346; Kasson 2000: 232; Bridger 2002: 430–36). There were, however, limits to Miles' commitment to realism. A crucial sequence in the film treated an infamous battle at Wounded Knee, South Dakota, in 1890 in which U.S. soldiers slaughtered Indian women and children. A promise to portray that accurately was part of what induced Indians to participate in the project. A reenactment of that event, on the ground on which it occurred, would be painful

under any circumstances, especially if it failed to convey the Sioux version of reality, yet that is precisely what happened. The battle sequence was filmed without women and children. That was too much reality for anyone except real Indians.

The second problem in establishing the film's claim to authenticity was visual. Part of the difficulty is apparent in one of the surviving still photos from the film, a long shot in which Buffalo Bill holds aloft the 'first scalp for Custer'. Unlike the real battle scene in 1876, only Cody and the dead body of Yellow Hair are in view, no other humans, no horses. The more serious visual problem, nonetheless, was one Cody confronted a year earlier in a biographical film about him, which required an actor to portray him as a young man. It was that the elderly Buffalo Bill did not look like the real Buffalo Bill, the commanding physical presence he was thirty-seven years earlier, the image of him familiar to the public. Even at a distance, the figure in the still is an overweight man in his sixties, not a lithe, powerful frontier hero just turning thirty. This may well have been especially problematic because Buffalo Bill was not only competing against his own younger image, but also against cowboy heroes in Western movies, like Broncho Billy Anderson, who made their own claims to be presenting the real West. Audiences voted with their tickets, staying away from *The Indian Wars*, but not from Western movies. In 1917, Essanay Studio, one-time home of Broncho Billy Anderson and itself about to collapse, attempted to profit from Cody's death by releasing a recut five reel version, described tepidly by one reviewer as a 'somewhat loosely constructed, but historically interesting photodrama' (Anonymous 1917b: 187). It was not a success.

If Buffalo Bill's claims to bring reality to the screen failed, how did magic fare? In some respects it did quite well. Students of early cinema have long commented on the presence of magicians among pioneering film makers, including the great French one, Georges Méliès, and the American, William N. Selig (Barnouw 1981; Musser 1990). Also well-known is the existence of a large number of early movies showing magic acts and so-called 'trick' films that used cinematic techniques to create magical effects. As early as 1908, one reviewer could dismiss a film entitled *Too Much Champagne* by saying that the series of which it was a part went 'back to the days when magical subjects were in high favor, and, except for several ingenious trick pictures, is not very interesting' (Rush 1983a: 14 March 1908). That familiarity with 'trick' pictures was part of the problem when a real magician like Houdini took to the screen a decade later.

But first: the man and his magic.

Harry Houdini began life in 1874 as Erich Weiss, a rabbi's son. The place of birth was Budapest, Hungary, a fact the family tried to conceal for purposes of establishing U.S. citizenship. Some accounts thus have him born in Appleton, Wisconsin, where he, his mother and brothers travelled in 1878 to rejoin his father. Later the family moved to New York City, where Erich practiced tricks with his half-brother and three brothers, one of whom had a long on-again, off-again career as a magician. He also read the autobiography of the great French magician, Jean Eugène Robert-Houdin. The stage name 'Harry Houdini' was his homage to Robert-Houdin, whom he would later denounce as a thief of earlier magicians' tricks. By the early 1890s he was on stage in a variety of magic acts, with various partners, including his wife, Bess Rahner, after the two married in 1894. By 1900 Houdini was a big-time performer, thanks to spectacular tricks and adroit self-publicity. He returned from a lengthy, successful European tour in 1905 as a major international star.

At this point, the question is 'what kind of magician was he?' The flip answer is that he was a very good and versatile one. Among his famous tricks were ones that are now familiar – changing places with his wife in a seemingly impossible manner, appearing to swallow a large number of needles, and making a sizeable object disappear in front of an audience's eyes. In his case, the object was an elephant.

His real claim to fame, however, was his ability to escape from all kinds of restraints in incredible fashion and under death-defying circumstances, as in a famous escape from a padlocked milk can filled with water. Among his bits of self-promotion while on tour was to make a well-publicised jump into a local river while manacled, freeing himself underwater. Houdini challenged audiences (and the police) to figure out how he escaped, even performing some stunts nude, after a search of his body, to refute the charge that he used hidden tools in his escapes. He also accepted public challenges from people who thought they had a device that could defeat him. A few of these proved harrowing, even to Houdini.

A more involved answer to the question, 'what kind of magician was he?', is that he was a 'modern' one. The terms 'new' or 'modern' magic appear in sources from Houdini's time and somewhat earlier, including ones he wrote. They also appear, with a slightly different meaning, in the work of present-day scholars on the subject.

When Houdini and his peers thought of 'modern magic', they usually understood it in contrast to alchemy and frauds, like those perpetuated by the infamous Count Cagliostro (1743–1795), or to claims to possess supernatural powers. Houdini and his peers continually asserted that they used rational means to achieve incredible effects. 'Old magic', as an early twentieth-century authority put it, 'endeavors to transcend human knowledge by supernatural methods' (Evans 1906: xv). In contrast, part of Houdini's mission in life was, he declared, 'uncovering the natural explanation of feats that to the ignorant have seemed supernatural' (Houdini 1920: v). In 1920 Helen Bullitt Lowry, a writer on contemporary popular culture, noted that 'magic is now a profession and not a cult' and that 'the modern magician is a man of science' (Lowry 1920: 4). This view received benediction from an unlikely source: over a span of several decades the popular journal, *Scientific American*, ran occasional pieces explaining magic tricks and in 1924 invited Houdini to serve on a panel with a group of scientists commissioned to prove the truth or falsity of spiritualism.

Although respectful of the notion of magic as a kind of science for profit, my own definition of 'modern magic' is somewhat more complicated and less self-congratulatory. It largely follows one in a fine recent book by James W. Cook on fraud and magic in mid-nineteenth-century America. Cook gives four primary characteristics of 'magical modernism'. These, he claims, mark the chief differences between earlier magic and a new kind that arose in Europe in the early nineteenth century and arrived in America by the 1830s (Cook 2001: 167–69). I will eventually add a fifth item to Cook's list, as well as some complications and qualifications of my own.

His first characteristic of 'modern magic' is that it was pure entertainment, based on rational principles, with no goal other than to amuse. It had nothing to do with such realms of traditional magic as the spirit world, religion, every-day life, or fraud. 'My audiences come impressed with no belief that I am operating through any "uncanny" influences, as audiences once attended a magician's receptions', wrote the great Alexander Herrmann. 'They come first to be amused with what only seems incredible, and next to discover the sources of its seeming incredibility' (Herrmann 1893a: 475). Modern magic was a transaction between magician and audience, a matter to which we will return in explaining the failure of Houdini's film career.

A second, and related, characteristic of the modern magician was respectability. This meant wearing formal attire, not what an early Houdini biographer dismissed as 'flowing robes and ... superfluous hocus-pocus' (Kellock 1930: 12). Respectability also meant incorporating women into acts, often as objects upon which male magicians performed their magic. Each of the three most important magicians working in late nineteenth-, early twentieth-century America – Alexander Herrmann, Harry Kellar, and Houdini – sometimes worked with his wife as a partner in a bit of on-stage domesticity. A reviewer noted of the Herrmanns' act that 'It is at all times enjoyable, clean and wholesome' (Anonymous 1896: 7).

This portion of the definition of 'modern magic' only partly applies to Houdini. He believed in the importance of respectability and was conscious of the difficulties he personally faced, as a magician and a Jew, in establishing his own. It was essential for him, in his assault on Robert-Houdin, to refute his former idol's boast of being 'the first magician to appear in regulation evening clothes' and to place credit on the performer to whom he believed it was due (Houdini 1908: 9). Yet Houdini's body, not his clothing, was central to his act. Short, but well-muscled, he was not afraid to display his naked or nearly naked body. In doing so, he was less a modern magician than a participant in a late nineteenth-, early twentieth-century discourse on masculinity and male and female bodies.[2]

The third characteristic of modern magicians follows logically from the equation of magic with science and respectability: they cast themselves as professionals, much like members of many other emerging occupational groups in the United States in the late nineteenth century. This meant setting standards for performances and denouncing colleagues who failed to meet them, an activity at which Houdini excelled. Being professional also meant establishing organisations and journals for magicians. The Society of American Magicians appeared in 1902 and still exists. Houdini himself published a professional journal entitled *Conjourers' Monthly Magazine* and spoke of his career as his 'professional life' (Houdini 1908: v; Silverman 1996: 126–30).

Cook's fourth characteristic is that 'modern magicians championed a vast assortment of bold new aesthetic techniques' that transcended national borders. This appears to be

what some magicians themselves saw as most significant about what they were doing. Robert-Houdin, for example, defined his own modernity by citing the innovative tricks he performed (Robert-Houdin 1859; Evans 1928: 8). He was part of an impressive international group of magicians who, over the course of the nineteenth century, developed what still largely comprises the basic Western repertoire of illusions and magical tricks. Of the stellar ones working in the United States when Houdini took the stage, only Harry Kellar was American-born, his first great escape being from his hometown, Erie, Pennsylvania.

I will now add a fifth characteristic of modern magic to Cook's list. It largely lacked *context.* I mean that in two quite different senses of the word. One missing context is *narrative.* Very few modern magic tricks were part of a coherent story. A partial exception were Houdini's escapes, which had a beginning, a middle and an end. But most tricks like 'the Vanishing Elephant' just happened, and not necessarily in relation to any other illusion performed by the magician at any other point in the act.

Lack of a narrative structure distinguished 'modern magic' from some forms of the old magic, frauds, for example. But it also distinguished 'modern magic' from other kinds of nineteenth-century American popular performances that likewise relied on deception. I especially have in mind hoaxes and tall tales – attempts to trick the public or to challenge it with information that may or may not be true, and if true, would be miraculous. Among the more notorious hoaxes were reported sightings of life on the moon and stories of a balloon ship crossing the Atlantic (Harris 1973: 68–70). Among the famous tall tales was the boast of a real person, Davy Crockett, that he was half-man, half-alligator. Although hoaxes and tall tales resembled modern magic in defying rational explanation, they came as stories with a narrative structure, such as one of birth and growth, or of travel and discovery. Tricks and illusions by magicians were rarely embedded in such narratives. This would pose a problem for placing magic at the centre of feature-length films.

There is another sense in which modern magic lacked *context* and this point is fundamental in defining its modernity. The sixteenth and seventeenth-century English magic analysed so brilliantly in Keith Thomas' *Religion and the Decline of Magic* is a catalogue of what nineteenth-century magicians thought of as the 'old magic', minus frauds (Thomas 1971).

Thomas' work reveals magic as a system of thought, an internally coherent way of viewing the world and acting within it. Modern magic had no such intellectual and material context; it consisted of disconnected fragments, specific performances. In renouncing 'superstition' and opting for entertainment and a 'scientific' and 'professional' model, 'modern magic' also renounced comprehensiveness and coherence.[3]

The theory and practice of modern magic, moreover, contained inconsistencies. The model of magician-as-professional implies possession of special knowledge and the existence of a special place – presumably the stage – in which the professional applies it. That is how it worked then, and does today, with doctors, members of the bar and most other professionals, but not necessarily with magicians. Herrmann, Kellar and Houdini occasionally explained their simpler secrets to amateurs. Among Houdini's books is one on how to perform tricks with paper and Kellar sometimes wrote articles for the *Ladies' Home Journal* bearing titles such as 'The Easy Tricks of a Famous Magician' and 'How I Do My Tricks' (Burlingame 1891; Kellar 1897; Houdini 1922; Kellar 1907a; Kellar 1907b; Kellar 1907c). All three performed off the stage, in public places, sometimes impromptu, with Herrmann being especially fond of playing tricks on unsuspecting bystanders, behaviour scarcely imaginable in a physician, although perhaps conceivable in a member of the bar.

A further discrepancy between modern magic as concept and as practice merits examination before we come to how it fared on the silver screen. It has to do with the relationship between modern and old magic, which presumably was one of discontinuity, both in time and in content. Yet the two often shared the same stage. Moderns like Houdini competed for bookings with Asian magicians dressed in traditional garb and performing ancient tricks. So generally respected were Chinese magicians that a few white performers made careers impersonating them, one of whom took his act so seriously that he spoke to reporters through a translator. Herrmann, Kellar and Houdini themselves sometimes blurred the line between old and new magic when they wrote historical and anthropological accounts about Asian, Indian and even Native American magic, all of which they insisted rested on rational principles, just like modern magic. Herrmann sniffed that European magicians had 'duplicated every trick of the Oriental and improved upon it'. Kellar, a bit more humbly, likewise denied that there was 'anything supernatural' in

'Hindoo magic', while admitting that there were a few things in it 'I am unable to explain' (Herrmann 1891: 93; Kellar 1893a: 86). Even Houdini's polemical assault on his former hero, Robert-Houdin, raised questions about the modernness of the moderns. Much of his attack on Robert-Houdin was that the latter was 'a mere pretender, a man who waxed great on the brainwork of others, a mechanician who had boldly filched the inventions of the master craftsmen among his predecessors' (Houdini 1908: 3). In another book Houdini speculated that a popular magic trick of his day, 'fire eating', 'must have been known in very early times' (Houdini 1920: 5). The performer in Houdini valued innovation in magic; the self-taught scholar in him located himself in a longer history of magic. In that history, the line between the old and new, ancient and modern, was much less distinct.

Those caveats aside, Houdini saw himself as a modern magician and so he was. Yet his own insistence on that point obscures what was equally important about him and about Buffalo Bill: their performance practices were deeply rooted in the nineteenth century, in the era before motion pictures. The modernity of Houdini's magic and the modernity of cinema were not necessarily identical in nature or entirely congruent. And that takes us to Houdini's undistinguished film career. We cannot avoid the wretched movies of Harry Houdini any longer. His magic played little better on the screen than Buffalo Bill's reality.

Given the popularity of trick and magic films, and France's pioneering role in producing them, it is not surprising that Houdini's first movie was made in Paris at some point between 1901 and 1905. Although under five minutes long, it had a bit of a story and featured our hero escaping from a Paris jail (Silverman 1996: 95–96). He appeared in other filmed stunts over the years, pictures that, like Buffalo Bill's early ones, fall into Tom Gunning's category of 'the cinema of attractions', featuring spectacle, tricks and theatrical effects rather than narrative (Gunning 1993; Gunning 1994). But Houdini's mercifully short career as a silent movie star began in 1918, a year after Buffalo Bill's death and five years after *The Indian Wars*. It ended in 1923, with *Haldane of the Secret Service*, a disappointing flop. Although movies changed between *The Indian Wars* and *Haldane*, it was the inability of each man to construct an effective cinematic narrative – whether based on a claim of authenticity or one of magic – that is most striking.

The first of Houdini narrative films was a fifteen-part serial, *The Master Mystery*, complete with a hair-raising escape in each episode (he played a United States Justice Department undercover agent), a bizarre robot villain, and a seductress named De Luxe Dora. A reviewer described the story-line as 'weird and improbable', hastily adding, 'but not nearly so perplexing as some of the feats performed by Houdini' (Anonymous 1983b: 15 November 1918). Although one commentator called the serial an 'unintentional farce', it was a fairly promising beginning in every respect, including at the box office. It even did well internationally, playing for over a year in the British Isles (Steadman 1977: 130; Silverman 1996: 261–62). He followed *The Master Mystery* in 1919 with *The Grim Game*, about which the *New York Times* review was guardedly positive. 'The familiar feats, with which he [Houdini] has entertained audiences for so many years', it noted, 'were more baffling than ever'. For good measure, the reviewer added, 'It looked real enough'. (Anonymous 1919: 11). Those words were a bit truer – and more problematic as an omen for Houdini's future movies – than audiences realised. The freshest and most spectacular stunt in *The Grim Game* was an unplanned airplane crash that occurred while the cameras were running. The real Houdini was not in that sequence. In his own bit of film fakery, the director used doubles for the most dangerous tricks.

There followed four more feature films. *Terror Island* (1920) employed technology as well as magic – a futuristic submarine was a central element of the story. There were also the standard Houdini escapes from manacles, containers, chains and boxes, including a sequence with him untying knots with his feet. A reviewer for the show business journal, *Variety*, felt that 'in the main it is only an excuse for bringing Houdini back to pictures to familiarize picture fans with the same accomplishments he has made equally familiar to vaudeville' (Step 1983: 30 April 1920). The act was getting old.

Very little information exists about the next Houdini picture, *Soul of Bronze* (1921). His most authoritative biographers do not mention it and *Variety* could not be troubled to review it. Even that vast warehouse of trivia, the Internet, is largely silent about the film.

Houdini's last two movies were interesting failures. By 1920 he was taking his film career very seriously, at the expense of his live performances (Christopher 1969: 158–65; Silverman 1996: 262). In the summer of that year he formed his own production company and began to write the screenplay for its first film, *The Man from Beyond*, which appeared in 1921. Houdini's close control over this movie makes it all the more peculiar. Its plot relies on reincarnation or migration of souls. A reviewer said it 'deals in a rather stumbling way with the problem of the hereafter' (Rush 1983b: 7 April 1922). With such a theme Houdini appeared to be endorsing spiritualist beliefs that he actively combated in public. In a remarkable sequence, a scantily-clad and somewhat pudgy Houdini emerges from a block of ice where his character was frozen for a century. With tenuous logic, *Variety's* reviewer said of the scene, 'Simply as an illusion the passage here had a certain shocking realism' (Rush 1983b: 7 April 1922). This was film trickery, not the kind of escape that made him famous.

One heart-stopping scene in *The Man from Beyond* did merit praise – a 'sensational rescue of the heroine in the Niagara [Falls] rapids'. The language used by reviewers, however, shows confusion over what to make of it. Harriet Underhill, writing in the *New York Tribune*, said 'There is no fake about this; Houdini actually does it' (Christopher 1969: 165). It was, for her, vintage Houdini the modern magician. *Variety*'s reviewer described it as a 'whale of a stunt'. 'Modern magic', maybe, but the word 'stunt' implied movie magic and an inability to distinguish between the two (Rush 1983b: 7 April 1922). Musing about the picture as a whole, the *New York Times* fell back on the same word, used even less charitably. *The Man from Beyond* 'is a stunt picture', the reviewer declared, 'but the trouble is it is not all stunts' (Anonymous 1922: 15).

Houdini's career-ending film was *Haldane of the Secret Service*, based on his own short story. He also directed the movie and starred as a dashing American Secret Service agent, Harry Haldane, locked in battle with an evil Chinese villain. *Haldane* had ambitions. It included on-location sequences in Paris, London and Glasgow. Publicity for the film evoked a comparison with Sir Arthur Conan Doyle, a hint that Houdini was trying to out-do his onetime friend by creating his own 'super detective' (Silverman 1996: 289).

The review in *Variety* was devastating. 'With all due respect to his [Houdini's] famed ability for escapes', it read, 'the only asset he has in the acting line is his ability to look alert'. The one big escape sequence was 'a poorly staged affair showing the star free[ing] himself from a giant water mill'. With a bit of New York chauvinism, the reviewer commented on the low turnout for the film's opening and speculated that 'Broadway filmgoers were wise to how bad a film this one is'. He allowed for the possibility that 'Way out in the sticks they may flock to see this one because of the name Houdini.' He added, 'But they won't like it' (Anonymous 1983a: 1 November 1923).

Houdini starred in no other movie before his early death three years later.

It is possible to argue that Houdini was simply a poor actor who made bad movies. In the United States that, however, has never been a barrier to successful film or political careers. Two more fundamental sets of issues were at work in Houdini's failure. One has to do with an uneasy relationship between modern magic and movies. The second has to do with how film both built upon earlier forms of popular culture, like magic acts and Wild West shows, and changed the rules of the game, sometimes in ways not fully apparent to performers who came from nineteenth-century American performance traditions.[4]

There are hints of what I have in mind about modern magic and movies in comments from reviewers who did not know what to make of Houdini's stunts. Even people connected with Houdini's first major attempt at being a movie star, *The Master Mystery*, were concerned about how audiences would view his tricks – whether they would see them as Houdini's magic or the camera's. One solution proposed for *The Master Mystery* was to shoot him performing his deeds in an uninterrupted close-up to forestall viewers' suspicions that they might be watching clever editing rather than real magic (Silverman 1996: 261–62).

A number of reviewers and commentators grasped the problem with filming magic. One noted about *The Grim Game* that 'with one exception Houdini's stunts do not seem any more unusual than those given the screen by serial stars such as Antonio Moreno and Charles Hutchinson', neither of whom was a magician, or even played one, during long film careers. The same reviewer praised the airplane crash scene – with which Houdini had nothing to do – then added 'but the star's muscle contracting stunts are not effective in pictures for the reason no one is certain he is doing what he seems to do' (Leed 1983: 29 August 1919). Houdini himself eventually conceded the point. '*No* illusion is good in a film', he wrote, 'as we simply resort to *camera* trix, and the deed is did' (Silverman 1996: 241).

For a magician like Houdini, cinema made the reality of illusion as problematic as the reality of reality had been for Buffalo Bill. Audiences simply had better trickery available.

If the story ended here it would be a straightforward one of the failure of two types of live performance to translate well into film. It was that, but the unhappy movie careers of Buffalo Bill and Harry Houdini are also emblematic of a deeper change in American popular culture brought about by cinema. That brings me to the mystery guest I mentioned at the outset. He is P.T. Barnum, the United States' greatest show business entrepreneur of the nineteenth century, a man whose name lives on in the United States in a circus and as a brand of sweet biscuit.

Barnum was born in 1810 and died in 1891. Over the course of that long life he was involved in a wide range of promotions and amusements that transformed American popular culture. Among his ventures were museums, tours for entertainers like the great Swedish soprano Jenny Lind, exhibits of human curiosities like the famous Siamese Twins, Chang and Eng Bunker, and the midget, Tom Thumb (who had an audience with Queen Victoria), and, most famously, the circus.

Barnum was also a student of his own promotions and audiences. He was, for example, among those nineteenth-century commentators who grasped the difference between the old magic and the emerging new, or modern, magic. He denounced the old as 'humbug' – a word often applied to him, signifying fraud and preying upon superstition. He admired the new to the point of paying a visit to Robert-Houdin, watching him perform several times, and buying an automaton from him (Barnum 1866: 212; Barnum 1972: 135–36; Harris 1973: 99; Kunhardt Jr., et al. 1995: 66, 73).

Barnum's importance here, however, is not for his views on magic, but rather as a benchmark against which to measure a subtle but significant shift in popular culture that was well underway by the time Buffalo Bill and Harry Houdini took to the screen. In making the point, I am drawing on a key insight into Barnum's career that Neil Harris put forward over thirty years ago. Beneath the diversity of Barnum's enterprises, Harris detected 'a certain unity ... an approach to reality and to pleasure. The objects inside the museum, and Barnum's activities outside, focused attention on their own structures and operations, were empirically testable, and enabled – or at least invited – audiences and participants to learn how they worked.' Harris labelled Barnum's technique the 'operational aesthetic' and noted that it was 'an approach to experience that equated beauty with information and technique' (Harris

1973: 57, 72–89; Cook 2001: 9). Information and technique were Buffalo Bill and Harry Houdini's stock-in-trade.

Barnum's first big show business promotion was a prime example of the operational aesthetic. In 1835 he went on the road with what he billed as 'The Greatest Natural and National Curiosity in the World'. She was an elderly African American woman purported to have been the nurse for a young George Washington. By her calculation (or Barnum's), she was 161 years old. The point to the exhibit was not simply to display a living relic of the past, but also to challenge audiences to decide the truth or falsity of the claim by viewing her, walking up to her, even talking to her (Reiss 2001).

There were many reasons why the 'operational aesthetic' worked for Barnum and made sense in nineteenth-century America. At issue here are not its causes, but its consequences. One was a more relaxed distinction between authentic and inauthentic, representation and reality, than our contemporary one. Probing that distinction, pondering it, questioning it, was part of the entertainment. Joy Kasson noted this at work in the Wild West Show when she wrote 'Audiences understood that its spectacle was fiction but approved its claims to authenticity' (Kasson 2000: 221; Griffiths 2001: 100). There are, however, signs that the line between authenticity and inauthenticity began to harden in the final decades of the nineteenth century, when scholars like Lawrence Levine and Miles Orvell and others find a broad-gauged assault on 'inauthentic' cultural forms. In one odd example, U.S. art museums began to remove plaster casts of ancient sculptures in favour of exhibiting inferior, but genuine, ones (Levine 1988: 165; Orvell 1989).

At this point, two unrelated things converged. The first was a movement in American culture to value authenticity over inauthenticity and to draw the line between them more sharply; and the second was the birth of movies, with their power to simulate both reality and magic. When that happened, claims to authenticity like Buffalo Bill's lost whatever coherence – or tolerance – they had under the 'operational aesthetic'. In the Wild West Show, he was the real Buffalo Bill, wrinkles and all. On the movie screen he was an old man playing a young Buffalo Bill. In Houdini's case, film even made the reality of modern magic questionable.

An absolutely crucial feature of the 'operational aesthetic', and one that film also undermined, was that it depended upon an element of contingency or unpredictability and on an active audience whose engagement was part of the show. To be sure, in the Wild West Indians never won the wars, Custer never survived Little Big Horn, and Yellow Hair never scalped Cody, but there were elements of unpredictability in Buffalo Bill's shows, nonetheless. One of his managers noted that 'accidents sometimes happen to the most skillful riders', and sharpshooters missed targets. One hapless cavalryman in the Fifth Royal Irish Lancers had a fatal heart attack while performing in the show (A Staff Correspondent 1893: 53; Anonymous 1894a: 2). The suspense was even greater in modern magic and performers occasionally died while doing dangerous tricks. It was not a foregone conclusion that Houdini would survive his stunts, even for the magician himself. As Addie Herrmann noted about the modern magic she and her husband practiced, 'Sometimes our tragic [life-threatening] performances result unfavorably' (Herrmann 1893b: 483). Striking a less sombre note, her mate described the operational aesthetic in practice when he wrote about the modern magician's audience. 'Our spectators come, not to be impressed with awe, but fully aware that his causes and effects are natural', he claimed. 'They come rather as a guessing committee, to spy out the methods with which he mystifies' (Herrmann 1891: 95). In 1938 a retired conjurer, looking back on his career, recalled 'All I have to say [to audiences] is that my trick is a good one and I challenge you to discover how I do it' (Anderson 1938: 280). Movies made contingency and participation in the performance – central components of the 'operational aesthetic' – more limited and difficult.

My point here is a fairly straightforward one, but also one that helps us to understand the difficulty of bringing both Buffalo Bill's version of realism and Houdini's magic to the screen. More important, it further helps us to understand a shift in U.S. popular culture. Movie audiences could be rowdy, disrespectful and participatory in their own way, but they could not join in the show, question the performers on the screen, or follow the action in real time. They also knew that the movie was not going to change from one viewing to the next. Without live performances, the 'operational aesthetic' ceased to be operational.

Early evidence of its decline appears in a variety of places, including the 1902 *Picture Catalogue* in which the American Mutoscope & Biograph Company explained its corporate philosophy regarding 'Trick Pictures', a category that included magic tricks. 'A trick picture that gets a laugh is doubly good', it proclaimed, 'and we have worked on the theory that the public is more interested in mirthful magic than in mere mystery' (American Mutoscope 1902: n.p.). 'Mere mystery' is, however, precisely what Houdini did in his live escape act and what he failed to create adequately in his films. Performing off-screen and at his best, Houdini was the 'operational aesthetic' embodied. As it receded, some of the old performance practices lost their power and the terms of engagement between audience and performance shifted. However modern Houdini's magic might have been, however much he and Buffalo Bill might have been innovators in live performances, when it came to movie careers, their brands of authenticity and magic were things of the past.

Acknowledgments

For help, support, encouragement, and constructive criticism I would like to thank Paul Carrington, Kate Jones, Caleb McDaniel, participants in the University of Glasgow's 2002 Arts and Humanities Research Institute Summer Term Seminar, Amy Wygant, members of the Johns Hopkins University History seminar, and Gayle Mowbray Walters.

Notes

1. I express my reservations about use of the term 'modernity' in film studies, and, by extension, in other studies of late nineteenth-century popular culture in Walters forthcoming.
2. Useful commentaries on late nineteenth-century American conceptions of masculinity, one of which discusses Houdini's body, are Bederman 1995 and Kasson 2001.
3. 'Old' magic persists, of course, and is compatible with modern media in some cultures. See, for example, Meyer 2003, and the essays in Kapferer 2002.
4. During 2002 locates magic at the very heart of modernity and gives a somewhat different reading of the failure of Houdini's film career.

References

American Mutoscope & Biograph Company. 1902. *Picture Catalogue*. New York: American Mutoscope & Biograph Company.

Anderson, G.B. 1938, December. 'The "Mentalist" Rackets', *Forum and Century*, C, 280–85.

Anonymous. 1894a. 13 May. 'Delighted Twenty Thousand', *New York Times*, 2.
Anonymous. 1894b. 9 September. 'The Greatest Summer Show', *New York Times*, 12.
Anonymous. 1894c. 3 October. 'To Close Saturday Night', *New York Times*, 6.
Anonymous. 1896. 7 November. 'Professor Herrmann', *National Police Gazette*, LXIX, 6–7.
Anonymous. 1897a. 18 April. 'Buffalo Bill's Wild West', *New York Times*, 16.
Anonymous. 1897b. June. 'People Talked About', *Peterson Magazine*, VII, 613–16.
Anonymous. 1900. 25 May. 'Biggest Moving Picture Ever Attempted', *New York Times*, 1.
Anonymous. 1917a. 21 January. 'Written on the Screen', *New York Times*, 6.
Anonymous. 1917b. March. No Title, *Current Opinion*, LXII, 187.
Anonymous. 1917c. 29 April. 'Written on the Screen', *New York Times*, 77.
Anonymous. 1919. 26 August. 'The Screen', *New York Times*, 11.
Anonymous. 1922. 4 April. 'The Screen', *New York Times*, 15.
Anonymous. 1983a. 'Haldane of the Secret Service'. *Variety Film Reviews, Vol. 2: Variety Film Reviews, 1921–1925*, 1 November 1923. New York and London: Garland Publishing, Inc.
Anonymous. 1983b. 'The Master Mystery'. *Variety Film Reviews, Vol. 1: Variety Film Reviews, 1907–1920*, 15 November 1918. New York and London: Garland Publishing, Inc.
A Staff Correspondent. 1893, 22 July. 'Chicago and the West', *Forest and Stream: A Journal of Outdoor Life, Nature Study, Shooting*, XLI, 52–53.
Barnouw, E. 1981. *The Magician and the Cinema*. New York: Oxford University Press.
Barnum, P. 1866. *The Humbugs of the World: An Account of Humbugs, Delusions, Impositions, Quackeries, Deceits and Generally, in All Ages*. London: J.C. Hotten.
Barnum, P. 1972. *Barnum's Own Story: The Autobiography of P.T. Barnum Combined & Condensed from the Various Editions Published During His Lifetime by Waldo R. Browne*. Gloucester, MA: Peter Smith.
Bederman, G. 1995. *Manliness and Civilization: A Cultural History of Gender and Race in the United States, 1880–1917*. Chicago: University of Chicago Press.
Boyne, J. 2001. *The Congress of Rough Riders*. London: Widenfeld & Nicolson.
Bridger, B. 2002. *Buffalo Bill and Sitting Bull: Inventing the West*. Austin: University of Texas Press.

Buffalo Bill's Wild West Show. 1902. *Buffalo Bill's Wild West and Congress of Rough Riders of the World: Official Programme.* Philadelphia: Partington Advertising Co.

Burlingame, H.J. 1891. *Leaves from Conjurers' Scrap Books: Or, Modern Magicians and Their Works.* Chicago: Donohue, Henneberry & Co.

Christopher, M. 1969. *Houdini: The Untold Story.* New York: Crowell.

Cook, J.W. 2001. *The Arts of Deception: Playing with Fraud in the Age of Barnum.* Cambridge, MA: Harvard University Press.

During, S. 2002. *Modern Enchantments: The Cultural Power of Secular Magic.* Cambridge, MA and London: Harvard University Press.

Evans, H.R. 1906. *The Old and the New Magic; with an Introduction by Paul Carus.* Chicago: The Open Court Publishing Company.

———. 1928. *History of Conjuring and Magic.* Kenton, Ohio: International Brotherhood of Magicians.

Griffiths, A. 2001. 'Playing at Being Indian: Spectatorship and the Early Western'. *Journal of Popular Film and Television* 29(3): 100–11.

Gunning, T. 1993. '"Now You See It, Now You Don't": The Temporality of the Cinema of Attractions'. *The Velvet Light Trap* 32: 3–12.

———. 1994. 'The Whole Town's Gawking: Early cinema and the Visual Experience of Modernity'. *The Yale Journal of Criticism* 7(2): 189–202.

Harris, N. 1973. *Humbug: The Art of P.T. Barnum.* Boston: Little, Brown.

Herrmann, C. [Chevalier Alexander]. 1891. July. 'The Art of Magic', *North American Review* CLIII: 92–98.

Herrmann, A. [Alexander]. 1893a. October. 'Necromany Unveiled'. *Lippincott's Monthly Magazine*, 475–81.

Herrmann, A. [Addie]. 1893b. October. 'Confessions of an Assistant Magician'. *Lippincott's Monthly Magazine*, 482–83.

Houdini, H. 1908. *The Unmasking of Robert-Houdin.* New York: The Publishers' Printing Company.

———. 1920. *Miracle Mongers and Their Methods.* New York: E.P. Dutton & Company.

———. 1922. *Houdini's Paper Magic.* New York: E.P. Dutton & Company.

Kapferer, B., ed. 2002. *Beyond Rationalism: Rethinking Magic, Witchcraft and Sorcery.* New York and Oxford: Berghahn Books.

Kasson, J.F. 2001. *Houdini, Tarzan, and the Perfect Man: The White Male Body and the Challenge of Modernity in America.* New York: Hill and Wang.

Kasson, J.S. 2000. *Buffalo Bill's Wild West: Celebrity, Memory, and Popular History.* New York: Hill and Wang.

Kellar, P.H. [Professor Harry]. 1893a. January. 'High Caste Indian Magic'. *North American Review* CLVI: 75–86.

———. 1893b. November. 'Magic among the Red Men'. *North American Review* CLVII: 591–98.

Kellar, H. 1897. November. 'How I Do My Tricks'. *The Ladies' Home Journal* XIV: 5.

———. 1907a. September. 'The Easy Tricks of a Famous Magician'. *The Ladies' Home Journal* XXIV: 27.

———. 1907b. October. 'The Easy Tricks of a Famous Magician'. *The Ladies' Home Journal* XXIV: 25.

———. 1907c. November. 'The Easy Tricks of a Famous Magician'. *The Ladies' Home Journal* XXIV: 27.

Kellock, H. 1930. *Houdini: His Life Story*. New York: Blue Ribbon Books.

Kunhardt Jr., P.B., P.B. Kunhardt III, P.W. Kunhardt. 1995. *P.T. Barnum, America's Greatest Showman*. New York: Alfred A. Knopf.

Langman, L. 1992. *A Guide to Silent Westerns*. Westport, CT, and London: Greenwood Press.

Lears, T.J. 1981. *No Place of Grace: Antimodernism and the Transformation of American Culture, 1880–1920*. New York: Pantheon Books.

Leed. 1983. 'The Grim Game'. *Variety Film Reviews, 1907–1920*, 29 August 1919. *Variety Film Reviews, vol. 2*. New York and London: Garland Publishing, Inc.

Levine, L.W. 1988. *Highbrow/Lowbrow: The Emergence of Cultural Hierarchy in America*. Cambridge, MA: Harvard University Press.

Lowry, H.B. 1920. 31 October. 'Magicians as Men of Science'. *New York Times* (Book Review Section), 4.

Meyer, B. 2003. 'Ghanaian Popular Cinema and the Magic in and of Film'. In *Magic and Modernity: Interfaces of Revelation and Concealment*, eds. B. Meyer and P. Pels, pp. 200–22. Stanford: Stanford University Press.

Moses, L. 1996. *Wild West Shows and the Images of American Indians: 1883–1933*. Albuquerque: University of New Mexico Press.

Musser, C. 1990. *The Emergence of Cinema: The American Screen to 1907*. Vol. 1 of C. Harpole, ed., *History of the American Cinema*. New York: Charles Scribner's Sons.

———. 1994. 'Rethinking Early Cinema: Cinema of Attractions and Narrativity'. *The Yale Journal of Criticism* 7(2): 203–32.

Orvell, M. 1989. *The Real Thing: Imitation and Authenticity in American Culture, 1880–1940*. Chapel Hill: University of North Carolina Press.

Reddin, P. 1999. *Wild West Shows*. Urbana: University of Illinois Press

Reiss, B. 2001. *The Showman and the Slave: Race, Death, and Memory in Barnum's America*. Cambridge, MA: Harvard University Press.

Robert-Houdin, J-E. 1859. *Memoirs of Robert-Houdin: Ambassador, Author, and Conjurer*. Ed. D.R.S. Mackenzie. Philadelphia: George G. Evans.

Rush. 1983a. 'Too Much Champagne'. *Variety Film Reviews. Vol 1: Variety Film Reviews, 1907–1920*, 14 March 1908. New York and London: Garland Publishing, Inc.

———. 1983b. 'Man from Beyond'. *Variety Film Reviews, Vol. 2: Variety Film Reviews, 1921–1925*, 7 April 1922. New York and London: Garland Publishing, Inc.

Silverman, K. 1996. *Houdini!!!: The Career of Erich Weiss*. New York: HarperCollins.

Stedman, R.W. 1977 [1971]. *The Serials: Suspense and Drama by Installment*. Norman: University of Oklahoma Press.

Step. 1983. 'Terror Island'. *Variety Film Reviews, Vol. 1: Variety Film Reviews, 1907–1920*, 30 April 1920. New York and London: Garland Publishing, Inc.

Thomas, K. 1971. *Religion and the Decline of Magic: Studies in Popular Beliefs in Sixteenth- and Seventeenth-Century England*. London: Weidenfeld & Nicholson.

Walsh, R.J. in collaboration with M.S. Salsbury. 1928. *The Making of Buffalo Bill*. New York: A.L. Burt Co.

Walters, R.G. forthcoming. 'When Theory Hits the Road'. In *Beyond the Bowery: The Cinema in Rural America from Its Origins to the Multiplex*, eds. K. Fuller-Seeley and G. Potamianos. Berkeley and Los Angeles: University of California Press.

Chapter 10

The Search for a New Dimension: Surrealism and Magic

Alyce Mahon

Magic was a stimulus to thinking. It freed man from fears, endowed him with a feeling of his power to control the world, sharpened his capacity to imagine, and kept alive his dreams of higher achievement (Seligmann 1997: 322). Magic might be defined as a way of thinking that looks to invisible forces to influence events, effect change in material conditions, or present the illusion of change. Magic involves secret knowledge and revelation, and, on a more banal level, may be based on a trick of the eye and/or sleight of hand. For the Surrealists, magic was 'the means of approaching the unknown by other ways than those of science or religion' (Ernst 1942: 15). It offered a means of engaging with people without resorting to the dominant means of collective 'faith', namely science and religion. In their art, writing and collective exhibitions, the Surrealists turned to magic, alchemy, occultism and voodoo as a means of looking at the world through new, marvellous eyes. The Surrealists found aspects of their own Surrealist vision of the world within the domain of magic: the alchemical union of opposites, the pursuit of the seemingly irrational, the appreciation of the collective unconscious and the states of childhood and femininity. They saw themselves as the magicians of the modern day.

Magic as a Counter-Cultural Force

The Surrealists' interest in magic was largely born of their revolutionary stance on subjective liberty, and their fascination with the unconscious and chance. They took a stand against scientific determinism and the rational Cartesian tradition typical of the education system of the Third French Republic. Theirs was a generation reared on rationalism, but it was also one that was exposed to a counter-cultural fascination with the occult and its creative powers amongst a burgeoning bohemian world in Paris. This late nineteenth-century fascination with the occult tapped into mediaeval sources but was emphatically romantic in tone, with Surrealist forefathers like Gérard de Nerval (1808–55) and Charles Baudelaire (1821–67) exploiting alchemical motifs and the daemonic undertones of occultism to their own poetic ends. Such writers' interest in the occult dramatically influenced the Surrealists in their search for a new bohemian tradition, one that was born out of the carnivalesque imagery of Hieronymus Bosch, the libertine philosophy of the Marquis de Sade and the *érotisme noir* of Baudelaire, and saw its role as a revolutionary agent against the institutions of the Family, Church and State.

Equally, the Surrealists' fascination with magic was linked to their fascination with sexual desire, taboo and its transgression, in offering a means to uncover an anti-Catholic tradition in France. Magic offered a radical new avenue for spiritualism without the trappings of the Church. The Surrealists were anti-clerical and atheistic and happily replaced Catholic iconography with an alchemical iconography. They imbued primitive and banal objects with sacred and/or fetishistic powers, rejecting the Western art tradition and recognising the significance of non-Western art traditions in the process. One only has to look at the Surrealist map of the world, as published in *Variétés* in 1929, to see that the Surrealists did not merely reject Western hierarchies but actively replaced them with their own geopolitics. The map's scale is such that the powers of Germany, France and Britain are overshadowed by the Celtic power of Ireland, while New Guinea, Mexico and Peru dominate as lands of archaic but also contemporary significance. In this way, the Surrealists' interest in magic intersected with their interest in anthropology and their desire to create a very different cultural geography and 'museum' of mankind. They did not merely want to take inspiration from magic, but also to pay homage to those peoples who had never lost faith in the power of magic.

Magical Beginnings

A 1922 painting by Max Ernst entitled *Rendezvous of Friends* depicts the founders of the Surrealist movement as a hermetic society. The group is presented before an icy landscape, signifying the Tyrolean Alps, where Ernst first met the Parisian Dadaists who would soon launch themselves as Surrealists, namely, André Breton, Paul Eluard, Max Morise, René Crevel, Paul Desnos and Benjamin Péret. Crevel, Desnos and Péret are positioned at either end and in the centre of the group, because they were gifted 'Sleepers', capable of falling into a creative trance during séances organised by the group, as explained by Breton in his essay 'Entrée des mediums', published in the group's review *Littérature* in November 1922. The only woman present is Gala Eluard, who stands to the right of the group. She had attended some of the group's experimental séances and her mask-like face and position of her body, which turns away from the group, denote her role as muse. She would retain this status, as later acknowledged by Salvador Dalí, who became her lover in 1929 and whom she eventually married in 1958, when he designed a Tarot deck for her in which her portrait appeared in the guise of the *Empress* card, one of the most powerful cards of the Major Arcana. Precursors to Surrealism are also portrayed in the painting: the contemporary Italian painter Giorgio de Chirico, his classicism denoted by his column-like body, the Renaissance painter Raphael, depicted as an Apollonian painter in his romantic cap, and the nineteenth-century Russian novelist Dostoyevsky, who is shown bearing Ernst in his lap and who is thus made a sort of Dionysian father-figure. The emphatic hand gestures of all portrayed may be a reference to sign language, and by extension to Ernst's father who taught in a school for the deaf, but it also acts as a unifying pictorial device.

In *Rendezvous of Friends*, the Surrealist is presented as the modern-day magician, the offspring of Mercury himself. This is signified by the diagram for an underground fortification beside Ernst, a possible allusion to Khunrath's Amphitheatre of Eternal Wisdom, which housed the dragon of the Greek god Hermes (the Roman God Mercury) (Warlick 2001: 67). Further allusions to Hermes/Mercury are found in references to the arts of music, architecture and astronomy: Crevel plays an imaginary organ, Arp touches a building, and Max Morise touches a red sphere. Breton, the group leader and orchestrator of rituals, wears a red magician's cape and touches a solar-eclipse-like form suggestive of the planet Mercury. The colour red denotes the Philosopher's Stone, and also alludes to the tradition of alchemy within the fine arts, recalling, for example, Cennino Cennini's reference in *The Craftsman's Handbook* (c.1390) to the alchemical qualities of the brilliant red pigment, vermilion, which could be purchased from Florentine apothecaries. That solar-eclipse-like form is also an alchemical symbol of unison of male and female, King and Queen, and lends a peculiarly Surrealist dimension to the image since these artists were concerned with the union of opposites, of the sexes, and the seemingly contradictory states of the real and the surreal.

The painting unites several aspects of Surrealism in its infancy, notably the movement's fascination with alchemy, the psyche and the concept of the 'group' in and of itself. Hermeticism was central to their creative vision, just as it had been a significant aspect of Surrealist literary forefathers: the Comte de Lautréamont, Arthur Rimbaud, Alfred Jarry, Raymond Roussel, and Guillaume Apollinaire. Presaging Surrealism, these authors turned to hermeticism and occultism as a means of rejecting and subverting rationalism and materialism.

In 1924, when the first Surrealist manifesto was published in Paris to launch the movement, the Surrealists' view of themselves as modern-day magicians was made clear. The manifesto dramatically claimed a magical power for Surrealism, ending with a Surrealist composition entitled 'Secrets of the Magical Surrealist Art'. These 'Secrets' included a guide on how to write 'automatically' (without the trappings of conscious intent or reason), how to write 'false novels', and how to catch the eye of a woman you pass on the street (the instructions are simply given as a series of dots). Magic and Surrealism were deemed to share the same spirit, since 'the mind which plunges into Surrealism relives with glowing excitement the best part of its childhood' (Breton 1994a: 39). Aside from these secrets, the subversive potency of magic was revealed as Western civilisation was rejected and the forbidden and inexplicable embraced:

> Under the pretence of civilisation and progress, we have managed to banish from the mind everything that may rightly or

> wrongly be termed superstition or fancy; forbidden is any kind of search for truth which is not in conformity with accepted practices (Breton 1994a: 47).

By the time of the second Surrealist manifesto of December 1929, the Surrealists' allusions to magic were more specific. Breton paid homage to the Symbolist poet Rimbaud in claiming that Surrealism was also about the 'Alchemy of the word', and he made direct reference to the alchemist Nicolas Flamel and to the underworld in the guise of 'Hermes'. Indeed, magician and poet were one in their role as initiate, as Breton stated:

> I would appreciate your noting the remarkable analogy, in so far as their goals are concerned, between the Surrealist efforts and those of the alchemists: the philosopher's stone is nothing more or less than that which was to enable man's imagination to take a stunning revenge on all things [...] (Breton 1994a: 174).

To make this relationship all the more emphatic, he continued, writing in upper case for emphasis, 'I ASK FOR THE PROFOUND, THE VERITABLE OCCULTATION OF SURREALISM' (1994a: 178). Magic, alchemy and occultism are presented as intertwined in their subversive power to transform the world and to change life.

As indicated by Breton's references to Flamel, numerous contemporary texts on alchemy were influential on the Surrealists' understanding of magic. Amongst them were Eliphas Lévi's *Histoire de la magie* (1860) which was key to the French occultist revival; Herbert Silberer's *Probleme der Mystik und Ihrer Symbolik* (1914) which depicted the union of the sexes (King and Queen) as a process of individuation and rebirth; Fulcanelli's *Les Mystères des cathédrales* (1926) which claimed that alchemical secrets were to be found on the walls of Gothic cathedrals, and *Les Demeures philosophales* (1930) which interpreted hermetic symbolism through linguistic associations; and Grillot de Givry's *Le Musée des sorciers, mages et alchimistes* (1929) which addressed witchcraft, alchemy, tarot and astrology and was illustrated with reproductions of prints and paintings by Lucas Cranach, Pieter Bruegel the Elder, Bosch, David Teniers, Hans Baldung Grien, Goya and Rembrandt, as well as other anonymous prints and diagrams. Sigmund Freud, whose theories on dream, taboo and the primitive were key to Surrealist texts and imagery from the start, had also discussed magic. In *Totem and Taboo* (1913), Freud wrote of magic in the chapter 'Animism, Magic and the Omnipotence of Thought'. Here he explained that sorcery and magic were often used as a means of gaining control over omnipresent spiritual entities. He explained magic as an art that 'disregards spirits and makes use of special procedures and not of everyday psychological methods', and that is 'the earlier and more important branch of animistic technique' (Freud 1990: 135). He also wrote that magical acts 'have played a large part among primitive peoples of every age' (Freud 1990: 137). Later, in his essays and lectures in the 1930s, published as *Psychology and Alchemy* in 1944, Carl Jung also linked alchemy to the process of individuation, the relationship between the conscious and the unconscious, and the role of dreams for the manifestation of mandala symbolism.

Alchemical Desire

Desire resonated with alchemical significance for the Surrealists since the alchemical process offered the perfect analogy for the ideal sexual union. Alchemy is an ancient science that involves the production of an elixir to gain immortality, or the transmuting of base metals into gold. The latter procedure is composed of two essential ingredients, philosophic sulphur and philosophic mercury, which are each separated and purified before being united. Most importantly for the Surrealists, this binding of the two essential ingredients, sulphur and mercury, had typically been characterised since ancient times in terms of the binding of the masculine and the feminine, the King and Queen, or the sun and moon. When considering alchemy in light of Surrealism it is this poetical union rather than chemical procedure that is afoot.

Alchemy was explored in automatic texts as well as in the moving and still image. Man Ray's 1928 film *L'Etoile de mer* was inspired by a poem/scenario by Robert Desnos who was in turn inspired by a starfish which he perceived as 'the very embodiment of a lost love' (Desnos 1996: 208). The poem's stream-of-consciousness style, half automatic, half symbolist, allowed Man Ray to improvise in his film technically and thematically, while retaining the alchemical symbolism. The film is centred on the theme of voyage, a sea voyage, a voyage into the unknown, a voyage in *amour fou* (mad love). The ideal outcome of the voyage is alchemical fusion, the male protagonist finding the ideal female, who 'completes' him. Within this

quest, alchemical symbols abound, including the four elements. One of the elements, water, dominates in the form of the sea and denotes the feminine, rebirth and that pictorial tradition made famous by the Florentine painter Sandro Botticelli in the *Birth of Venus* (1485), born of the sea. The star, in contrast, is male, in denoting air and fire, and the celestial power to influence events, and is also the symbol of the seventeenth card of the tarot. Both feminine and masculine symbols are then united as a starfish whose nature and five arms/points represent the hermaphrodite, the union of opposite sexes. This union is symbolised at the end of the film in the simple form of the starfish placed in a glass container: water and fire are united in the alchemist's vessel.

Another example of the Surrealists' marriage of film and alchemical symbolism is found in Luis Buñuel and Salvador Dalí's film *Un Chien andalou* (1929). Here the optical illusion intrinsic to film as a medium in itself was exploited as the hermetic symbolism of the polarities of blindness and inner sight, hypnotic gaze, and psychic abilities were used in both the editing and narrative process. The notorious opening scene of the film, the slicing of a young woman's eye by her lover, not only violates the act of seeing for the spectator and the woman and suggests the theme of Oedipal castration, but it also promotes the idea of 'inner', hermetic sight too. In classical narrative cinema, montage collaborates in film to orient the eye and implement vision; here montage is used to disrupt the *mise en scène*, to destabilise the eye and continuous vision. Through optical illusionism, i.e., the supposed slicing of a woman's eye but the actual slicing of a dead cow's eye, continuity is replaced with the uncanny. As a result the familiar becomes unfamiliar and a new, magical way of looking at the world, initiated by the art of Surrealism, occurs. Again, we find that woman is the key to this new, marvellous, alchemical vision. She alternately stands as sexual victim and seductress, a role which is symbolically indicated by a sequence in the film where a man's hand crawling with ants (denoting lust), cuts to a woman's armpit (denoting the fetish, the object of desire), which cuts to a sea urchin (denoting the feminine and the sea and so the element of water), which cuts to the head of a woman seen from above (again reminding us that woman, the object of desire, is also the vessel), and then cuts to a severed hand (denoting impotence or castration before the potent female). Alchemical union has not yet been found, but woman is undoubtedly the means to that end.

Occult Knowledge

The association between magic and the feminine, specifically woman as alchemical vessel, and the aspiration for a new way of looking at the world inspired by greater knowledge of magic, reached a crescendo during and after the Second World War. By the time Hitler invaded Paris, the majority of the Surrealists, including Breton, Max Ernst, André Masson, Roberto Matta and Yves Tanguy, had fled the capital and were organising their escape from France too. They journeyed to the United States, via the South of France. Marseilles, in 'Free France', was the point of departure for ships to the United States and here, in 1940–41, a number of Surrealists gathered. They partook of activities organised by Breton while awaiting his visa in a villa called 'Air Bel', run by the 'Emergency Rescue Committee', set up to rescue German refugees and Jewish and Communist intellectuals from the Nazis.

During this time, Breton devised a game that again reinforced the Surrealists' faith in the power of magic even at this critical moment in history, *Le Jeu de Marseille* (*The Marseilles Game*). It was a Surrealist deck of cards based on the Tarot of Marseilles, a deck that dated back to the Renaissance as a tarot design, and was famously engraved by Nicolas Conver in 1760. The Surrealists replaced the traditional King and Queen cards with their own totemic figures, the Genius and the Mermaid, and the Joker with the Magus in the person of Alfred Jarry's Ubu. They devised four new suits for the deck: the flame (signifying love), the black star (signifying dream), the wheel (signifying revolution), and the lock (signifying knowledge). The face cards were replaced by a number of Surrealist forefathers, including Freud, Sade, Lautréamont, the German romantic poet Novalis, the sixteenth-century occultist Paracelsus, Baudelaire, Hegel, the Mexican revolutionary Pancho Villa, the seventeenth-century romantic writer known as 'the Portuguese nun', and the medium and 'outsider' artist known as Hélène Smith (Elise Müller, 1861–1929). There were also literary characters, namely Stendhal's female heroine Lamiel, and Lewis Carroll's Alice in Wonderland. Lots were drawn to decide on who would design which card and, with some exchanging between individuals, a new deck of cards was devised accordingly. Significantly, Breton designed the Paracelsus card.

Max Ernst was acknowledged as the 'Magician' of the Surrealist group in the April 1942 special 'Ernst' edition of the

New York-based periodical *View* (an edition which also included articles by Seligmann and emblematic drawings that would later appear in his 1948 book *The Mirror of Magic*). However, Breton became increasingly fascinated by magic in the 1940s, culminating in the publication of his *L'Art magique* in 1957. This was a lengthy history of the relationship between magic and art from ancient to modern times in which Breton ends his analysis of the polemical role of magic with a chapter on 'La magie retrouvée: le surréalisme'. Breton's friendship with René Alleau, president of the Société Alchimique de France, and with Fulcanelli's disciple Eugène Canseliet were major factors here, as was his exposure to indigenous art in New York and beyond, and the general renewed interest amongst postwar French intellectuals in Gnosticism and magic, as indicated by such publications such as Jules Monnerot's *La Poésie moderne et le sacré* (1945).

It was during his exile in the United States that Breton wrote *Arcane 17* (1944) in which he voiced his hope for mythical and alchemical renewal after the war. The title of the book indicates Breton's fascination with the occult. The title referred to the seventeenth card of the tarot deck, the 'star' card, which suggests hope in following the fifteenth and sixteenth cards which denote the devil and his deeds (e.g., war). Breton personified this hope in Mélusine, the mythological nymph figure of fifteenth-century French folklore who, through love, becomes a cursed mortal. Mélusine is both woman and serpent, water sprite and French virago: she is of the mythological and mortal world, between the human and the divine. Breton depicts alchemy and hermeticism as part of a feminine power of rejuvenation, and political rejuvenation at this dark moment of history. He writes:

> [T]he time has come to value the ideas of woman at the expense of those of man, whose bankruptcy is coming to pass fairly tumultuously today. It is artists, in particular, who must take the responsibility, if only to protest against this scandalous state of affairs, to maximise the importance of everything that stands out in the feminine world view (Breton 1994b: 61).

In the unsettled social and political climate during and after the Second World War, Breton, and the Surrealist group, turned to magic as the link between the individual and cosmic forces, psychology and alchemy, and as a means of offering alternative avenues for cultural and spiritual rebirth. They also turned to magic as a peculiarly feminine force, a means of offering a new dimension to life.

Initiation

The culmination of the Surrealists' collective interest in magic and its subversive, political potential, was found in their major, international exhibition held in the Galerie Maeght in Paris in 1947. The exhibition was their first in postwar Paris, and was dedicated to the 'Great Transparent Ones' who would indicate to man that he was 'perhaps not the centre, the cynosure of the universe' as described by Breton in the 1942 'Prolegomena to a Third Surrealist Manifesto' (1994a: 293). In the gallery design and installations, the Surrealists intended to initiate the public into a magical worldview.

Breton's notion of initiation was influenced by the recent publication of René Guénon's *Aperçus sur l'initiation* (1946) in which initiation was presented as a 'rebirth' and a 'regeneration'. Initiation involves a ceremony, ritual or test through which knowledge is gleaned; accordingly, the layout of the gallery space in the 1947 exhibition led the public from the street into a microcosmic Surrealist world through a series of initiatory stages. It fell to Marcel Duchamp, hailed by Breton as 'le grande animateur occulte' (Breton 1969: 246) and the Austrian-born architect Frederick Kiesler, to create an atmosphere of initiation. They designed a labyrinth of rooms, in which totemic objects, sculptures, paintings and installations were on show. Of course, the manipulation of space itself, so that it took on a labyrinthine form, had anti-rational, feminine and magical overtones, being mythologically linked to the Minotaur, to Ariadne's forbidden, mad love. It also evoked the 'vever' of Voodoo magic, a symbolic design sprinkled with flour on the ground (in the peristyle) at or before the beginning of a ceremony, a magic that Breton had discovered during his wartime visit to Haiti and which lay behind much of the symbolism of the paintings by Cuban artist Wilfredo Lam who had joined the movement just before the outbreak of the war.

In the gallery space, a series of stages was mapped out for the spectator, beginning with a room of so-called 'Surrealists despite themselves' who were major influences on the Surrealists (Bosch, Blake, Carroll), and to 'momentary Surrealists' (de Chirico, Masson, Picasso, Dalí). The spectator then proceeded up a flight of twenty-one steps, designed on the sides to appear like the spines of books. Each book title corresponded in signification to the twenty-one major arcana of the tarot, and each was dedicated to one of Surrealism's revolutionary forefathers

(Isidore Ducasse, Rousseau, Baudelaire, Sade). In sum, on entering the gallery, the spectator was effectively taking the first step in initiation.

The spectator then entered the Room of Superstitions, envisaged by Duchamp as a white grotto and designed by Kiesler as a space of 'continuity-Architecture-painting-Sculpture' (Kiesler 1947: 131). It was a room which was intended to expose man's psychic need for ritual and superstition and the essential role the arts had to play in satisfying that need. It also symbolised the breakdown of man's relationship with Nature, one that Kiesler was eager to rebuild. This was symbolically staged in a curving path which had tall dark cloth hangings and was bathed in a green-blue light, like a primeval forest. Max Ernst's *The Black Lake* was on the floor as were sculptures that typified Surrealism's renewed interest in Native American and Oceanic cultures, such as Kiesler and Etienne Martin's *The Totem of Religions* which stood at over six feet like a primitive crucifix.

Next to *The Totem of Religions* was *The Green Ray*, a peephole view designed by Duchamp and constructed by Kiesler which paid homage to magic and the pre-scientific mind. It was an optical illusion using sheets of blue and yellow gelatine to produce the optical phenomenon, a flash of green similar to that which appears just as the sun sets. The work referred to a story by Jules Verne, *Le Rayon vert* (1882) in which a young woman decides between two lovers, a scientist and an artist, on the basis of her quest for the green light which appears on the horizon before sunset. When the scientist informs her that this phenomenon is no more than an optical illusion, she chooses the artist. The installation was intended to encourage the spectator to abandon reason and scientific logic and look through the innocent eye.

The next initiatory space was the Rain Room, devised by Duchamp, with a central billiard table and curtains of artificial rain that poured down on artificial grass. On leaving the Rain Room, and before entering the next initiatory stage and space, the spectator was greeted by Jacques Hérold's sculptural rendition of Breton's *Great Transparent One*. The sculpture embodied the astral and the symbolic with a cavernous, wailing face, triangular breasts and the solar appendages of a star and crescent at its collar bone. It was a fragmented, crystalline sculpture in which Hérold intended to represent the mutilated form of the postwar world. However, it also suggested the power of rejuvenation in its alchemical qualities.

A piece of coal in its left hand suggested hope as an alchemical reference to the fire which turns base metals to gold, and a plate holding two eggs at its feet suggested the unification of opposites (the two hemispheres of the earth).

Hérold's sculpture led the way into the final stage of initiation, the Labyrinth of Initiation. This was a rectangular room divided into twelve octagonal spaces, based on the votive altars of pagan cults and each dedicated to a Surrealist mythical being or object susceptible to being endowed with mythical life. The altars were adorned with signs and minerals of the zodiac. One, entitled *The Secretary Bird or Serpentine*, was devoted to Max Ernst and the Virgo zodiac sign. It held Victor Brauner's painting *The Lovers* (1947) which represented two figures from the tarot, the 'Street Performer/Magician' with his coins, chalice, sword and staff, and the 'Papesse' (female pope) with her attributes, the tiara, pontifical habit, book and throne. The words Liberty, Magic and Destiny (*Liberté, Magie, Destin*) are printed to the left of the figures, the words Future, Present, Past (*Avenir, Présent, Passé*) to their right. This painting insisted on the cycle of life and the rejuvenating, liberating power of magic at this historical moment when people were still suffering from the trauma of the War. As Breton explained in the exhibition catalogue, this was an exhibition intended as a 'spiritual parade' before which the individual had to judge his/her own faith (Breton 1947: 13–19). The exhibition, like Surrealism itself, strove to create 'the gold of time' out of the 'base metal' of the postwar world.

Select Bibliography

Arp, J. 1947. 'L'Oeuf de Kiesler et la "Salle des Superstitions"'. *Cahiers d'art* no. 22: 281–86.

Bauer, G. 1984. 'Max Ernst's Gëmalde Au Rendez-vous des amis'. *Wallraf-Richartz-Jahrbuch* 45: 231–55.

Batache, E. 1978. *Surréalisme et tradition: La Pensée d'André Breton jugée selon l'oeuvre de René Guénon*. Paris: Editions Traditionnelles.

Breton, A. 1947. 'Devant le rideau'. *Le Surréalisme en 1947*. Paris: Galerie Maeght.

———. 1969. *Entretiens*. Paris: Gallimard.

———. 1991. *L'Art Magique*. Paris: Editions Phébus.

———. 1994a. *Manifestoes of Surrealism*, trans. R. Seaver and H.R. Lane. Michigan: Ann Arbor.

———. 1994b. *Arcanum 17*, trans. Z. Rogow. Los Angeles: Sun & Moon Press.

Desnos, R. and Man Ray. 1996. 'Manuscript Scenario for *L'Etoile de Mer*'. In R.E. Kuenzli, ed., *Dada and Surrealist Film*. Cambridge MA: MIT Press.
Ernst, M. 1942. 'Some Data on the youth of M.E. as Told by Himself'. *View* 2(1): 28–30.
Frederick Kiesler, artiste-architecte. 1996. Paris: Centre Georges Pompidou.
Freud, S. 1990. 'Totem and Taboo'. In *The Origins of Religion*, vol. 13. London: Penguin.
Guénon, R. 1946. *Aperçus sur l'initiation*. Paris: Editions Traditionnelles.
Hedges, I. 1996. 'Constellated Visions: Robert Desnos's and Man Ray's *L'Etoile de Mer*'. In R.E. Kuenzli, ed., *Dada and Surrealist Film*. Cambridge MA: MIT Press.
Kiesler, F.J. 1947. 'L'architecture magique de la salle de superstitions'. *Le Surréalisme en 1947*. Paris: Galerie Maeght.
Legge, E. 1987. 'Posing Questions: Ernst's "Au Rendez-vous des amis"'. *Art History* 10: 227–43.
Mahon, A. 2005. *Surrealism and the Politics of Eros, 1938–1968*. London and New York: Thames & Hudson.
Markale, J. 1983. *Mélusine, ou, l'androgyne*. Paris: Editions Retz.
Pech, J. 1983. *Max Ernst: Au Rendez-vous des amis*. Brühl: Max Ernst Kabinett.
Seligmann, K. 1946. 'Magic and the Arts'. *View* 7: 15–17.
———. 1948. *The Mirror of Magic: A History of Magic in the Western World*. New York: Pantheon Books.
———. 1997. *The History of Magic and the Occult*. New York: Random House.
Warlick, M.E. 2001. *Max Ernst and Alchemy: A Magician in Search of Myth*. Austin: University of Texas Press.

Notes on Contributors

Mark Brummitt has degrees in both theology and performance. His doctoral thesis, a critical theoretical reading of Jeremiah, was researched at the School of Divinity, University of Glasgow. He writes for *Reviews in Religion and Theology* (Blackwell), has co-written an article for *Sense and Sensitivity*, a collection of essays in memory of the biblical scholar Robert Carroll, and has contributed to a volume entitled *Derrida's Bible*. He is currently the Old Testament Teaching Fellow at The Partnership for Theological Education in Manchester.

John Gager is William H. Danforth Professor of Religion at Princeton University, and the author of *Moses in Greco-Roman Paganism* (1972), *Kingdom and Community: The Social World of Early Christianity* (1975), *The Origins of Anti-Semitism* (1983), and *Curse Tablets and Binding Spells from the Ancient World* (1992).

Nicholas Hammond is Reader in Early Modern French Theatre and Thought at Cambridge University and Director of Studies in Modern Languages at Gonville and Caius College. The editor of the *Cambridge Companion to Pascal*, he is the author of books on the *Pensées* and seventeenth-century literature. His most recent book is *Fragmentary Voices: Memory and Education at Port-Royal* (Tübingen: Biblio 17, 2004). He is currently working on gossip on early modern France.

David S. Katz holds the Abraham Horodisch Chair for the History of Books in the Department of History, Tel Aviv University. He has published widely in religious and intellectual history, taking in adamic language, Christian Hebraists in seventeenth-century England, and religious toleration, with a special emphasis on early modern Anglo-Jewish history and the reception of the English Bible. His most recent book is *God's Last Words: Reading the English Bible from the Renaissance to Fundamentalism* (Yale University Press, 2004).

Alyce Mahon is University Lecturer in History of Art and Fellow of Trinity College, Cambridge. Her most recent publications include *Surrealism and the Politics of Eros, 1938–1968* (Thames & Hudson, 2005), and *Eroticism and Art* (Oxford University Press, 2005).

Justin Meggitt is Staff Tutor in Theology and Religious Studies at the Institute of Continuing Education, Cambridge University, an Affiliated Lecturer in New Testament at the Faculty of Divinity, and a Fellow of Hughes Hall. He is the author of *Paul, Poverty and Survival* (Edinburgh, 1998), which has been widely praised for its fundamental rethinking of the economic and social conditions of the Pauline churches in the first-century world. His more recent publications are concerned with the relationship between ancient popular culture and the development of Christianity, and his chapter forms part of his current book-length work in progress: *Christ and the Universe of Disease.*

Sara Melzer teaches at the University of California, Los Angeles, in the Department of French and Francophone Studies. She has published books on Pascal, women and the French Revolution, and the role of the body in seventeenth- and eighteenth-century politics. She is completing a book entitled *Colonizer or Colonized? The "Hidden" Colonial History of Early Modern France.*

Ronald G. Walters is Professor of History at the Johns Hopkins University. His longstanding interests include nineteenth- and twentieth-century American popular and commercial culture, and the radical and reform movements of the nineteenth century. He is the author of *The Antislavery Impulse: American Abolitionism After 1830* (1976, 1984), and *American Reformers* (1978, 1997).

David Weston is Keeper of Special Collections and Assistant Director at Glasgow University Library.

Amy Wygant lectures in early modern literature and culture at the University of Glasgow. She is the author of *Towards a Cultural Philology: Phèdre and the Construction of 'Racine'* (European Humanities Research Centre, 1999) as well as numerous articles on witchcraft and demonology, tragedy, opera and psychoanalysis. Her current book-length project is *Medea, Magic, and Modernity*.

Index

A

Abbeville, father Claude d', 141
amulets, 90
Ashmole, Elias, 172

B

Barnum, P.T., 213–15
Barthes, Roland, 14, 137
binding spells. *See* curse tablets
bin Laden, Osama, 12–13, 14
Bombastus von Hohenheim, Theophrastus. *See* Paracelsus
Brecht, Bertolt, 58, 60–61, 63–64, 67nn. 19, 20, 21, 27, 28
Breton, André, 223, 224, 225, 228, 230
  Arcane 17, 229
  Great Transparent One, 231–32
  Le Jeu de Marseille, 228
Buffalo Bill, 200–3, 209, 212, 214, 215–16
  Congress of Rough Riders of the World, 201–2
  and George Armstrong Custer, 201, 203, 215
  Indian Wars, 202–3, 209
  Wild West Show, 201, 202, 214
Buñuel, Luis
  Un Chien andalou, 227

C

Caliostro, 205
Cody, William F. *See* Buffalo Bill
Crockett, Davy, 207
culture (France)
  and assimilation, 137, 138–39, 139–43
  and protection, 147–50
  and seduction, 143–44
  and transformation, 145–47
curse tablets
  and amulets, 83–84
  and business rivalries, 77–78
  and lawsuits, 76–77
  and love/sex, 78–81
  and pleas for justice and revenge, 82–83
  and public competitions, 74–75

D

Dalí, Salvador, 223, 230. *See also* Buñuel, Luis
de Lancre, Pierre 20, 137–38, 150–55

Desnos, Robert. *See* Ray, Man
disease and illness, 99–104
Duchamp, Marcel, 230–32

E

Eluard, Gala, 223
Ernst, Max, 228–29, 231, 232
  L'Art magique, 229
  Rendezvous of Friends, 223–24
eschatology, 36–38
exorcisms, 91, 92–97. *See also* healing

F

Ferguson, John
  Bibliotheca Chemica, 162–63, 164–65, 175–76
  and James Young, 162, 164, 167, 175
  and John Millar Thomson, 164
  and the occult revival, 174–75
  and Thomas Anderson, 163
  and William Thomson, Lord Kelvin, 163
fire eating, 209
Flamel, Nicolas, 173, 179, 225
Fludd, Robert, 170
frauds, 207
Frazer, James George, 2, 16, 20, 25, 33–35, 50–52, 52n. 9, 56, 66n. 9
  and William Robertson Smith 33–34
Freud, Sigmund, 25–26, 225–26

G

Geber. *See* ibn Hayyan, Jabir
Glamour Magazine, 8
grimoires, 17, 72

H

healing
  Arthur Kleinman on, 98–99
  and medical anthropology, 97–98
  and non-Jews, 106–7
  and social class, 107–8
  and therapeutic strategies, 104–5, 107, 109
Herrmann, Alexander, 205, 206, 208, 215
hocus-pocus, 206
Houdini, Harry, 204–16
  Grim Game, 210, 212
  Haldane of the Secret Service, 211–12
  Man from Beyond, 211
  Master Mystery, 210, 212
  Soul of Bronze, 210
  Terror Island, 210
humbug, 213

I

ibn Hayyan, Jabir, 163–64, 164, 168, 169, 172
infanticide. *See* Medea and infanticide

J

Jeremiah
  chapter 13, 62–63, 64–65
  chapter 18, 59–60, 61–62
  chapter 19, 57–59
Joachim of Fiore, 38–42, 51
  and the Spiritual Franciscans, 41
  and John Nelson Darby, 44
Jung, Carl Gustav, 161, 180, 226

K

Kellar, Harry, 206, 207, 208–9
Koresh, David, 51–52
Kiesler, Frederick, 230–32

L

L'Hermite, Tristan, 185–87
liliths, 84, 85n. 15
Lindsey, Hal, 42–46, 47, 49, 51
  and Randy Weaver, 46

M

Maier, Michael, 171, 172
Malleus maleficarum, 3–4
Medea
  and Aeson, 188–93
  and infanticide, 194
  and Jason, 193, 194, 195
Montesquieu, Charles, baron de, 121, 136–37

N

Naxagorus, Ehrd de, 193–94
Newton, Isaac, 35, 167

P

Paracelsus, 162, 171
Pascal, Blaise, 118, 119, 146–47
Pascal, Jacqueline, 118
petites écoles, 120–23. *See also* Racine, Jean
philosopher's stone, 165, 166, 224
Priestley, Joseph, 21

R

Racine, Agnès de Sainte Thècle, 118
Racine, Jean, 118, 120–21
  Abrégé de l'histoire de Port-Royal, 127
  Andromaque, 123–24
  Athalie, 128–31
  Britannicus, 125–26, 131
  Esther, 127–28, 131
  Phèdre, 123, 124, 126
  and Saint-Cyr, 126–27
  schooling, 123
Ray, Man
  L'Etoile de mer, 226–27
Reagan, Ronald, 46–49. *See also* Lindsey, Hal
  and Billy Graham, 46–47, 49
  and Donn Moomaw, 46
  and James Mills, 47–48
  and Jerry Falwell, 48
  and Jim Bakker, 48
  and Nancy Reagan, 49
Revlon, 9–10
Robert-Houdin, Jean Eugène, 204, 206, 207, 209, 213
Roddick, Anita, 9
Rosicrucians, 162, 170
Rowling, J.K., 182
  Harry Potter and the Order of the Phoenix, 180, 187
  Harry Potter and the Philosopher's Stone, 179–80, 187
  Harry Potter and the Sorcerer's Stone, 181–82

S

Society of American Magicians, 206

T

tarot, 223, 232. *See also* Breton, André, *Le Jeu de Marseille*
Trismosin, Salomon
  Aureum vellus, 183–84, 187
  Toison d'or, 184–85
Tuke, Thomas, 4–5

V

voces magicae, 71, 73, 80